CONTINENTAL PIETISM AND EARLY AMERICAN CHRISTIANITY

CONTINENTAL PIETISM AND EARLY AMERICAN CHRISTIANITY

EDITED by F. ERNEST STOEFFLER

William B. Eerdmans Publishing Company

Copyright © 1976 by Wm. B. Eerdmans Publishing Co.
255 Jefferson Ave. S.E., Grand Rapids, Mich. 49502
Printed in the United States of America

Library of Congress Cataloging in Publication Data

Main entry under title:

Continental pietism and early American Christianity.

    1. Pietism—United States—Addresses, essays, lectures. 2. Sects—United States—Addresses, essays, lectures. I. Stoeffler, F. Ernest.
BR1652.U6C66   280'.0973   75-46511
ISBN 0-8028-1641-X

LIST OF CONTRIBUTORS

DONALD F. DURNBAUGH
Professor of church history at Bethany Theological Seminary, Oak Brook, Ill. His publications include *The Brethren in Colonial America* (1967) and *The Believer's Church: The History and Character of Radical Pietism* (1968).

FRANKLIN H. LITTELL
Professor of religion at Temple University, Philadelphia, Penna. His publications include *The Origins of Sectarian Protestantism* (1964). Recently he co-edited *The German Church Struggle and the Holocaust* (1974).

MARTIN H. SCHRAG
Professor of the history of Christianity and chairman of the division of religion and philosophy, Messiah College, Grantham, Penna. He is the co-author of *The Ministry of Reconciliation* (1973) and the author of *History of the Swiss Mennonites from Volhynia* (1974).

F. ERNEST STOEFFLER
Professor of religion at Temple University, Philadelphia, Penna. His publications include *The Rise of Evangelical Pietism* (1965) and *German Pietism During the Eighteenth Century* (1973).

JAMES TANIS
Director of Libraries at Bryn Mawr College, Bryn Mawr, Penna. His publications include *Dutch Calvinistic Pietism in the Middle*

Colonies (1967) as well as contributions to professional journals.

THEODORE G. TAPPERT

Was professor of the history of Christianity at the Lutheran Theological Seminary, Philadelphia, Penna. He was co-editor of *The Journals of Henry Melchior Muhlenberg* (1942–1958). He also translated and edited Jacob Spener's *Pia desideria* (1964). The essay in this volume is his last and was completed with great difficulty.

JOHN R. WEINLICK

Dean emeritus of Moravian Theological Seminary, Bethlehem, Penna. His publications include *Count Zinzendorf* (1956) and *The Moravian Diaspora* (1959).

CONTENTS

INTRODUCTION   8

1. THE INFLUENCE OF PIETISM IN COLONIAL
   AMERICAN LUTHERANISM *by Theodore G. Tappert*   13
2. REFORMED PIETISM IN COLONIAL AMERICA
   by James Tanis   34
3. THE IMPACT OF PIETISM UPON THE
   MENNONITES IN EARLY AMERICAN
   CHRISTIANITY *by Martin H. Schrag*   74
4. MORAVIANISM IN THE AMERICAN
   COLONIES *by John R. Weinlick*   123
5. RADICAL PIETISM IN AMERICAN
   HISTORY *by Franklin H. Littell*   164
6. PIETISM, THE WESLEYS, AND METHODIST
   BEGINNINGS IN AMERICA *by F. Ernest Stoeffler*   184
7. THE BRETHREN IN EARLY AMERICAN
   CHURCH LIFE *by Donald F. Durnbaugh*   222

   EPILOGUE   266
   INDEX   272

INTRODUCTION

by F. Ernest Stoeffler

To give a universally satisfactory definition of pietism would be quite impossible at this time. According to Heinrich Heppe (*Geschichte des Pietismus und der Mystik in der Reformirten Kirche der Niederlande,* 1879) the term was first used in reference to the followers of Philipp Jakob Spener at Frankfurt am Main in 1674. For some years thereafter it was applied in this narrow sense, and there are people today who, for one reason or another, would wish to restrict its meaning in this way.

A much broader understanding of the term has been gaining ground ever since the early days of the eighteenth century. Already in August Hermann Francke's time his orthodox opponents lumped together a number of related religious developments under the umbrella of Pietism. This was done much to the chagrin of Francke and the theologians of Halle. The latter could not stop the trend, however, since the similarities in thought and practice, as well as in attitude and religious self-understanding, between the Spener-Francke movement and these other developments were simply too obvious to be ignored. Furthermore, the historical continuity between them was decidedly visible.

Presently Heppe, as indicated above, found Pietism in the Reformed churches of the Netherlands and W. Hadorn in the Reformed churches of Switzerland. When Albrecht Ritschl wrote his three-volume *Geschichte des Pietismus* (1880–1886) there was no doubt in his mind that he was dealing here with an identifiable historical phenomenon which cuts across confessional and national boundaries. In time others began to see the striking similarities and historical connections between the piety of certain other groups—the Puritans in England and America, the Jansenists in France, Hasidism within the Jewish tradition—and that which was practiced by acknowledged Pietists.

In the light of these developments we may spell out, if not a definition then at least a working concept of Pietism as follows: It is an historical movement within Protestantism which has its major roots in the Zwingli-Butzer-Calvin axis of the Reformation, which began to show its first characteristic evidences within English Puritanism and the Reformed churches of the seventeenth century, which influenced Lutheranism through Arndt, Spener, Francke, Bengel, and their followers, was radicalized by men like Gottfried Arnold and Konrad Dippel, romanticized by Lavater, Jung-Stilling, and others, and perpetuated within and without the major communions of Continental Protestantism for an indefinite period of time. Through the Wesleys it helped to shape the evangelicalism of Great Britain. In America it combined with and revitalized the older Puritan tradition to form the basic religious ethos of a host of Protestant denominations. Like all such movements it has produced a variety of form and expression, yet it can be recognized as historically distinct from other movements within Protestantism such as Orthodoxy, Rationalism, etc. Wherever it is found its ethos is manifested in a religious self-understanding which the author has characterized elsewhere as experiential, biblical, perfectionistic, and oppositive.

The importance of the rise of Pietism for the Protestant experience in general has only recently begun to dawn upon us. In the grip of Orthodoxy both the Reformed and the Lutheran churches on the Continent had often lost touch with the vital concerns of religion, concentrating their efforts on the attempt to answer questions which were no longer being asked, and to solve problems which were widely felt to bear little relationship to man's workaday experience. Under the circumstances large numbers of nominal Protestants treated their churches with benign neglect, respectfully accepting them as institutions to which one turns to be baptized, married, and buried, but which should not be expected to enter vitally into life's concerns.

Not until the advent of Pietism did this state of affairs begin to change significantly. During much of the seventeenth century, and throughout the eighteenth, it engendered a new spirit of religious devotion. As a result of Pietist fervor many sections of Continental Protestantism found themselves oriented once again toward man's individual and corporate needs. Religious faith began to be regarded as a live option by large segments of the population which had hitherto thought of it as little more than a cultural relic. Preaching and pastoral work were revitalized. An entirely new hymnody came into existence and devotional aids were made widely available for private and family worship. There was a new vision of a Christian's responsibility toward community and nation, a new sensitivity to the needs of the disadvantaged, the sick, and the dying, and a new awareness of the dire necessity of adequate educational institutions. Not only that, but for the first time during its existence Protestantism began to think seriously of a worldwide witness to its faith in word and deed.

The purpose of this volume is to point out a little more fully than has hitherto been the case the importance of the movement under discussion for the religious experience of America. Largely because of the dramatic nature and intellectual vigor of the early Puritan experiment in New England Americans have been led to assume that the only significant religious impulses which have helped to shape their culture came out of Puritanism. Supported by prominent sociologists like Max Weber, as well as by many historians, and by a certain ethnic orientation which has its roots in colonial attitudes, this has become an ingredient of a national mythology which is based partly on fact and partly on fancy.

During the sixties we witnessed the rise of a rather new phenomenon in the collective self-understanding of Americans. The reference here is to the dawning of an ethnic consciousness which, as it matures, will undoubtedly force a revision of the assumptions implicit in the old melting-pot notion of what is truly American. The profound implications of pluralism will have to be progressively applied to the study of our national origins as well as to other areas of common concern. This will mean that the contributions to American life which have been made by various racial and ethnic groups must be given far more weight than heretofore. So must religious movements which are not directly related to Anglo-Saxon traditions.

The essays in this volume originate in an awareness of this newer, and presumably truer, look at ourselves and our history. By design they are exclusively concerned with the matter of religious origins. As such they are not meant to call into question the fact of our Puritan heritage, or challenge its influence, for better or for worse, upon our culture and our institutions. They are merely intended to point out in an initial way, and in one volume, that there were other such influences, specifically that of Pietism, which rightfully share in the glory and the shame of what happened in our history. It is hoped that future research will correct and/or supplement our present studies, which, like all efforts at historical interpretation, offer only tentative conclusions.

The word "early" in the title of the book has been introduced deliberately so as to keep flexible the period of time covered in each esssay. In the nature of the case this must vary somewhat with each subject. Generally speaking we are concerned with the eighteenth century, the golden age of Pietism. In the chapter on Methodism, a late arrival on the American scene, the cut-off date is about 1825.

The essays have been written by a group of scholars each of whom has a certain professional interest in the subject he has covered. Their enthusiastic cooperation is greatly appreciated by the editor.

CHAPTER ONE

THE INFLUENCE OF PIETISM IN COLONIAL AMERICAN LUTHERANISM

by Theodore G. Tappert

SEVERAL DIFFERENT NATIONAL ORIGINS WERE REPRESENTED among the Lutherans in North America during the colonial period. New Sweden was established on the Delaware River in 1638, and the early colonists included many Finns as well as Swedes. Although colonization by Sweden ceased after the Dutch and then the English conquered the territory within a short generation, about a thousand of the Swedish and Finnish colonists and their descendants survived to petition in 1693 that ministers be sent from the homeland to restore public worship in the Swedish manner and tongue.

The Dutch colony on the Hudson River, which was founded in 1624, had a similar fate when the English conquered it in 1664. As in the old country, so in New Netherland, most of the original Dutch settlers were Reformed in their religious adherence, but Lutherans among them were sufficiently numerous to petition for a pastor in 1649. By the close of the century Dutch Lutheran services were held in several places along the Hudson River.

Although there were some German settlers who accommodated themselves to the Swedish services on the Delaware or to the Dutch services on the Hudson, they were too few in number and too scattered geographically to permit the introduction of regular public worship in their own tongue. A settlement of German colonists was established in Germantown (now part of the city of Philadelphia) in 1683, and Lutheran services appear to have been held there for a time.[1] After this more Germans arrived in the New World. Most of these early arrivals came to be known as "sect people"—for example, Mennonites, Dunkers, Quakers, and small clusters of mystics and chiliasts—and these were followed by such "church people" as Lutherans and German Reformed, who continued to come in larger or smaller waves from about 1710 to the American Revolution.[2] The German-speaking Lutherans who thus found their way to the New World far outnumbered the Swedish and Dutch-speaking Lutherans who had preceded them. They were also more scattered geographically, for they settled along the entire Atlantic seaboard from Nova Scotia in the North to Georgia in the South.

THE COMING OF LUTHERAN PIETISTS TO AMERICA

The major problems that confronted these people, insofar as their external religious life was concerned, were the supply of competent ministers and the provision for public worship. Unlike the Anglicans and Congregationalists, the Lutherans could not count on aid from the colonial governments—at least not after the conquest of New Sweden in 1664. Under these circumstances the colonists turned to their home countries for help. Over a period of about a century the Dutch-speaking Lutherans on the Hudson River secured a few ministers from the Lutheran consistory in Amsterdam, Holland, and most of these were actually supplied by the nearby Lutheran consistory of Hamburg, in Germany. The Swedish-speaking Lutherans on the Delaware River were provided with ministers from Sweden, and the expenses of the voyage to America were defrayed by the crown, but there were often long periods of time when some of the colonists were without the services of a minister. There was no similar government in Germany to which the German-speaking colonists could turn, and accordingly they appealed for help to charitable societies,

---

1. Cf. Theodore E. Schmauk, *A History of the Lutheran Church in Pennsylvania*, vol. 1 (1903), pp. 82–101. (Volume 2 was never published.)
2. See the frequently cited contemporary description of the principal methods of German colonization in William J. Mann *et al.*, eds., *Nachrichten von den vereinigten Deutschen Evangelisch-Lutherischen Germeinen in Nord-Amerika*, new edition, 2 vols. (1886–1895), vol. 2, pp. 194–204. Hereafter this work is referred to by its common designation, *Hallesche Nachrichten*.

foundations, and individuals in their homeland. For example, appeals were sent to the ministers of Lutheran congregations in London who had access to the British Society for the Promotion of Christian Knowledge; to the mission-minded Samuel Urlsperger in Augsburg who made it possible for refugees from Salzburg, in Austria, to find a haven in Georgia; to a small group of persons gathered around John C. Velthusen in the North German university town of Helmstedt, who provided some men and materials for Lutheran settlers in North Carolina. By far the most productive response to appeals, however, came from leaders of the institutions founded a generation earlier in Halle, Saxony, by August Hermann Francke. As a matter of fact the spirit and practices of Halle informed most of the others who helped the distressed and forsaken Lutherans in North America. From Halle in particular, it was reported, the need was made known "among Evangelical Christians whose faith is carried out in practice and shows itself in charity." The persons whose faith thus expressed itself in practice were identified with "those whom the world called Pietists."[3]

This is not to suggest that, without exception, all who ministered faithfully to the Lutherans in colonial America were Pietists. Obviously the ministers in the earliest Swedish and Dutch churches were unacquainted with the type of piety that was later inculcated in Europe by Philipp Jakob Spener and August Hermann Francke.

From 1703 to 1723 Justus Falckner, who had been a disciple of Francke in Halle, ministered in the Dutch congregations along the Hudson River. He was followed, however, by William Christopher Berkenmeyer and a number of other clergymen who had been secured from the Lutheran consistory in Hamburg, notorious for its opposition to Pietism. Yet even in the second quarter of the eighteenth century, when Berkenmeyer (1725–1751) exercised a strong antipietist influence, more and more of the ministers were sympathetic to Pietism. How they were often regarded by opponents becomes apparent from the bracketing of "Quakerism, Pietism, religious syncretism, and feigned hypocrisy."[4]

Although there was no trace of Pietism in the Swedish

---

3. Theodore G. Tappert and John W. Doberstein, eds., *The Journals of Henry Melchior Muhlenberg*, 3 vols. (1942–1958), vol. 2, p. 128.
4. Arnold J. H. van Laer, tr., *The Lutheran Church in New York, 1649–1772: Records in Amsterdam, Holland* (1946), p. 194.

colony on the Delaware during the seventeenth century, later Swedish ministers were aware of the official hostility toward Pietism on the part of both church and state in Sweden.[5] Warnings were repeatedly sent abroad from the homeland to urge the colonists to beware especially of the Moravians, whose preachers were said to be insinuating themselves into vacant congregations and causing disorder.[6] The attitude of the Church of Sweden is reflected in the fact that among the books sent to the colonists for their instruction and edification were Swedish translations of Ernest S. Cyprian's *Reasonable Warning Against the Error that all Religions Are Equally Good,* with an introduction referring to the Moravians, and John Walch's *Thoughts Upon the Sect of Herrnhuters.*[7] In 1744 the ecclesiastical consistory of Uppsala sent a long letter to a prominent Swedish layman on the Delaware to explain what was objectionable in the "new religion" of the Moravians. Not only were the Lutheran standards of faith often repudiated, it was said, but "a so-called internal word, an inner light," is placed above the Scriptures. Moravians speak more "about Christ in us than about Christ for us." They tend to base the justification of the sinner not only on Christ's merits but also on man's merits and on his contempt for the world. The public ministry of the church they often hold in low esteem, and they are inclined to be separatistic or schismatic. Not all Moravians were identical in their beliefs, it was conceded, but their hymnal, which was taken to be more or less normative, contained "gross heresies" of this kind.[8]

Pietists who remained in the Lutheran church and did not separate from it were regarded with similar hostility in Sweden, where conventicles were forbidden by law. Exceptional was the conduct of Charles Magnus Wrangel, who was dean, or provost, of the Swedish clergy on the Delaware from 1759 to 1768. He warmly supported the evangelistic activity of George Whitefield[9] and had cordial relations with the German

---

5. Cf. Hilding Pleijel, *Der schwedische Pietismus in seinen Beziehungen zu Deutschland*(1935).

6. Israel Acrelius, *A History of New Sweden* (1759), tr. William M. Reynolds (1874), p. 333.

7. Acrelius, p. 368.

8. Amandus Johnson, ed., *The Records of the Swedish Lutheran Churches at Raccoon and Penn's Neck, 1713–1786* (1938), pp. 46–52.

9. Cf. William S. Perry, ed., *Papers Relating to the History of the [Anglican] Church in Pennsylvania, 1680–1778* (1871), p. 354.

Lutheran ministers who had been sent to America from Halle. His three Swedish colleagues on the Delaware were displeased with this and branded him a Pietist. Charges to this effect were sent to Sweden and led eventually to Wrangel's recall to his homeland. The most prominent of the German Lutheran clergymen, Henry Melchior Muhlenberg, recorded in his diary in 1765 how bitter the feeling between Wrangel and his colleagues had become.[10]

The situation among the German colonists was not altogether different. The first concrete reference to Pietism among German Lutherans came in connection with a dispute among some of the so-called Palatine settlers on the Hudson River in 1709. It was reported that "nineteen persons of the forty-seven of the said Germans have changed their Religion, become Pietists, and withdrawn themselves from the Communion of the Minister and ye Rest of ye said Germans."[11] Upon investigation by the civil authorities it was discovered that being a Pietist did not signify departure from the Christian faith, and that accordingly those who were so designated were not liable to prosecution. The fact of the matter is that as the eighteenth century advanced Pietism enjoyed more and more popular favor, and leadership among Lutherans was increasingly exercised by ministers and laymen of Pietist persuasion. When a synod (originally called a ministerium) was formed in 1748 it was controlled by clergymen molded by Halle Pietism and expressly excluded others.[12]

LUTHERAN PIETISTS AND THEIR OPPONENTS

These "others" were of various kinds. Some were "pretenders" who lacked theological education and ordination but gave themselves out to be clergymen. Also among them were men who had been dismissed from the pastoral office in Europe on account of their misconduct or incompetence or both. The scattered population and shortage of ministers in the colonies encouraged the neglected colonists to engage the services of such men, only to be disappointed more often than not. The

---

10. *The Journals of Henry Melchior Muhlenberg*, vol. 2, p. 282; cf. *Records of the Swedish Lutheran Churches at Raccoon and Penn's Neck*, pp. 86, 87.
11. Edward T. Corwin, ed., *Ecclesiastical Records, State of New York*, 7 vols. (1901–1916), vol. 3, pp. 1742, 1743.
12. Adolph Spaeth *et al.*, eds., *Documentary History of the Evangelical Lutheran Ministerium* (1898), p. 11.

major reason for organizing the ministerium, often called "the united pastors" or "the united congregations," was to bring some order into church life, beginning with the supply of an adequate public ministry.

There is abundant evidence in the literature of the eighteenth century that Pietist ministers sent to America under the auspices of "the Reverend Fathers in Halle" were frequent objects of ridicule and attack. Some critics of Henry Melchior Muhlenberg in New Hanover, Pennsylvania, said, "Since we have to hire a preacher for money, let's have a jolly one, for this Muhlenberg is too strict for us."[13] Rumors were circulated among the people that "the preachers sent from Halle are Pietists, secret Zinzendorfers, heretics, false Lutherans, seducers, dangerous people, etc."[14] Polemical tracts written by laymen as well as clergymen belabored "the Hallensians."[15] In Friesburg, New Jersey, "the united preachers" were said to be "scheming and practicing hypocrisy."[16] A minister in Virginia burned several boxes of tracts for the simple reason that the tracts had been printed in Halle.[17] Not all of the criticisms and charges came from pretenders and similar irregular ministers, for even a man of such acknowledged probity and orthodoxy as William Christopher Berkenmeyer in the colony of New York was suspicious of all men who were "infected with the plague of Pietism" and who engaged in "pietistic loose talk about love."[18] Still others attached to Pietist ministers such labels as enthusiasts, botchers of Babel, legalists, priests of Baal, and the like.[19]

The Pietists for their part had criticisms to make of their opponents. Some of these opponents were charged with leading dissolute lives. Pietists were offended by people who hunted, raced horses, or went swimming on Sundays.[20] In

---

13. *The Journals of Henry Melchior Muhlenberg*, vol. 1, p. 97.
14. *Ibid.*, vol. 1, p. 446.
15. *Ibid.*, vol. 2, p. 164.
16. *Ibid.*, vol. 2, pp. 284, 285.
17. Manuscript volume in the archives at the Lutheran Theological Seminary at Philadelphia, PM95, A1174–79, pp. 70, 71.
18. Simon Hart and Harry J. Kreider, trs., *Protocol of the Lutheran Church in New York City, 1702–1750* (1958), pp. 102, 185; John P. Dern, ed., *The Albany Protocol: W. C. Berkenmeyer's Chronicle 1731–1750* (1971), pp. xlvi, xlvii.
19. *Hallesche Nachrichten*, vol. 1, pp. 693, 694.
20. Samuel Urlsperger, ed., *Amerikanisches Ackerwerk Gottes, oder zuverlässige Nachrichten ... von Saltzburgischen Emigranten ... in Georgien,* 4 parts, (1754–1767), vol. 3, pp. 418, 419; *The Journals of Henry Melchior Muhlenberg,* vol. 2, pp. 89, 90.

1752 Henry Melchior Muhlenberg wrote a letter in English to complain:

> The state and condition of some English and German neighbors here [in Trappe, Pennsylvania] groweth worse because Abr. de Haven continues to abuse the granted license by enticing one after another into a dissolute and wicked life. Surfeiting, drunkenness, playing cards and dice, fiddling, dancing, cursing, swearing, fighting, scuffling, and such like will hardly cease on the Lord's days! He has had, several Sundays in my absence, horse racing before, during, and after divine Worship.[21]

Opponents of Pietism were assailed for considering "merriment, buffoonery, the customary dances of the world, and so-called Christian drinking parties on special occasions as permissible adiaphora."[22] Muhlenberg took his maidservant to task when she was invited to attend "a frolick" in the neighborhood, "where cornhusking will be rewarded with drinks, games, and dancing," and on another occasion he criticized his own daugher-in-law for having a tea party "according to the prevailing fashion," which he thought was "not according to the counsel and command of our Lord."[23] On the other hand, alcoholic beverages were consumed instead of water, partly because available water was often unsafe for drinking and partly because of inherited custom. It was the abuse rather than the use that was frowned upon. Beer was quite regularly brewed in the home.[24] Beer was often served at meetings of church councils or consistories in Dutch congregations.[25] A Swedish minister in New Jersey habitually drank a glass of wine after preaching.[26] In Georgia the judgment was expressed:

> Rum is a dangerous drink, but its use cannot be forbidden altogether on that account, for experience teaches that when it is taken with moderation it is beneficial to the health. To be sure, it might be better to substitute a light beer, but this is not easy unless one brews it oneself.[27]

---

21. Letter dated August 25, 1752, in archives referred to above in n. 17.
22. *The Journals of Henry Melchior Muhlenberg*, vol. 1, p. 382.
23. *Ibid.*, vol. 3, pp. 619, 746.
24. Cf. Samuel Urlsperger, ed., *Ausfürliche Nachricht von den Saltzburgischen Emigranten* (1735–1752), second continuation, pp. 704, 712; fifth continuation, p. 2353.
25. Hart and Kreider, eds., *Protocol of the Lutheran Church in New York*, pp. 27, 57, 206.
26. Johnson, *The Records of the Swedish Lutheran Churches at Raccoon and Penn's Neck*, p. 98.
27. Urlsperger, *Amerikanisches Ackerwerk Gottes*, vol. 1, pp. 466, 467.

What distinguished the Pietists in their own eyes not only from unbelievers but also from critics within the church was variously expressed. Many had only an external knowledge of the Christian faith, they said, without an experience of it. They were acquainted with the outer shell but not with the kernel. They had learned formal definitions of justification but gave no evidence of conversion or sanctification. They regarded religion as a matter of the head rather than of the heart, they thought of a code of Christian conduct as adiaphoral rather than as prescribed, and they looked upon the Christian life as passive rather than active. Muhlenberg once wrote of an elder who thought he was adhering to Lutheran doctrine, "who wanted to be saved by grace but expected to see God without sanctification." On another occasion he wrote about a woman who "has remained orthodox in historical understanding and sticks to the unaltered Augsburg Confession with an unaltered heart."[28]

Pietism appeared in various forms and degrees. Among the clergy John F. Handschuh and J. C. H. Helmuth might be classified as representative of an excessive or even morbid type of Pietism. Most of the clergy were moderate in comparison. Yet even these engaged at times in the interpretation of dreams and in the search for divine guidance by resort to biblical lottery. They cultivated what they called "edifying conversation," which was marked by sentimental allusions and pious embroidery known as "the language of Canaan."[29] They were not satisfied with a simple and direct statement of a person's death but wrote or said, "He laid aside his fragile tabernacle" or "He suffered a temporal but blessed death."[30] A man on his deathbed asked his pastor to send "thousands of greetings and kisses in the Spirit" to the "Reverend Fathers" in Europe.[31] Some of this extravagant language was a product of the culture of the age. It was reflected in such widely read devotional books as John Arndt's *True Christianity* and C. H. von Bogatzky's *Golden Treasure Chest of the Children of God* and in a variety of sermon collections and hymnals. It was often criticized by opponents as pretentious vanity and pious hypocrisy, even as the emphasis on holiness or sanctification evoked charges of legalism and works righteousness.

---

28. *The Journals of Henry Melchior Muhlenberg*, vol. 1, p. 326; vol. 3, p. 427.
29. Urlsperger, *Amerikanisches Ackerwerk Gottes*, vol. 3, p. 435; *The Journals of Henry Melchior Muhlenberg*, vol. 3, p. 516.
30. Urlsperger, *Amerikanisches Ackerwerk Gottes*, vol. 1, p. 2.
31. *The Journals of Henry Melchior Muhlenberg*, vol. 1, p. 374.

LUTHERAN IDENTITY IN RELATION TO OTHERS

The character of Lutheran Pietism in colonial America can best be illustrated by sketching a few selected aspects of its common life and activity. At the outset it is well to underscore the fact that these people regarded themselves as Lutheran. They expressed this in their high regard for Martin Luther. They thought of themselves as followers of the Reformer and declared that if he were to reappear Luther would certainly be a Pietist.[32] Official documents uniformly committed ministers and congregations to the Lutheran confessions or standards of faith. When the Swedish churches on the Delaware River appealed to Sweden for pastors they declared that they desired ministers attached to "the Lutheran religion, which we shall now confess before God and all the world."[33] When in response the archbishop of Uppsala sent several ministers to the Delaware in 1696, he directed them

> to preach God's Word, expound the prophets and other ca-
> nonical books of the Old and New Testaments as well as the
> Athanasian and Nicene Symbols and the true doctrines con-
> tained in the Augsburg Confession of faith, which they were
> to explain clearly and purely without any admixture of
> superstitious or false doctrines.... [They were] to adminis-
> ter the holy sacraments according to God's ordinances and
> instruct the children of the colonists in [Luther's Small]
> Catechism.[34]

In its records the Swedish church in Wilmington, Delaware, called itself "the Swedes Lutheran Church called Trinity" or "the Lutheran Church Called Trinity" to the close of the eighteenth century.[35] There is reason to expect an even stronger commitment on the part of the Dutch Lutherans on the Hudson River who were a minority in a predominantly Reformed environment. In fact, we find this reflected in an agreement made with a minister in which he is committed to "preaching the Holy Gospel purely according to the Holy Scriptures and the Symbolical Books of our Lutheran Church."[36]

---

32. *Ibid.*, vol. 1, pp. 317, 326, 360, 382.
33. Acrelius, *A History of New Sweden*, p. 187.
34. Thomas Campanius (Holm.), *Description of the Province of New Sweden*, tr. Peter S. DuPonceau (1839), pp. 94–96.
35. Horace Burr, tr., *The Records of Holy Trinity (Old Swedes) Church* (1890), pp. 473, 519.
36. *Documentary History of the State of New York*, 4 vols. (1850–1851), vol. 3, pp. 591, 592.

It was among the German-speaking Lutherans that Pietism was most deeply intrenched, but even here the consciousness of Lutheran identity was strong. When Peter Brunnholtz was ordained for service in Pennsylvania in 1744 he pledged

> to be faithful to the Word of God, pure and incorrupt, as this is contained according to the mind of the Spirit in the Scriptures of the holy prophets and apostles and as this was afterward repeated and clearly set forth in the three chief Creeds and especially in the confession of the Lutheran Church, namely, the unaltered Augsburg Confession, its Apology, the Smalcald Articles, the two Catechisms of Luther, and the particular Formula of Concord, all of which have been drawn with great diligence out of the Holy Scriptures and have been compiled to oppose all heresies.[37]

Similar testimonies to the binding character of the standards of Lutheran faith were inserted in congregational and synodical constitutions, property deeds, cornerstones, and the like. Ordinands were instructed to study the confessions, and on occasion the confessions were appealed to in theological colloquies between ministers of different communions.[38]

From such evidence it is safe to conclude that Pietism, as it appeared in colonial Lutheranism, did not materially alter the doctrinal content inherited from the Scholastics or Orthodoxists of the seventeenth century. What it did was to shift the emphasis from the head to the heart, from the Christ-for-us to the Christ-in-us. This in turn had an effect on the relation of churches to one another.

Friction between Lutherans and Moravians in the Middle Colonies has already been mentioned. This is at first sight puzzling in view of the great similarities between the two in the eighteenth century. It was just this likeness, however, that contributed to the friction, for it was felt that Nicholas Zinzendorf encouraged the separation of Lutherans from their own church to become Moravians. Zinzendorf reached Pennsylvania a year before Henry Melchior Muhlenberg, and these two leaders at once set out on a collision course. The result was an estrangement and controversy that lasted many years and deeply affected the two churches, especially in New Jersey,

---

37. *Hallesche Nachrichten*, vol. 1, p. 85.
38. *Ibid.*, vol. 1, p. 374; *The Journals of Henry Melchior Muhlenberg*, vol. 1, pp. 302, 303.

Pennsylvania, and Maryland. In the Southern Colonies, on the other hand, Moravians and Lutherans usually got along very well with one another.[39]

"CHURCH PEOPLE" AND "SECT PEOPLE"

Any discussion of Reformed-Lutheran relations must take into account the difference between the Dutch Reformed and the German Reformed churches in colonial America. In the Netherlands the Reformed people were members of the established church, enjoyed special privileges as such, and took the rather exclusive doctrinal position reflected in the decrees of the Synod of Dort (1619). The Lutherans in the Netherlands comprised a small minority, and the Lutherans on the Hudson River were also a small minority. They complained that they were discriminated against, and it was in fact not until after the English conquest of 1664 that they were permitted to have a minister of their own. The bad feeling that was thus engendered in the early years persisted for a long time. After extended controversy the Lutherans in Albany finally secured the right in 1674 to employ their own grave digger instead of being compelled to make use of the Reformed sexton.[40] A generation later, in response to requests by his parishioners, Justus Falckner prepared a book in which he set forth what he believed to be the distinctive teachings of Calvinists in comparison with those of the Lutherans,[41] and it was observed again and again that the greatest differences concerned predestination and the Lord's supper.[42] Still another generation later, in 1734, William C. Berkenmeyer complained that, because they outnumbered Lutherans, the Dutch Reformed insisted on having everything their own way.[43] Intermarriage and the Pietist emphasis on experience rather than doctrine gradually softened the antagonism on both sides.

The coolness and even hostility which marked the rela-

39. Cf. Adelaide L. Fries *et al.*, eds., *Records of the Moravians in North Carolina*, 10 vols. (1922–1966), vol. 2, pp. 920, 921; vol. 3, pp. 1065, 1079, 1114, 1115, 1152; vol. 4, p. 2174; vol. 5, pp. 2400, 2060, 2323.
40. *Documentary History of the State of New York*, vol. 3, pp. 871, 872.
41. Justus Falckner, *Grondlyke Onderricht van Sekere Voorname Hoofdstucken der Waren, Loutern, Seligmakenden Chrystelycken Leere* ... (1708).
42. *Hallesche Nachrichten*, vol. 1, p. 207; vol. 2, pp. 25–27.
43. Simon Hart and Harry J. Kreider, trs., *Lutheran Church in New York and New Jersey, 1722–1760: Records in Hamburg* (1962), p. 57.

tion of the Lutherans to the Dutch Reformed was hardly evident in the attitude toward German Reformed ministers and lay people. Many of the German Reformed and Lutheran colonists had come from the same parts of southwestern Germany, crossed the Atlantic on the same ships, and settled side by side in the New World. When they established churches and schoolhouses in America they often shared in the construction and maintenance of common facilities, economy supplying the impulse and the *Simultankirchen* of western Germany providing models for the "union churches" in America. Because many of the Reformed and Lutheran people intermarried there was a tendency to avoid preaching on "theological differences" between these two churches without thereby completely obliterating the distinctions between Reformed and Lutheran teaching and practice. This was true even in the case of the short-lived (1787–1794) administrative union of Lutheran and Reformed churches in South Carolina called the Unio Ecclesiastica.[44] It was sometimes said that the only difference between the Reformed and the Lutherans was that in repeating the Lord's Prayer the former said "Unser Vater" and the latter said "Vater Unser."[45] Because other and more serious differences were actually acknowledged, the churches remained separate in spite of the common ownership of church property. Dissension occasionally occurred,[46] but as a rule Reformed and Lutheran clergymen and laypersons got along with one another as well as their respective leaders, Michael Schlatter and Henry Melchior Muhlenberg.[47] In passing it may be observed that the Heidelberg Catechism, which was the only standard of faith subscribed to by the German Reformed, was much more moderate than the decrees of the Synod of Dort, to which the Dutch Reformed subscribed in addition.

That it was not merely common nationality and language that account for the cordial relations between the German Reformed and the Lutherans becomes apparent when the so-called "sect people" are considered. The Mennonites, Dunkers, Seventh-day Baptists, and others spoke the

44. Cf. *The Journals of Henry Melchior Muhlenberg*, vol. 2, p. 452.
45. Spaeth, *Documentary History of the Lutheran Ministerium*, p. 98; *The Journals of Henry Melchior Muhlenberg*, vol. 1, pp. 51, 52.
46. *Acta historico-ecclesiastica, oder Gesammelte Nachrichten von den neuesten Kirchengeschichten*, 20 vols. (1735–1758), vol. 16, pp. 908, 909.
47. Cf. Henry Harbaugh, *The Life of Michael Schlatter* (1857), pp. 138, 139, 342–348.

same language and were of the same nationality but were regarded differently, partly because they had been condemned and sometimes exiled by Lutheran state churches in Europe and partly because of their divergent teachings and practices. When Muhlenberg reported to his European patrons in 1749 he wrote unsparingly of them.

> [Quakers] do not need to trouble themselves with the written Word of God and the sacraments. They do not have to pay a salary to any preacher. They wear the very plainest attire, and everybody is permitted to teach and prophesy when good ideas occur to him.... We also have others here who renounce all visible things, pretend to worship God in spirit and in truth, and call themselves "the Silent in the Land." These belong to no religious organization at all, allow themselves to be disciplined by nobody, have no compassion or feeling for other church members because they are separated from them, interpret the Bible according to their own good pleasure, obscure the plainest truths with their strange utterances, and find there great mysteries which ordinary people must leave unsolved.... [There are also the Ephrata Brethren.] They have a fertile tract of land, large common houses for single men, single women, and so on, and mills, breweries, and bakehouses erected by the sweat and blood of the self-denying adherents.... One hears nothing there about a righteousness apprehended by faith. If only they affect a righteousness of life by fasting, mortification, hard work, and a ridiculous manner of dress, turn over their goods and property to the common treasury, have themselves baptized by immersion in the community, and allow themselves, in their bodies and souls, to be governed for life by the chief taskmaster, then they are converts.... [Among the so-called Dunkards] little is required of converts beyond the memorization of a couple of verses in the Revelation of St. John pertaining to Babylon and the beast and the whore, the making of an outward sign of this, and submission to public immersion by them. Their lessons are suited to man's nature and are easy to learn. They need only to scoff at infant baptism, judge all others who do not agree with them (especially parsons and church people), and believe among other things that devils and the damned will be released again from hell. Conversion to the Mennonite religion is also very easy, convenient, and advantageous. It is probably one of the quietest groups.
>
> I must also lament over some in our own church, however, and confess that many have the illusion that they are already converted if they have performed the *opus operatum* of external worship ... although on other occasions they curse

enough and horrify heaven, get drunk, and engage in other worldly vanities. . . .[48]

The sharp criticism of the radical left gave Muhlenberg an opportunity to express a typically Pietist complaint about some of his fellow Lutherans. Otherwise it is manifest that what troubled Muhlenberg and his colleagues most was the rejection of infant baptism (or even of sacraments in general), the renunciation of an educated and salaried ministry, and the assumption that anybody could interpret the Scriptures correctly. It remains clear at all events that Lutheran identity was not merely an echo of ethnic or nationalist loyalty.

SIMILAR EVALUATIONS OF OTHER COMMUNIONS

Anglicans were representatives of a different nationality. The Swedish congregations on the Delaware discovered that they had something in common with neighboring Anglicans. Both the Church of Sweden and the Church of England were episcopal in their polity and liturgical in their practice of worship, and something of these similarities was preserved in the colonies. When in the eighteenth century the Anglican churches were often short of ministers they therefore requested Swedish Lutheran ministers who had a sufficient command of the English language to conduct services for them, and in return for this service the Society for the Propagation of the Gospel, centered in London, granted the Swedish ministers a stipend.[49] By the middle of the eighteenth century most of the descendants of Swedish-speaking colonists were no longer able to understand their mother tongue and demanded ministers who could speak English as well as their neighbors. When such ministers were sought unsuccessfully among the more recently arrived German Lutherans,[50] it was decided that henceforth their ministers should be "of the Lutheran or Episcopal

---

48. *Hallesche Nachrichten*, vol. 1, pp. 520–521.
49. E.g., Burr, *The Records of Holy Trinity*, pp. 142, 155, 257, 258, 264, 314, 319, 320, 323, 326, 327, 441–443; Acrelius, *A History of New Sweden*, pp. 214, 282, 285, 286, 294–296, 304, 305, 361, 362; T. E. Biörk, *The Planting of the Swedish Church in America, 1731*, tr. I. O. Nothstein (1943), pp. 26, 27; B. Elfoing, tr., "Extracts from the Journal of the Reverend Andreas Sandel, pastor in Philadelphia, 1702–1719," *Pennsylvania Magazine of History and Biography*, vol. 30, pp. 287–299, 445–452. *passim*.
50. Cf. Johnson, *Records of the Churches at Raccoon and Penn's Neck*, pp. 213, 219.

churches and hold their faith in the doctrine of the same."
This led eventually to the official transfer of the congregations
to the Protestant Episcopal Church.[51]

The German Lutherans were for the most part prevented by the barrier of language from having close relations
with Anglicans. In some Southern Colonies, especially in
Virginia, Lutherans were displeased with the limitations imposed on them by the Anglican establishments.[52] Peter
Muhlenberg, the oldest son of Henry Melchior Muhlenberg,
had to secure episcopal ordination in London in order to
minister effectively to the German Lutheran settlers in the
Shenandoah Valley of Virginia. Elsewhere relations were
friendly, notably in the case of clergymen located in the larger
towns and clergymen who were sympathetic to the Great Awakening. As a matter of fact, the cordiality which existed can
only be understood when it is remembered that this was long
before the Oxford Movement altered Anglicanism in a fundamental way. The evangelist George Whitefield may be taken
as a symbol of the ground on which Lutheran Pietists and
Anglican supporters of the Awakening could agree. On occasion Whitefield was invited to preach in Lutheran churches.
John Martin Boltzius, minister to the Salzburg Lutherans in
Georgia, wrote of Whitefield's visit to Savannah in 1740:

> He is a very warm person who is honorable toward God and
> man.... Whitefield preaches the gospel of Christ... with
> purity and great power. He does not speak from a written
> manuscript, as other preachers of the Anglican Church, but
> from the fullness of his heart.[53]

The next year, however, Boltzius wrote: "More and more his
manner and his unusual methods, of which I do not want to
single any out, displease me."[54] Friendliness led easily to
thoughts of absorbing the Lutherans of Pennsylvania and adjacent colonies into the Anglican Church. In 1764 the Anglican
missionary Thomas Barton wrote to England:

> The Germans in general are well affected to the Church of
> England and might easily be brought over to it. A law obliging

---

51. Nelson Rightmyer, "Swedish-English Relations in Northern Delaware,"
    Church History, vol. 15 (1946), pp. 101–115.
52. Spaeth, *Documentary History of the Luthern Ministerium*, pp. 92, 101, 102;
    The Journals of Henry Melchior Muhlenberg, vol. 2, pp. 374, 375.
53. Urlsperger, *Ausführliche Nachricht*, seventh continuation, pp. 369–371.
54. *Ibid.*, eighth continuation, pp. 726, 727.

them to give their children an English education... would
soon have this effect.[55]

In 1781, when the American Revolution confronted the
Anglicans with many problems on account of the ecclesiastical as well as political separation from the mother country,
William White, later to become the first bishop, discussed with
the Lutheran ministerium or synod "various matters which
could be profitable to friendly union," but the Lutherans
showed little interest. A proposal in 1797 that Lutherans and
Episcopalians in New York should unite likewise collapsed for
lack of interest.[56] Shortly after the close of the Revolution the
Anglicans, who desired to have bishops in their now independent Protestant Episcopal Church but seemed unable to get
consecration for American candidates in England, were assured through the intervention of John Adams that the Lutheran bishops in Demark were willing to administer episcopal
consecration to them. Resort to the Church of Demark became
unnecessary when consecration was finally secured from England.[57]

As in the case of the Anglicans, so in the case of the
Presbyterians, Lutheran Pietists expressed their basic sympathy with supporters of the Awakening like William Tennent
but criticized the arid traditionalism and inflexibility of the Old
Side Presbyterians.[58] Without attempting here to present a
detailed description of Lutheran attitudes toward Presbyterians, Quakers, Roman Catholics, Baptists, Methodists, and
others, it must suffice to state that the multiplicity of denominations in colonial America bewildered many people who had
not known such diversity in their homelands. "Each one claims
to possess the best medicine for the soul and the nearest road to
heaven."[59] The Rev. Christian Rabenhorst expressed the fairly

---

55. Perry, *Papers Relating to the History of the Church in Pennsylvania*, p. 367; cf.
   The Journals of Henry Melchior Muhlenberg, vol. 1, pp. 665, 666.
56. *The Journals of Henry Melchior Muhlenberg*, vol. 3, p. 427; Spaeth, *Documentary History of the Lutheran Ministerium*, p. 178; J. Nicum, *Geschichte des
   Evangelisch-Lutherischen Ministeriums vom Staate New York* (1888), pp. 76–
   107.
57. For the documentary evidence see Frank R. Manhart, "A Proposal to have
   the Lutheran Bishops of Denmark Consecrate Bishops for the Episcopal
   Churches in America," *The Lutheran Quarterly*, vol. 25 (1895), pp. 365–370;
   cf. Charles C. Tiffany, *A History of the Protestant Episcopal Church* (1895), pp.
   52, 351.
58. *The Journals of Henry Melchior Muhlenberg*, vol. 2, pp. 181, 571–574.
59. *Hallesche Nachrichten*, vol. 1, p. 504.

common conviction among Lutheran Pietists that there was a limit to openness and toleration when he wrote in 1752:

> In this dangerous land it is necessary that our auditors, adults and children, are carefully instructed in the wholesome teaching of our church concerning Baptism and the Lord's Supper, for both sacraments of the New Testament have many opponents here, some of whom despise them in theory and practice and others of whom attach a false meaning to them.[60]

At a meeting of Lutheran ministers in 1760 it was proposed that it would be helpful to the confused people if preachers would occasionally point out in an unpolemical way what the major denominational differences were. This would counteract any tendency toward theological and ecclesiastical indifferentism without becoming too exclusive and dogmatic.[61] It was on the whole characteristic of Pietists among the Lutherans to be less interested in party labels and other external distinctions than in conscious spiritual experience and "godly life."

PASTORAL MINISTRY AMONG LUTHERAN PIETISTS

Another area in which the character of Lutheran Pietism was made manifest was pastoral ministry. John Nicholas Kurtz wrote in his diary that pastoral visits among the people

> are necessary and useful here [in America], for they offer an opportunity to spread many a good word, one becomes more intimately acquainted with the condition of people's souls, one thereby awakens confidence in their hearts and minds, one secures materials for preaching and prayer, and one fulfills the duty of one's office and stops the mouths of blasphemers.[62]

Ministers labored under serious difficulties in realizing this goal of pastoral visitation. Except in the larger towns the people were widely scattered. Moreover, the shortage of ministers during the whole colonial period made it impossible for them to reach all the Lutherans. What the last of the Swedish clergymen, Nicholas Collin, wrote about his parish in New Jersey may be regarded as fairly typical.

---

60. Urlsperger, *Amerikanisches Ackerwerk Gottes*, vol. 1, p. 186.
61. Spaeth, *Documentary History of the Lutheran Ministerium*, p. 54.
62. *Hallesche Nachrichten*, vol. 1, p. 201.

The scattered location of the people causes a pastor unbeliev-
able toil; often he must travel four to five [twenty-five to thirty
English] miles in one day, especially during those times when
fevers, influenza, dysentery, and other illnesses rage, which
often cause great havoc in these districts. At times in the
summer one suffers terribly from a heat which kills both
people and animals, and frequently in the winter from pierc-
ing rain or a fearful cold, especially as one must travel on
horseback on miserable roads. Since many of the members are
sluggish and indifferent, or in some cases delinquent, they
must often be visited in their homes with admonitions and
reminders about going to church, about the baptism and training of their children, etc. Frequently it is necessary to ride in
great haste, day or night, a long distance to baptize a dying
child. . . . [63]

Pastoral visits were not social calls. "Whenever I entered
a home," Muhlenberg wrote when he was in New York, "I was
given an opportunity to speak of the condition of the individual's soul." On a visit to a woman he asked her if she was a child
of God. On another visit he asked a man to relate the story of
his life and the circumstances of his conversion.[64] Ministers
were always on the lookout for "evidences of the grace of God
working in people," "a true change of heart," or "traces of the
power of godliness."[65] On pastoral visits, as in preaching, the
aim was to produce a consciousness of sin, repentance, and
faith, culminating in a holy life. Moreover, as preaching was
often accompanied by tears of sorrow or joy (when J. N. Kurtz
preached on one occasion, for example, "many hearers wept,
and the floor was moistened as by a shower"),[66] it was not
uncommon for people who were visited in their homes to be
"deeply moved, sighing before God with tears."[67] Ministers
diligently recorded their experiences on pastoral visits. Many
individuals were troubled by their confessed want of faith or
inability to pray, and many others had scruples about sins (even
stealing an egg) committed in their youth.[68] Muhlenberg
sometimes made pastoral visits to admonish quarreling

---

63. Amandus Johnson, *The Journal and Biography of Nicholas Collin, 1746–1831*
(1936), p. 219.
64. *Hallesche Nachrichten*, vol. 2, pp. 21, 39, 40, 44.
65. *Ibid.*, vol. 2, pp. 24, 155, *et passim.*
66. Spaeth, *Documentary History of the Lutheran Ministerium*, p. 140.
67. *Hallesche Nachrichten*, vol. 1, p. 345; Urlsperger, *Ausfürliche Nachricht*,
ninth continuation, pp. 1017, 1032, 1036, 1040, 1063, etc.
68. *Ibid.*, tenth continuation, pp. 1859, 1862.

parishioners to be reconciled or to advise women on how best to treat unconverted husbands.[69] A not untypical entry of John Boltzius reads:

> Spent a pleasant hour with a man who has already been awakened several times but unfortunately relapsed into a state of security every time. Now more evidences of true repentance are to be observed in him than before.[70]

The greatest attention was given by Pietist Lutheran pastors to the sick and the dying. Parishioners were prepared for death more than for life. This is not to say that the health and well-being of the body were neglected or despised. On the contrary, in that day of primitive medical knowledge and skill clergymen often tried to diagnose illnesses and prescribe medication. This was especially true of Lutheran ministers who had some connection with Halle, where an apothecary had been established by August Hermann Francke about the year 1700. This was made possible through a gift of recipes of secret remedies, which were put up in powders, pills, and liquids, widely distributed in Europe, and then introduced into America by Lutheran ministers.[71] In the absence of physicians, especially able physicians, the ministers prescribed for all manner of illnesses: colds, fevers, pleurisy, catarrh, colic, epilepsy, smallpox, measles, malaria, rheumatism, constipation, delirium, gout, consumption, typhoid fever, hysteria, sea sickness, and many others. Some ministers also scrutinized urine, and others practiced phlebotomy. No doubt harm was sometimes done by these unschooled practitioners of medicine, but physicians of that time did not have a very good record either. But as Muhlenberg once put it, "Books and medicine belong to our concern and calling, the one for the soul and the other for the body."[72]

With their inherited anthropology which divided man into two parts, body and soul, it was the latter that was of major interest to colonial Lutheran ministers. Every sickness was interpreted as a visitation from God. The divine purpose was to punish sins, to make hard hearts repentant, or to warn people that they were facing eternity. Sick persons were urged

69. *Hallesche Nachrichten*, vol. 2, pp. 27, 46, 385.
70. Urlsperger, *Ausfürliche Nachricht*, first continuation, p. 300.
71. W. Germann, ed., *Heinrich Melchior Mühlenbergs Selbstbiographie, 1711– 1743* (1881), pp. 209–210.
72. *The Journals of Henry Melchior Muhlenberg*, vol. 3, p. 543.

to examine themselves spiritually while there was still time. To this end the pastors engaged the sick in conversation, read from the Scriptures, exhorted, prayed, and even sang hymns. Often they spent hours at a time at the bedside of the sick and dying. They directed their efforts to "awakening" the impenitent and comforting the penitent with the consolation of the Gospel. Muhlenberg, among others, wrote rather full accounts of many cases of pastoral ministry, almost a hundred of which were published as "remarkable examples."[73] Such faithful pastoral ministry was characteristic of Pietism. It was said that people were able to see "the differences in teaching, catechization, visitation of the sick, etc. between Halle pastors on the one hand and [antipietist] pastors . . . on the other."[74]

Many other testimonies to the character of Lutheran Pietism in colonial America could be discussed. Suffice it to mention that congregations generally felt an obligation to care for their own poor and needy. The orphans' home founded in Halle by August Hermann Francke became the model for a similar, if more modest, institution established in 1738 by the Salzburg Lutherans in Georgia, and homes of the same sort were contemplated in Pennsylvania. Patients in hospitals, residents of almshouses, and prisoners in jails were visited and ministered to according to their need. In 1750 the Lutheran ministerium appointed a guardian to protect the interests of children orphaned at sea on their voyage to America, and in 1764 the German Society of Pennsylvania was organized with a prominent Lutheran layman as its first president but with interdenominational membership to protect German newcomers from injustice and cruel treatment. Similar societies were organized in Charleston (1766), Baltimore (1783), and New York (1784). Meanwhile Lutherans were very active in providing for the education of children in parish schools and played some part, although not a major part, in the evangelization of American Indians and black slaves.

Pietism, as we have seen, involved the hearts as well as the heads of many Lutheran colonists. It was marked by activity, enterprise, and concern for fellowmen. It is doubtful whether Lutheranism would have been established in the New World as effectively under the influence of the Scholasticism which preceded or the Rationalism which followed Pietism.

---

73. See *Hallesche Nachrichten,* vol. 2, pp. 445–493, 501–520, 588–615, 637–648, 672–680, 722–730.
74. *The Journals of Henry Melchior Muhlenberg,* vol. 2, p. 424.

SELECTED BIBLIOGRAPHY–CHAPTER ONE

Beck, Walter H., *Lutheran Elementary Schools in the United States* (1939)

Bittinger, Lucy F., *German Religious Life in Colonial Times* (1906)

Eisenberg, William E., *The Lutheran Church in Virginia* (1967)

Evjen, John Oluf, *Scandinavian Immigrants in New York, 1630–1674* (1916)

Fortenbaugh, Robert, *Development of the Synodical Polity of the Lutheran Church in America to 1829* (1926)

Hammer, Carl, *Rhinelanders on the Yadkin: the Story of the Pennsylvania Germans in Rowan and Cabarrus [Counties in North Carolina]* (1943)

Jacobsson, Nils, *Svenskar och Indianer. Studier i svenskarnas insats i den tidigare protestantiska missionens historia* (1922)

Knittle, Walter A., *Early Eighteenth Century Palatine Emigration. A British Government Redemptioner Project* (1937)

Kreider, Harry J., *Lutheranism in Colonial New York* (1942)

Mackinnon, I. F., *Settlement and Churches in Nova Scotia, 1749–1779* (1930)

Maurer, Charles L., *Early Lutheran Education in Pennsylvania* (1932)

Nelson, E. Clifford, ed., *Lutherans in North America* (1974)

Pellens, Eberhard, *Die Beziehungen der Evangelisch-Lutherischen Kirchen von Hannover und Braunschweig zur ev.-luth. Kirche in North Carolina in der 2. Hälfte des 19. Jahrhunderts* (1961)

Schomerus, Rudolf, *Die verfassungrechtliche Entwicklung der lutherischen Kirche in Nordamerika von 1638 bis 1792* (1965)

Society of the Colonial Dames of America, *Church Music and Musical Life in Pennsylvania in the Eighteenth Century*, 2 vols. (1926)

Voigt, Gilbert P., *German and German-Swiss Element in South Carolina, 1732–1752* (1922)

Ward, Christopher, *The Dutch and Swedes on the Delaware* (1930)

Wentz, Abdel Ross, *A History of the Evangelical Lutheran Synod of Maryland* (1920)

———, *A Basic History of Lutheranism in America*. Revised edition (1955)

Wuorinen, John H., *The Finns on the Delaware, 1638–1655* (1938)

CHAPTER TWO

REFORMED PIETISM IN COLONIAL AMERICA

by James Tanis

REFORMED PIETISM ARRIVED IN NEW ENGLAND WITH THE PIL-
grims and in the Middle Colonies with the founding Dutch.
Both traditions were deeply indebted to the earliest Dutch
Pietists and both continued to be influenced by pietistic strains
in later seventeenth-century Dutch thought. Belatedly paral-
leling the course of Puritanism in England, Dutch Pietism
found its first and foremost early spokesman in Willem Teellinck (1579–1629). Prototypical of men in each succeeding
generation, Teellinck's Pietism was a popular piety for the
layman, a piety which tended at times toward both mysticism
and asceticism. Though sharing with Teellinck and his followers a common core of Puritan ethics, a more scholarly, more
systematically orthodox Pietism soon developed in the theology of Gysbertus Voetius (1589–1676), a younger friend of
Teellinck and later a professor at the University of Utrecht.

Among the guidebooks for young students at seventeenth-century Harvard was Voetius' *Exercitia et Bibliotheca
Studiosi Theologiae*, first published in Utrecht in 1644, revised there in 1651 and later reprinted in both Frankfurt
and Leipzig. The fat little volume reveals Voetius' great
twofold concern: true godliness and right learning. Among his
first writings had been a Dutch text entitled *The Test of the Power
of Godliness* (1628).[1] This also had been the thrust of his inau-

---

1. Gysbertus Voetius, *Proeve van de cracht der godtsalicheyt* (1628). The work
   was also written to refute attacks on the Synod of Dort and to defend its
   theological position.

gural oration on assuming the professorship at Utrecht: "Concerning Piety Conjoined with Knowledge." Nearer the end of his life, he developed this theme still further in his *Exercitia Pietatis* (1664), a work of nearly nine hundred pages designed for the use of the youth in the academies. Though none of his works was translated into English, his Latin texts were widely used by the Reformed throughout Europe and America. A century later, the German Lutheran bibliographer Johann Georg Walch still refers to the *Exercitia Pietatis* as the foremost such work produced among the Reformed.[2]

In his *Exercitia et Bibliotheca,* Voetius refers frequently to the eminently practical theology of Teellinck together with that of Jean Taffin (1528 or 1529–1602) and Godefridus Cornelisz Udemans (1581 or 1582–1649). The direct influence of Udemans, whose works were published only in Dutch and German, was largely confined to the Middle Colonies. On the other hand, the Huguenot Taffin, onetime chaplain to Willem the Silent, was widely read in the original French and, as well, in numerous Dutch and English translations. His *The Amendment of Life* (1595) and *Of the Marks of the Children of God* (1590) were not only translated into English but the latter work passed through at least five English editions. In introducing one of Teellinck's biblical expositions, Voetius rightly praises Taffin as a decisive forerunner. Voetius cites as well the crucial role of the English Puritans in the development of Dutch piety.

Numerous Puritan writings were translated into Dutch and widely read in the Middle Colonies. William Perkins (1558–1602) and William Ames (1576–1633) were the most influential of such figures in the early period. In 1607 Teellinck, on his return from studying with the Puritans in England, translated for his Dutch parishioners a little pious tract of Perkins which was still being reprinted in the 1650s. It was Perkins' pupil William Ames, however, who was most responsible for introducing the best of Perkins' thought to the Netherlands. Ames, who exchanged English restraint for Dutch liberty in 1610, early came into contact with Teellinck, Udemans, and Voetius. Teellinck was himself associated with circles of English Puritan piety. He married an English wife, maintained close contacts with friends in the British Isles, and his son Maximilian pastored the English congregation in Vlissingen. There was a deepening of these relationships at the Synod of Dort. Udemans was vice-president of the Synod; Voetius, then

---

2. Johan Georg Walch, *Bibliotheca theologica selecta* (1758), vol. 2, p. 1177.

only 29, was active in making preparations for the Synod and in generating the theological productions of the back rooms; and Ames served as theological counsel to the president of the Synod. For Ames and Voetius particularly, these roles confirmed the clear distinctions which they held between dogmatic truths and practical instructions for the new life.

An enticing yet ultimately unanswerable question comes to the fore: What were the sources, what were the impulses which gave rise to Continental Pietism and how do they illuminate colonial American thought? Albrecht Ritschl's suggestions of medieval precedents are borne out by extensive quotations from St. Bernard, Thomas à Kempis, and other medieval authors found in the writings of the Pietists. The influence of the Brothers of the Common Life has often been singled out. The pervasiveness of this movment has been seen in areas where Reformed Pietism later found congenial ground. Calvin came under their tutelage when studying in Paris. One finds no totally satisfactory bridge, however, from medieval Catholicism to colonial Reformed Pietism. As one searches the early years of the Reformed tradition itself, one finds but few evidences of convincing substance. Zwingli's strong emphasis on a transcendent doctrine of the Spirit is one critical evidence, Calvin's highly developed doctrine of the Holy Spirit another. Yet, though these Reformers are occasionally cited in colonial American writings, their doctrine of the Spirit is not directly connected to the Spirit-filled theology of Reformed Pietism at its high-water marks.

THE ENIGMATIC ROLE OF THE HUGUENOTS

One problem in uncovering the sources of American Reformed Pietism lies in the enigmatic role of the Huguenots. No other large group of colonial Americans obscured its traces by cultural assimilation as effectively as did the French Protestant emigrés. This was equally true of their experience in England and the Netherlands and only slightly less true in Germany. Evidences of their previous acculturation in each of these areas can be traced in the Colonies as well. Who thinks of Priscilla Mullins (daughter of Guillaume Molines) as a Huguenot maiden?—even though her "Speak for yourself, John" may seem more French than English. Even John Alden was probably of Huguenot ancestry. This openness to assimilation sharply contrasted with the attitudes of the English. The Pilgrim congregation at Scrooby so feared the loss of its English identity that it sailed to America. The Huguenots by contrast frequently adopted Dutch or English patronymics. For example, "du Bois" became "van den Bosch" or "Forest," as "Molines" became "Mullins." Nonetheless, from Mayflower passengers to the Faneuils and the Reveres, Huguenots played an important role in establishing the Reformed traditions of New England. The French pulpit Bible given to the French Church in Boston by Queen Anne remains as a lone relic of a vibrant tradition.

The French Protestants who came to America exhibited little of the rigid piety of New England's Puritans and little of the precision of the most extreme Middle Colony Dutch Pietists. Huguenot piety, nonetheless, was so deeply imbedded in their faith that they had been willing to give up family, friends, property, and homeland to follow their Reformed beliefs. On analysis, their piety differed most from their Puritan and precisionistic neighbors in the quality of its openness, rather than in its basic structure, for all owed much to the theology of the Frenchman, Jean Calvin. It was no mark or lack of personal commitment or devotion, therefore, that the Huguenots held moderation and freedom as basic marks of the Protestant way. These premises, lessons learned from experience rather than from dogmatic theology, marked the Huguenot experience in each of the early colonies. Their idea of moderation at times conflicted with the more stringent teachings of the Puritans and the Pietists. In New England, Cotton Mather objected to the Huguenot celebration of Christmas; a little later, George Whitefield objected to the levity which the French had introduced into Charleston, South Carolina. French piety clearly differed from English and Dutch piety; hence it is unfortunate that the theological evidences for it in colonial America have left little trace.

Some glimpses do remain in the writings of Andrew Le Mercier (1692–1763), "pastor of the French Church at Boston," who argued well for "the rules of benignity, honesty and moderation." Pious moderation for him, however, was no detached affair of indifference. In his *A Treatise Against Detraction*, Le Mercier wrote: "It is the misfortune of the Roman Catholics to have zeal without knowledge; it is the sin of most Protestants to have knowledge without zeal; we shall be virtuous and happy if we have both together."[3] In this work Le

---

3. Andrew Le Mercier, *A Treatise Against Detraction* (1733), p. iv.

Mercier proceeds from "knowledge" and "zeal" to matters of conscience. He follows Puritan and Pietist models in his extensive section on "cases of conscience." Le Mercier's position is that of his Puritan and Pietist contemporaries when noting to the reader: "As to the work itself, some people will perhaps blame me for being too particular, and mentioning trifling things, but I must beg of them to consider that to write treatises of morality in a general way only, and to write nothing, is almost the same thing. If we pretend to convince and convert men, we must do it by entering as it were into their very heart, and making them sensible of all their mistakes, and as they are very various, and numerous in order to examine and confute them, we are obliged to be very particular. . . ." Le Mercier had a mastery of the French language but soon his English translations further proved his ability with words. In 1747, toward the end of his ministry, he published a lengthy poem entitled *The Christian Rapture* in which the piety of his beliefs is revealed:

> *Unhappy me! How longs my Soul to go,*
> *Whence rise these Springs, and where these waters flow.*
> *Tir'd with the Chace, and scorch'd with noon-tide Beams,*
> *So pants the weary Stag for cooling Streams.*
> *While in this Vale of Miseries we live,*
> *We all these Pleasures insincere receive.*
> *Heav'n is the Place,—Thou, God, who'rt all in all,*
> *O take us up and burn this worthless Ball.* [4]

As post-Revolutionary American piety took shape, the Huguenot contribution continued to be a great influence. John Jay, grandson of Pierre Jay who fled France after the revocation of the Edict of Nantes, was to be the founder of the American Bible Society. He was supported in the work by other French-Americans. Yet, like Priscilla Mullins Alden, John Jay is not thought of as a Huguenot but as "an American" and probably as one of English descent. As one studies the outlines of American Pietism, one senses that, in spite of the vagaries of the sources, theological structures were as importantly influenced by French Huguenots as were cultural, economic, and political structures. Dutch Reformed New York was heavily Huguenot from the beginning. Peter Stuyvesant's wife was the daughter of a Huguenot pastor, and director Pieter Minuit was himself a Huguenot and an elder in the New Amsterdam Church. (Minuit, however, had come to New

---

4. Andrew Le Mercier, *The Christian Rapture* (1747), p. 4.

Netherlands from exile in Germany, where he had been a deacon in the Reformed Church of Wesel.) Well into the eighteenth century, services in the Dutch Reformed churches were conducted in both French and Dutch. The call to Cornelius van Santvoort (1686–1752), the Pietist pastor of Staten Island from 1718 to 1742, expressly stated that he was to preach both in Dutch and French. Among the foremost New York pastors was Gualtherus Du Bois (1671–1751), domine of the Collegiate Church from 1699 to 1751. One of the many Dutch Reformed of Huguenot ancestry, Du Bois' father, Pieter Du Bois, had been a student at the University of Utrecht under Voetius. In young Gualtherus the Pietism of Voetius was still evident, though mixed with the spirit of moderation more typically Huguenot. The Classis of Amsterdam wrote to the consistory of New York about their new pastor: "We feel assured that this man, with God's blessing, will do good service in your church. Since he is an enemy to all partiality, we have good hope that he may prove a blessed instrument to calm all your disturbances both by precept and example."[5] Repeated testimony bore out this sentiment over a ministry of fifty-two years. The modified Voetian Pietism of Du Bois was later to contrast starkly with the radical Pietism of the fiery Raritan pastor, Theodorus Jacobus Frelinghuysen (1692–1747 or 1748). Nonetheless, Du Bois joined Frelinghuysen to grace the platform when George Whitefield held his New York revival.

Before moving on to a closer examination of Dutch Reformed Pietism in the Colonies, a proper understanding of both that background and that of the Huguenots requires a more detailed appraisal of the groundwork laid by Jean Taffin. Taffin was not a Pietist; rather, he was a pious Huguenot. Parallels abound between his thought and that of the English Puritans. He laid great stress on the need for a new morality, though this was not linked to the Pietist emphasis on rebirth. Taffin's Reformed faith was born with the Reformed movement itself; his family was numbered among the first refugees; one brother at least met death in the struggle. A devout Calvinist, he differed with many other orthodox Calvinists who felt that religious peace was not in accord with Reformed theology. He had been a moderating influence at the Synod of

---

5. *Ecclesiastical Records [of the] State of New York* (1901–1916), p. 1304. Volumes 1 through 6 are paged continuously so that volume numbers are not given in the citations. Volume 7 is the index volume. Hereafter cited as *EcR*.

Emden in 1571, and in 1573 he went into the service of Willem of Orange as chaplain. In 1578 he helped establish the brief religious peace between the Protestants and Roman Catholics. Again he served as moderator in the 1590s when pastoring in Amsterdam during the early years of accusation against Jacobus Arminius. Though an exponent of Calvin's doctrine of predestination, Taffin, like Calvin, did not place it among the major dogmas of the Reformed Church. In spite of subtle theological differences, Taffin and Arminius remained friends until Taffin's death, and Taffin's body reposed at the home of Arminius until burial.

Taffin's piety is best understood in the context of his tortured life. Piety which is tempered in the flames has a power of its own. What might seem simply moralistic when heard from a bystander is spiritual food when poured out of the heart of a refugee. *The Marks of a Child of God and Consolations in their Afflictions to the Faithful in the Netherlands* was written when Taffin was fleeing from Antwerp and heading north to Emden. In addition to the five editions in English, this work appeared in at least seven French editions, eleven in Dutch, and one in Latin. In it, Taffin treats of the inner witness of the Holy Spirit and the peace of assurance, though he does not tie it to regeneration as do the later Pietists. In spite of personal moral imperatives which greatly influenced the earliest Pietists, he also stressed the importance of communal prayer-life, church attendance, and the use of the sacraments—matters of less concern to many Pietists.

Taffin's last major work, *A tract on the Amendment of Life*, appeared in French, Dutch, English, Latin, and German. It dealt extensively with Christian conversion in the light of the impending Kingdom of God. Heinrich Heppe called it Taffin's major work and described Taffin himself as "the earliest exponent of 'the practice of piety' or Pietism in the Netherlands."[6] Heppe, however, most often interpreted Pietism as a corrective to Orthodoxy (or what is now being called Orthodoxism). Taffin shows that Pietism's basic thrusts grew up together with Orthodoxism. As dogmatics and systematics were first fully developed in the seventeenth century, so too, full-blown Pietist edificatory literature was first developed

---

6. Heinrich Heppe, *Geschichte des Pietismus und der Mystik in der Reformirten Kirche, namentlich der Niederlande* (1879), pp. 95–97.

fully in the seventeenth century. Yet not only the roots but clear shoots of both dogmatic and pietistic literature had appeared in the sixteenth century—of the latter, none was more central, none more influential than Taffin's *A tract on the Amendment of Life*. In addition, even his personal motto could have been adopted as that of the emerging Pietist movement: "A dieu ta vie, en Dieu ta fin."

LABADISM AND REFORMED PIETISM

Reformed Pietism in seventeenth-century America was basically a movement within the established churches. A significant though relatively obscure exception was the Labadist movement. Taking its direction from Jean de Labadie (1610–1674), Labadism was a mixture of various extreme Pietist views. A Jesuit until nearly thirty, de Labadie embraced the Reformed church as he moved steadily, if slowly, away from the ecclesiology of both Rome and Geneva. From Switzerland and France he passed on to the Netherlands where he shared for a time in the Pietist fellowship directed by Voetius. Moving beyond the church-related conventicles of early Pietism, he sought to establish separate communities for his followers. His radical ideas were seen as a threat to the church, and candidates for the ministry in parts of the Netherlands and Germany were specifically required to abjure the doctrines of de Labadie. Even in Pietist communities where Teellinck and Udemans were commended as providing "a necessary rule of life," the teachings of de Labadie were feared and scorned. In 1679 and 1680 two young Labadists set out for the New World where they aroused the same fears that were felt so strongly in the Old World. Jaspar Danckaerts, one of the two, left behind a revealing journal of his impressions, detailing life in the Colonies. Danckaerts and his companion, Peter Sluyter, sailed to America in search of a site for a new Labadist community. On their exploratory trip they sought to attract as little attention as possible, so they engaged in no public evangelistic ventures but sought to win converts by their personal witness and testimony to individual acquaintances. They attended services in the towns they visited so as not to attract attention by their absence, though they were generally very critical of what they observed. Danckaerts descriptively summarized worship in Boston: "There was no more devotion than in other churches, and even less than at New York; no respect, no reverence; in a word, nothing but the name of independents; and that was all."[7]

New Englanders in general they discounted, having found them as unreliable as any Colonists "although they wished to pass for more upright persons." Of all the ministers they visited in colonial America, only the aged John Eliot of Roxbury, "Apostle to the Indians," received their praise. Since Eliot spoke neither French nor Dutch and the Labadists but little English, in conversation they largely fell back to Latin. Eliot spoke of his work with the Indians, and the Labadists of their new movement. At their departure Eliot praised God that a reformation had begun in Holland, for he deplored the decline of the church in New England, and especially in Boston. Danckaerts and Sluyter departed with a copy of Eliot's Indian Bible and they left with him the Latin edition of de Labadie's *Declaratio*.[8]

Wherever they travelled, from Massachusetts to Maryland, they sought quietly to win converts, to spread their Pietist doctrines, and to circulate their numerous publications. Jean de Labadie was a prolific author and his works were frequently translated. Danckaerts mentions his own efforts to supply on-the-spot translations of requested texts. By the time the two Labadist emissaries returned to the home community in Friesland, they had mapped out land for a community in Maryland and had left behind in New York a small group of converts. In 1683 Danckaerts and Sluyter returned, secured the land, and established a community of about one hundred Labadists. The community maintained its strength for twenty years, at which time the mother church in Friesland "was scattered." The American colony survived for another twenty years, until after the death of Sluyter in 1722. The radical Pietism of the Labadist teachers distorted many of the doctrines of Reformed Pietism beyond recognition. Yet its presence in the Colonies made orthodox Reformed Pietists suspect, as Pietist practices disturbed more conservative and more staid churchmen.

---

7. Jasper Danckaerts, *Journal of a Voyage to New York and a Tour in Several of the American Colonies in 1679–80,* tr. and ed. Henry C. Murphy (1867), p. 380. Issued as vol. 1 of the *Memoirs* of the Long Island Historical Society. Reissued in slightly revised form in Scribner's series "Original Narratives of Early American History" (1913).

8. *Ibid.,* p. 383.

AMERICAN ROOTS OF DUTCH REFORMED PIETISM

The roots of Reformed Pietism within the church itself were laid by the New Jersey pastor, Guiliam Bartholf (1656–1726). Bartholf (or Bertholf) had come to North Jersey as a cooper at a time when there were no settled Dutch pastors west of the Hudson River. In addition to his coopering, he undertook the tasks of lay-reader and of comforter-of-the-sick. Bartholf had been reared in the Dutch village of Sluis, near Middleburg on the southern border of the Netherlands. Middleburg in Zeeland was the heartland of Reformed Pietism. Here Willem Teellinck had preached the awakening doctrines of self-examination and regeneration. Here he had mediated the Puritanism of William Perkins. Sluis had also been the parish of Voetius' Utrecht colleague, Jodocus van Lodenstein (1620–1677) and later of his beloved pupil Jacobus Koelman (1630–1695). The ardent Pietist zeal of Koelman was communicated to his young parishioner, Guiliam Bartholf. First directly through Bartholf and later indirectly through Theodorus Jacobus Frelinghuysen, Koelman was to have the greatest influence of any single Dutch Pietist on the developing points of issue among the Dutch Reformed Pietists in the Colonies. Indeed, Koelman himself almost accepted a call to New Netherlands in 1682, a move which would have considerably altered this chapter.

Koelman, like Teellinck, translated many English and Scottish Puritan works for the Dutch readers. These works were as avidly read in the Middle Colonies as were the original English texts in New England. Indeed, through Koelman's translations printed in the Netherlands, two works by Thomas Hooker passed from Connecticut to the Netherlands and back across the sea into the hands of the Dutch settlers in Jersey. Danckaerts mentions encountering one of Koelman's translations in New York. Koelman actually veered for a time toward Labadism, so advanced were his views against unregenerated churchmen, as well as against ceremonialism and formalism in worship. He early became disillusioned with de Labadie, however, and wrote two of the more cogent works against the Labadist position. Nonetheless he continued to run into difficulties with the civil and ecclesiastical authorities in the Netherlands, first because of his position against state interference in matters of the church and later because of his Pietist preaching and writing.

Bartholf, brought up in this Koelmanist atmosphere, had imbibed the full spirit of it. On the urging of the pastorless congregations of Hackensack and Acquackanock (now Passaic), Bartholf returned to Sluis for examination and ordination. The formalistic pastors in New York sought to block his ordination, but Sluis was in the Classis of Walcheren in the Synod of South Holland. The Dutch churches in the Middle Colonies were under the jurisdiction of the Classis of Amsterdam in the Synod of North Holland. The Classis of Walcheren ignored the urging of both the Classis of Amsterdam and the Synod of North Holland not to ordain Bartholf. By the time he returned to the Colonies in 1694, Bartholf has been ordained, thus becoming the first settled Reformed pastor in New Jersey. At the time of his ordination, the records of the Classis of Amsterdam referred to him not only as a Koelmanist but also as a Labadist.[9] The former he was; the latter he was not. Bartholf was reported as claiming in true Koelmanist fashion that he had turned to the Classis of Walcheren for ordination because half of the Classis of Amsterdam were unregenerated men.[10] His spirit of cooperation in New Netherlands, however, voided such earlier remarks. In seeking to stop his ordination, one New York pastor had referred to Bartholf as a "schismatic" of a "very restless spirit" and stated further that "by such persons much disquiet would be brewed, and much trouble caused to the churches and especially to the ministers." In due course, Bartholf won from his adversaries their confidence and respect as "a very honorable and pious man." Bartholf was zealous and untiring in his labors, travelling about, preaching, performing the sacraments, and even establishing new congregations. His contemporaries wrote of him: "His piety was deep, his judgement and tact superior, his grasp of the Bible clear and strong, his preaching reverent and spiritual, his intercourse with people cordial and magnetic."[11] Obviously Bartholf's activities kept him so occupied in New Jersey that he had no time to spread his Pietist views in New York. Bartholf's warm and mild-tempered ways no doubt also helped overcome

---

9. *EcR*, p. 1100.
10. *EcR*, p. 1107.
11. Edwin T. Corwin, *A Manual of the Reformed Church in America . . . 1628–1902*, 4th ed., rev. and enl. (1902), p. 318.

the problems in his initial relationships with those New York pastors who had objected to his circuit-riding activities.

Bartholf's call had read, "To preach on water and on land and by the way." This he did with vigor, though one man could scarcely cover the whole of East Jersey, and so the congregations along the Raritan sought a settled pastor who could minister to them as Bartholf ministered to the congregations of the Passaic River Valley. Finally in 1720 young Domine Frelinghuysen arrived from the Old World to develop even more intensely the Reformed Pietism first planted by Bartholf.

Meanwhile, New York had attracted two young men of strong Pietist leanings: Bernhardus Freeman (1662–1743) and Cornelius van Santvoort. Freeman first pastored in Schenectady and later on Long Island, and van Santvoort first on Staten Island and later in Schenectady. Both their appointments, as too the later appointment of Frelinghuysen, were the direct result of the efforts of two ardent Dutch Pietists, one a pastor and the other an Amsterdam merchant, Willem Bancker. Bancker's American brother, a layman in the Albany church, was urging the appointment of pastors for the vacant colonial churches. Freeman, though a tailor and formally untutored, was an astute young man. Through the intervention of Willem Bancker, he sought ordination at the hands of the relatively independent Classis of Lingen (then on the eastern-most border of the Netherlands, though now a part of Germany).[12] The ordination and appointment of Freeman were irregular if not illegal; hence, his relationships with the other New York clergy were clouded at the outset. Unfortunately, they continued to be a problem until his death in 1743.

In his early years in Schenectady Freeman ministered to the Indians, learning the Mohawk language and translating religious materials for the use of the Indians. In addition to his Mohawk publications, he wrote *The Mirror of Self-Knowledge,* a book of moral precepts, and *The Scale of God's Grace,* a volume

---

12. *EcR,* p. 1341. At the time of Freeman's ordination the Classis of Lingen was not "outside the Netherlands" as usually stated, nor was the town of Lingen in Westphalia. Graafschap (or county) Lingen was a part of the Netherlands under Prince Willem III until it passed to King Friedrich I of Prussia in 1702. Though the Classis was not a part of any Dutch Synod, it was in close contact with the Dutch Synods, particularly those of North and South Holland where it was regularly represented. Whether Freeman, ordained by the Classis of Lingen, was a resident of that county or of Westphalia, as usually stated, is not presently known.

of thirty Pietist sermons.[13] Though Pietist in content, the sermons were actually dull and would scarcely have given rise to the evangelistic fervor which marked true awakening-preaching.

Van Santvoort, in contrast to Freeman, was a well-bred, highly educated pastor whose ministry was marked by as great an absence of conflict as Freeman's was marked by conflict. Van Santvoort had studied at the University of Leiden where the dominant influence was Johannes à Marck (1655–1731), the leader of one of the two major schools of Voetian theology. À Marck was neither preacher nor enthusiast but his dogmatic and exegetical works supplied the theological structure underlying much Pietist thought. In addition to his theological influence on van Santvoort, à Marck remained his personal friend throughout his life.

Van Santvoort had also been a close personal friend of Mathias Gargon (1661–1728), a pastor of the Walloon church and rector of the Latin school at Vlissingen, near Middleburg in Zeeland. Gargon was a person of literary ability, an historian as well as a theologian. Among his major theological writings was a popular two-volume work entitled *The Crucified and Glorified Christ* presented in thirty-one edifying addresses.[14] Gargon also prepared Dutch translations of numerous works, including one of the commentaries of the German-born Pietist Friedrich Adolph Lampe (1683–1729). Van Santvoort had assisted Gargon in his literary endeavors and had himself mastered the art of translation. During his Staten Island ministry he prepared a one-volume synopsis in Dutch of à Marck's massive three-volume Latin commentary on the book of Revelation. Initially the effort was undertaken in response to the apocalyptical interest of New York's governor William Burnet (1688–1729). Burnet had published a book in 1724 on portions of the book of Daniel, a copy of which he had presented to van Santvoort.[15]

Van Santvoort was called to Staten Island to minister to both the Dutch and the French, and he regularly held morning

---

13. Bernardus Freeman, *De spiegel der self-kennis* (1720) and *De weegschaale der genade Gods* (1721).

14. Mathias Gargon, *De gekruiste en verheerlijkte Christus* (1719, 2d ed. 1725).

15. William Burnet, *An Essay on Scripture-Prophecy, Wherein it is Endeavoured to Explain the Three Periods Contain'd in the XII Chapter of the Prophet Daniel. With some Arguments to make it Probable, That the First of the Periods did Expire in the Year 1715* (1724). The capitalization of the title follows the original. Van Santvoort's synopsis of à Marck was entitled *Ontleding der*

services in Dutch and afternoon services in French. He also spoke fluent English, so that he was frequently called upon to fill pulpits in other churches. In 1742 he left Staten Island for Schenectady where he ministered until his death ten years later. For van Santvoort as for Freeman, evidence for the depth of their Pietist commitment is best discovered in the books they wrote to defend their colleague Frelinghuysen.

Frelinghuysen had come to New Netherlands shortly after van Santvoort. Soon their common interests laid the foundation for their continuing friendship. Their personalities were so different, however, that they were not as close friends as Freeman and Frelinghuysen. (Indeed it was through Freeman that Frelinghuysen met Eva, a young girl of Huguenot parentage, who was to become his wife.) Freeman and Frelinghuysen also shared an antipathy to the New York clergy, particularly Domine Henricus Boel (1692–1754) and his cohorts, Boel was the epitome of all the formalistic, legalistic, and antipietistic modes of the time. In the hands of the congenial Bartholf, Pietist doctrine had been difficult for Boel to oppose. And furthermore, as noted above, Boel's senior pastor, Gualtherus Du Bois, was of a mildly Pietist nature, having absorbed much of the Voetian position from his father. Frelinghuysen, on the other hand, was a man of a much more radical Pietism than Du Bois and of a much more irascible personality than Bartholf.

Frelinghuysen was born a Westphalian German, the son of a German Reformed pastor. He grew up in the Pietist atmosphere created in the Lower Rhine by the followers of Voetius and the Utrecht pastor Jodocus van Lodenstein. The Reformed churches of the Lower Rhine—as those of Lingen and East Friesland to the north—were deeply influenced by the theology of the Dutch Reformed. Though they abjured the teachings of de Labadie, the Westphalian Reformed responded to the waves of influence which came from both the Dutch Pietists at the University of Utrecht and also those Pietist voices from the German Reformed of the University of Herborn. Most articulate of these latter forces had been Wilhelm Dieterici who in 1679 published the first major German Reformed Pietist work, *The True Internal and External Christ.*[16]

Openbaringe van Johannes; Getrokken uit de Uitlegginge over de Openbaringe, en eenige andere Werken van Johannes à Marck (1736).

16. Wilhelm Dieterici, *Der wahre inwendige und auszwendige Christ* (1679–1682).

Though accused of Labadism, Dieterici refuted the charge; and his work, reprinted again in 1739, carried into the eighteenth century the strongest voices of Puritanism, of Voetian Pietism and the proto-Pietism of Jean Taffin. Building on these youthful influences, Frelinghuysen studied first in Hamm where the Pietist feelings of the village pastor encouraged Frelinghuysen to move on to the University of Lingen, then firmly in the hands of Voetian Pietists. Arriving in Lingen in 1711, just a dozen years after Freeman's ordination there, Frelinghuysen was soon to work through the theology of à Marck. Lingen's professor of theology, Johannes Wilhelmius (1671–1754), had prepared a Dutch translation of à Marck's *Medulla,* a weighty precis of his massive *Compendium.* So popular was this work that it was still being reprinted in Dutch a century later. The last Latin editions were published in Philadelphia in 1824 and 1825 respectively. Here in Lingen Frelinghuysen first mastered the Dutch language as well as à Marck's Dutch theology. He was also introduced to the basic structures of Dutch Pietist preaching, though these were to be much more finely honed in his first pastorate.

East Friesland, the field of Frelinghuysen's brief but deeply formative fourteen months of ministry, had long been marked by the influences of Dutch Reformed Pietism, even though it was technically a German province. Frelinghuysen's parish was just outside Emden, the commerical capital of the area. Here Jacobus Koelman had spread his teachings during visits early in the 1680s. In the years following, ardent Pietists assumed major pastorates. Many of these East Frisians took their places at the head of the most radical churchly Pietists. Works by men like Eduard Meiners (1691–1752) and, particularly, Johan Verschuir (1680–1737) were to be among the most avidly read volumes in New Jersey's Pietist congregations. East Frisian Pietism, rather than the milder forms of Voetian Pietism, was decidedly the theology brought by Frelinghuysen to the New World. It was akin to Koelmanism. In fact, Koelman's followers wrote the catechism with which they supplemented the older standards. Each still defended his position on the basis of the Heidelberg Catechism. In the Netherlands the Heidelberger was used together with the Belgic Confession, and in East Friesland with the Emden Catechism. These earlier standards lent themselves to both Puritan and Pietist explication while, at the same time, the opposing forces of social moderation and theological formalism built on the same standards. Indeed it was the breadth of the Reformed position as set forth in the Heidelberg Catechism that made possible the co-existence of such diverse attitudes within one denomination.

Frelinghuysen left two principal legacies from which to reconstruct his thought and its influence. The first is a series of twenty-two Dutch sermons printed during his lifetime, five of which appeared in 1731 in an English translation by his lay assistant, Hendrik Visscher (1697–1779). The second is a series of publications about him, written in part by friends and in part by foes. To these should be added the references to him found in the writings of such contemporaries as Gilbert Tennent, Jonathan Edwards, and George Whitefield. Since none of these sources provides a structured theological position, for this one must turn to those writings which he most heartily commended. Chief among them is Verschuir's *Truth in the Inmost Parts, or Experimental Divinity*.[17] The latter part of this title became not only the general title by which the book became known but also the name for that type of religion deemed essential for salvation. It was the theology of rebirth, refined by the rigors of precisionistic, puritanical moralism. Proponents of this theology were dubbed *de fijnen* ("the sanctimonians").

The theology of *de fijnen* was shaped not only by Voetian piety but also by a theological mixture created by men like Johannes d'Outrein (1662–1722). D'Outrein was one of a group of young theologians who sought to combine the more vibrant typological exegesis of Johannes Coccejus (1603–1669) with the Pietism of Voetius. He was a prolific writer and his works were popular among the New World Dutch as well as among those in the Old World. Frequently used for the instruction of children as well as adults was his *Short Sketch of Divine Truths*,[18] a work which went through at least fifteen editions and was even translated into Malay for use on the mission field. Particularly prized by both Coccejans and Voetians was d'Outrein's oft-reprinted commentary on the

---

17. Johan Verschuir, *Waarheit in het binnenste, of Bevindelyke godtgeleertheit* (1736). This work passed through at least four eighteenth-century editions, and was still being reprinted in the nineteenth and twentieth centuries.

18. Johannes d'Outrein, *Korte schets der goddelijke waarheden* (1687).

Heidelberg Catechism. All editions after the first included the annotations of the German Reformed Pietist, Fredrich Adolph Lampe.[19]

In addition to those theologians already mentioned, the most influential Dutch Pietists still to be noted are Herman Witsius (1636–1708), the Brakels, father Theodorus (1608–1669) and son Willem (1635–1711), and Abraham Hellenbroek (1658–1731).

The early works of Witsius were treasured by Pietists of all persuasions. Koelman praised especially his *Controversy of the Lord with his Vineyard*, a "very edifying, persuasive and soul-stirring tract."[20] Frelinghuysen also praised "the renowned Witsius" and particularly his *Controversy*. Indeed, most points of Frelinghuysen's theology, as one deduces it from his sermons, are consistently paralleled in the imaginative earlier Dutch works of Witsius. Witsius had early imbibed the thought of Teellinck and Udemans; these teachings were later reinforced by studies under Voetius and his colleagues. But as d'Outrein had moved away from the pedantic preaching of the Coccejans to embrace the piety of the Voetians, so Witsius had moved away from the Scholasticism of Voetius' theology to embrace the convenant theology of Coccejus. D'Outrein enthusiastically recommended Witsius' *Controversy*.

The Brakels contributed mightily to colonial Pietism; probably more tattered copies of their works survive than of any others. Theodorus à Brakel gave Reformed Pietism some of its most beloved writings, chief among them *The Steps of the Spiritual Life*.[21] The work has scarcely been out of print since it first appeared in 1670 and no known count has been made of its editions. German translations appeared in Switzerland and in Germany. The elder Brakel's writings contributed a strong mystical tone to the Pietist approach of his followers. The precisionism of others is spiritualized in *The Steps of the Spiritual Life*. Though further popularized by his son Willem, this spiritual precisionism emerges full-blown in the writings of Lampe, most importantly in the *Milk of Truth,* where Lampe

---

19. Johannes d'Outrein, *Het gouden Kleinoot van de leere der waarheid die naar de godsaligheid is; vervattet in den Heidelbergschen Catechismus* (1719).
20. Herman Witsius, *Twist des Heeren met syn wÿngaert* (1669). The *Twist* passed through at least seven editions in its first century and was still reprinted in 1892.
21. Theodorus à Brakel, *De trappen des geestelijcke levens* (1670).

presents a detailed structuring of the order of salvation.[22]

Willem à Brakel prepared an elaborate three-volume theology, *The Reasonable Service of God,* frequently referred to by Frelinghuysen.[23] It was the most extensive Dutch Pietist theology and the first of a long series of theologies to be written in vernacular Dutch rather than scholastic Latin. The "eminent practicality" of Brakel was praised. In the volume Brakel sought through knowledge of one's self to restate Calvin's doctrine of the knowledge of God. The work stressed all the major points of Pietist doctrine from rebirth to moral precisionism. In the course of his writing Willem à Brakel refuted Arminianism, Labadism, and other "errorists." Yet in spite of refutations, the wide-ranging arguments of his mystically tinged position cracked many of the doors his followers were to open.

Of all Reformed Pietist writings, Abraham Hellenbroek's works received the broadest distribution in eighteenth-century American English-language editions. Hellenbroek's early years of ministry had been undistinguished; but, in his seventh year, "it pleased the All-Sufficient One to reveal himself to [Hellenbroek's] soul as a reconciling God."[24] He became the Voetian preacher of his time. In spite of a scattering of the usual antiquarianisms of his time, his preaching was simple and had great popular appeal. Typical of his style, his theology, and his filial piety was his *General Lamentation in the Streets of Rotterdam Over the Very Venerable, God-fearing and Learned Man, Wilhelmus à Brakel.*[25] His first work to appear in

22. Friedrich Adolph Lampe, *Milch der Wahrheit* (1718). According to Heppe (*Geschichte der Evangelischen Kirche von Cleve-Mark und der Provinz Westphalen* [1867], pp. 237–238) not only was this work widely distributed alongside the Heidelberg Catechism but in some places it even replaced it to some degree. This work is placed in a larger theological context in the author's "The Heidelberg Catechism in the Hands of the Calvinistic Pietists," pp. 154–161 in the *Reformed Review* (vol. 24, 1971).

23. Willem à Brakel, *Redelijke godsdienst* (1700). The work passed through at least twenty eighteenth-century editions and, as well, has been reprinted since.

24. *Biographisch Woordenboek van Protestantsche Godgeleerden in Nederland* (1907–1943), vol. 3, pp. 639–640. The quotation is from Domine Alardus Tiele's funeral sermon for Hellenbroek.

25. Abraham Hellenbroek, *Algemeene Rouw-klagt in de straaten v. Rotterdam* (1711). This was certainly one of the most frequently reprinted of funeral sermons. The author has a seventh edition of 1737, as well as a "new edition" printed in 1854.

English was *A Sermon . . . from Canticles Chap. II, Ver. 15. Take us the Foxes, the little Foxes that spoil the Vines: for our Vines have tender Grapes.* The text was actually excerpted from a homiletical commentary and not originally designed as a sermon. Its interest lies not only in the probing content of Hellenbroek's work but in the fact that the text was translated by Hendrik Visscher (Frelinghuysen's lay associate) and published in Boston in 1742 (at the height of the Great Awakening) appended to a treatise by Gilbert Tennent. Hellenbroek's treatise was a strong attack on unregenerate corrupting clergy and, as such, fit well into the judgmental position of the Voetian Pietists—a position embraced and expounded most eloquently in Tennent's *The Danger of an Unconverted Ministry*.

Most popular of all Hellenbroek's works was his catechism. The Dutch text passed through innumerable editions and was still in use in the twentieth century. The first American edition appeared in New York in 1765. Like his *Sermon* the catechism was translated by a layman, Petrus Lowe, "a builder by trade." Entitled *Specimen of Divine Truths,* the work sought to change catechizing from a mental exercise to a spiritual exercise. "Be not content that your Ears only have heard, but endeavor after a hearty Experience of those Things. . . . And above all, it is thy Duty to shew, that those Truths you have made Profession of, do not consist in Words but in Power, and that, in an Holy Conversation, for as much as it is a Doctrine leading to Godliness."[26] Hellenbroek's *Specimen* passed through at least nine editions before the end of the eighteenth century and numerous editions in the nineteenth century. Its ardent piety had a lasting influence on the Reformed church both early in the widely used Dutch editions and after 1765 in the English-language editions. A number of the editions had been printed in New Brunswick, the seat of Dutch Reformed Pietism, by the publisher Abraham Blauvelt. Among additional works proposed by Blauvelt was a five-volume English translation of Willem à Brakel's *Reasonable Service,* but this work never appeared.

These then were the chief Pietist voices heard among the Dutch of the Middle Colonies. Their influence came through their books and through the pious laymen, who, as well as the domines, had accepted their teachings. The great contribution of the Reformed Pietists of the Middle Colonies

---

26. Abraham Hellenbroek, *Specimen of Divine Truths* (1765), p. viii.

was not to be found in their originality—evidence of which is singularly lacking—but in their adding to the American stream that theology which marked the Pietists of the Netherlands and of northwestern Germany. Unfortunately, the thousands of Dutch Pietist sermons preached in the Middle Colonies have largely disappeared, except for the printed sermons of Freeman and Frelinghuysen.[27] It is to these sermons, then, that one must turn to reconstruct the outlines of Dutch Reformed Pietism in the Middle Colonies.

"Experience" was the key to this theology, and both Freeman and Frelinghuysen laid great stress on the explication of "experimental divinity." The experience to be achieved was "rebirth"—the thrust of Frelinghuysen's awakening theology. "Consider your insignificance and unworthiness" and "learn to know your guilt." On the positive side, Frelinghuysen added that true religion "is righteousness, it is peace and it is joy in the Holy Ghost." Without the excruciating awareness of insignificance and guilt there could be no convicting of the sinner; without the affirmations of righteousness, peace, and joy, there could be no conversion. Rebirth was equally dependent upon both. It was, as well, the ultimate test. "The Spirit of God, which always knows best," asserted Frelinghuysen, "terms all unconverted as natural men, who are outside of God's fellowship, not united with Christ and not sanctified by his Spirit, godless and sinners, even though they lead modest and proper lives, yes, are even outwardly religious. All those who are still in a natural or unregenerate state are, without exception, godless and sinners."[28] It was a personal, not a corporate concern. As à Marck had written, "by regeneration . . . one is not to understand the renewing of the whole world . . . but of the change in the individual believer."[29]

The teachings of insignificance and guilt were easier to arouse in those who were economically and socially insignificant; this was certainly the plight of many of the Jersey Dutch settlers. On the other hand, the most forceful opposition to Frelinghuysen's preaching came from the well-established Dutch settlers—those farmers, lawyers, and clergy alike, who were described by Frelinghuysen as "in the sieve of Satan."[30]

27. These sermons are listed in detail in the author's *Dutch Calvinistic Pietism* (1967), pp. 182–185.
28. T. J. Frelinghuysen, *Een trouwhertig vertoog* (1729), p. 50.
29. Johannes à Marck, *Kort opstel der christene got-geleertheit* (1770), p. 582.
30. T. J. Frelinghuysen, *Versamelinge van eenige keur-texten* (ca. 1748), p. 582.

This meshed well with Frelinghuysen's observation that "the largest portion of the faithful have been poor and of little account in the world"[31] In those areas where Frelinghuysen's ministry first took root, poverty was often coupled with that enforced isolation created by the endless drudgery of eking a living out of the woods or out of the fields. In the towns this was paralleled by the weariness of long hours filled with servile labor. The resultant emotional starvation created a vacuum waiting to be filled by joy in the Holy Ghost and other rapturous episodes which might mark the way. Violent rebirth and all of its preparatory ferment helped restore sorely needed hope and provided revitalized nerve for the future.

Typical of Dutch Reformed converts was Hendrik Visscher, the poor son of an otherwise unknown Raritan riverside farmer. He was Frelinghuysen's right arm through the years of religious turmoil created by their radical Pietism. Visscher distinguished himself as lay preacher and as translator of the writings of both Frelinghuysen and earlier Dutch Pietists. Typical of younger pastors was Henricus Goetschius (John Henry), whom Frelinghuysen helped ordain in 1741. All three figures—Visscher, Goetschius, and Frelinghuysen—also demonstrate the interrelatedness of the various Reformed churches both on the Continent and in the Middle Colonies. As noted before, Frelinghuysen had been born a Westphalian German, the son of a German Reformed pastor; Visscher's father had been an emigrant from the German Palatinate; and Goetschius' father had been ordained a Swiss Reformed pastor. Yet it was among the Dutch Reformed "in this so guilty land, this wilderness of America" that all three were awakening leaders.

One of the inherent contradictions of that radical Pietism which remained within the Reformed church was the heightened effectual power of individual clergymen, while at the same time these men, joined by numerous laymen, violently attacked many who filled the ministerial offices. Already Lodenstein had preached and written extensively against "the present-day lack of spirituality among the pastors" and "the corrupted ways of the so-called spiritual profession." Koelman, in a lengthy preface to a Puritan tract designed to awaken the clergy, had also assailed the multitudinous faults of "the faithless, the hireling, and the gluttonous" clergy. To this

---

31. T. J. Frelinghuysen, *Drie predicatien* (1721), p. 10.

he added a prayer that God either "convert them or thrust them out." From the time of Frelinghuysen's arrival in New York, he had preached against the "unfaithful watchmen." At the ordination of Goetschius, Frelinghuysen provided theological underpinnings by quoting one of his Dutch professors: "As there always has been, and will be, a conflict between the seed of the woman and the seed of the serpent, so does the enmity discover itself principally in unsanctified ministers. . . ."[32] Such unnerving doctrines, coupled with the dearth of any kind of ordained clergy for many of the widely scattered settlements, increased the anxieties of the Colonists and made them more receptive to Pietism's call.

The preachers of rebirth confronted a homiletical problem; or, conversely phrased, a new method of preaching was a major factor in the revivals which were to mark this phase of Pietism's upsurge. It was a technique which Frelinghuysen had brought with him from East Friesland, one of the areas where the method had been extensively developed. Hendrik Visscher had described it as "drawing one matter out of another, thereby discovering the state and condition of his auditors to themselves."[33] Its origins lay, in part, in the philosophy of Petrus Ramus (1515–1572), and its perfecting owed much to many Puritans and numerous Pietists along the way. Using it himself as a carefully honed tool, Frelinghuysen instructed Gilbert Tennent in the method; soon it became a mark of awakening preaching in the Middle Colonies. Even George Whitefield claimed to have further developed his own preaching style as a result of its effectiveness. The old formal structures which Frelinghuysen had learned in school were a constant critique to him, but he was a man guided rather than bound by critiques. This kept his preaching from degenerating into ranting, even when his morning text was "Blow the trumpet in Zion."

For the Reformed Pietists, both on the Continent and in the Colonies, the central Reformed doctrines of election and certainty of faith were cast in a new form.[34] Pietists had long

---

32. T. J. Frelinghuysen, *Sermons* (1856), p. 373.
33. T. J. Frelinghuysen, *A Clear Demonstration of a Righteous and Ungodly Man, in their Frame, Way and End* (1731), p. v. The preface as well as the translation was by Hendrik Visscher.
34. For a fuller discussion of this pivotal shift, see the author's *Dutch Calvinistic Pietism*, particularly pp. 119–124.

struggled with these doctrines, particularly the classical statements of predestination. Though the churchly Pietists by and large assented to the decrees of the Synod of Dort, they continually struggled with the seeming contradictions implied in telling people on the one hand that they must be born again, but then telling them that the decisions regarding their ultimate salvation had already been made by God himself. One wonders what Frelinghuysen meant by affirming the decrees of Dort, while simultaneously remarking to his congregation that "in the day of judgment God will not deal with men according to election and reprobation but according to their obedience and devoutness." While decrying Arminianism, these rebirth theologians, like Arminius himself, fell to using the cogent arguments of a high doctrine of grace to restore some logic to a fundamental dilemma. At the same time, lacking the astute theological perception of Arminius, they found no solution other than vigorously denying the theological implications of their own experiential divinity. Concerning certainty of faith Frelinghuysen declared, "Is this your ground, that you firmly hold and do not doubt, but that Christ is your Saviour, and that you shall be saved . . . but know that this ground is false. . . . Oh! to the state of grace appertaineth somewhat else."[35] Assurance comes rather from the fruits of faith. So new uncertainties confronted the comfortable, and new opportunities were afforded those who had thought themselves lost among reprobates. Frelinghuysen's "summons to repentance" was clearly a break with Reformed theology according to Dort, in spite of his intention.

Another of Pietism's breaks with Reformed traditionalism involved the prominent role assigned to lay leaders. The most outstanding example was Hendrik Visscher, a mechanic by trade. Visscher's work as translator of Pietist texts has been mentioned, but his work in the church included not only translations of the works of others but zealous sermons of his own. His lay preaching at first encountered opposition from the conservatives but his theological competence gradually proved the day. From the outset he defended Frelinghuysen's Pietism; already in 1723 he wrote a defense entitled *A Warning to Lovers of the Truth*.[36] He was with the clergy at the

---

35. T. J. Frelinghuysen, *A Clear Demonstration*, p. 84.
36. This work is mentioned in the *Klagte* ("the complaint of some members of the Low Dutch Reformed Church, living on the Raritan"), pp. 33 and 59. It appears to have circulated only in manuscript and not in printed form.

forefront of the movement for the independence of the church from the Classis of Amsterdam and for forty years attended every major meeting moving in that direction. In a day when Pietism and Politics spoke the same language, he worked for national independence from England as well as ecclesiastical independence from the Netherlands. A delegate to the New Jersey Provincial Congress of 1775, he was elected its president, having forcibly set out the grievances of the Colonies. At the time of the Revolution, he was fully supported by his pastor, Johannes Leydt (1718–1783). Leydt's patriotic preaching inflamed his parishioners to a fever pitch of enthusiasm. A firm patriot himself, Leydt worked for independence and roused young men to join the army for freedom.

Another mark of these colonial Pietists was their zeal for higher education. Leydt, who had been Frelinghuysen's protégé, and ultimately his successor in New Brunswick, had been prominent among those laboring to establish Queen's College (now Rutgers). It was realized that ecclesiastical independence depended on the ability of the American church to train its own clergy. On the petitions for the establishment of this college, Leydt's name was invariably accompanied by Visscher's. An early sign of success was apparent in the royal charter of 1766; a further advance came in the provincial charter of 1770. As a newly created board sought a professor of theology, it turned to the University of Utrecht, asking for "a man of tried piety . . . and able to lecture upon Marckii *Medulla Theologiae Christianae.*"[37] Thus the writings of à Marck—so influential fifty years earlier in the thought of the elder Frelinghuysen, van Santvoort, and others—were now to continue to give form to the theological thought of future young candidates for the American ministry. Again and again colonial Pietism refutes the mid-twentieth-century stereotype of Pietism, for it was activistic, political, social, and educational.

Pietism also embraced a responsive group of learned women. The remarkable Anna Maria van Schuurman, Pietist leader of mid-seventeenth-century Netherlands, was paralleled in eighteenth-century America by the zealous Jufvrouw Dinah Hardenbergh (1725–1807). Born in Amsterdam, baptized Dinah van Bergh, she was the daughter of a wealthy East Indian merchant and was raised in the midst of fashion and refinement. At a young age she became "the subject of divine

37. *EcR*, p. 4274.

grace" and was "remarkable for her attainments in Godliness and unusual exercises of faith."[38] Later she met John Freling-huysen (1727–1754), son of Theodorus Jacobus, while he was studying at the University of Utrecht. He proposed marriage to Dinah but was at first opposed by her parents. Indeed, only after the greatest soul-searching, coupled with a sense of God's direct intervention, did she herself consent. A manuscript of twenty-four finely written pages survives in which Dinah describes wrestling with herself on the spiritual aspects of marriage with John. After marriage, they sailed to the Colonies and settled in Raritan (present-day Somerville), New Jersey. Not long after she gave birth to their second child, John was taken ill and died. Meanwhile, Jacob Rutsen Hardenbergh (1738–1790) had come to Raritan from Kingston, New York, to study with John Frelinghuysen. The latter's sudden death led to Hardenbergh's early ordination in 1758, at which time he succeeded his mentor in the pastorate. The widow Dinah was preparing to return to the Netherlands when Hardenbergh, thirteen years her junior, persuaded her to stay in Raritan and marry him. Both husband and wife were forceful leaders in the church, sharing their piety and learning. They supported each other in the work of the ministry. Between her husband's morning and afternoon services, Dinah would gather with the women to further expound the texts and elaborate on matters of doctrine. The Hardenberghs were also involved in the political life of the colony and became strong supporters of the Revolution. They were close personal friends of George and Martha Washington, whose headquarters were near their home and who regularly attended their church. So ardent and valuable a patriot was Hardenbergh that the British placed a hundred pounds on his head; the domine slept with a musket beside him during much of the War. The British burned his church to the ground.

Like Leydt in New Brunswick, the Hardenberghs worked hard for the creation of the College; Hardenbergh himself became its first president. During all of this time, Dinah continued her unique ministry alongside her husband. She maintained an extensive correspondence, seeking "to be an Example to others in Doctrine, Rebuking, Direction, Comforting and Sanctification." In her early years she kept a

---

38. Richard H. Steele, *Historical Discourse . . . of the First Reformed Dutch Church, New-Brunswick, N.J.* (1867), p. 80.

spiritual diary, parts of which have been preserved. No document better details the ruminations of the Pietist spirit: "It was the beginning of the year 1747. Midnight had passed; and I continued in earnest wrestlings, and drew near with a renewed dedication of myself to God, yielding myself unreservedly to Him and His ways and His service and His people. It was my inmost desire that I might receive larger measures of the renewing grace of the Holy Ghost—that my old and sinful nature might be more fully broken, the depravity of my heart subdued and the precious image of the Lord Jesus be more fully transferred to and impressed upon me, and all things become more and more new."[39] Later in life her counsel was sought by domines young and old. She wrote to them humbly, yet as a bishop in her concern for the church—and for the College which was to her an extension of the church. She was a pastor to pastors. In the thought of Jufvrouw Hardenbergh christological development became more and more pronounced and sacramental devotion played a larger part than in earlier American Reformed Pietism. The change was only one of emphasis, yet it marked a gradually changing thrust from the bolder doctrines of the Spirit to the sweeter doctrines of the Lord Jesus. In this her thought was to find closer affinities with Lutheran Pietism and to mirror the emerging piety of the Wesleys. It also anticipated developments which were to take place in the Dutch Reformed Church in the nineteenth century.

THRUSTS OF GERMAN REFORMED PIETISM

German Pietism in the Colonies was initially propagated through separatistic and sectarian groups, many of which espoused extreme modes of radical Pietism. Churchly Pietists among German Reformed Colonists were at first frequently absorbed into Dutch Reformed communions, as was the case with Hendrik Visscher and, even in Europe, with Frelinghuysen himself. The thrusts of Dutch Pietism had been a major source of German Reformed Pietism so that Pietists easily moved from one national group to the other.

Until the eighteenth century there was only a small

---

39. *Sketch, and a Translation from the Dutch, of the Diary of Dinah van Bergh* (1869), p. 63. Page numbers are taken from a typescript copy of the original manuscript. This translation is interlarded with the editor's evaluations.

number of German immigrants to the Middle Colonies, and these were frequently sectarians who had accepted William Penn's invitation to find refuge and freedom in Pennsylvania. Following the devastation of much of the Palatinate by French forces in the last quarter of the seventeenth century, suffering and starvation created new masses of Protestant refugees. Switzerland and the Netherlands absorbed thousands of poverty-stricken Germans, and thousands more fled to England. Queen Anne soon found thirty thousand Palatines looking for freedom in the British Isles or for passage to the Queen's American Colonies. These so-called Palatines soon included in their number large groups of Germans from surrounding parts of the Rhine country and even many German-speaking Swiss. It was estimated that half of these immigrants were either Reformed or nominally so, yet when the first of the Palatines arrived there was not a single German Reformed congregation in any of the Colonies.

Though the formal beginning of the German Reformed Church in America was the establishment of the Philadelphia Church in 1727 under Georg Michael Weiss (1700–1761), a few individual ministers had migrated to the Colonies during the preceding two decades. Eminent among them was the Swiss Pietist Samuel Güldin (1660–1745). Güldin (later Americanized to Guldin) came from the region of Bern, where he helped to establish the Pietist movement. In 1690, before his pietistic development, Guldin had visited and studied briefly in the Netherlands. Dutch Pietist influences had early been disseminated in Switzerland by German translations of Udemans' writings. The first of these was Udemans' exposition of the *Song of Solomon*, translated by Hans Heinrich Meyer and published in 1667 together with a treatise on prayer by his son (Hans) Jacob Meyer (d. 1710). The Meyers were pastors in turn of the Reformed parish in Winterthur. Numerous additional translations of Udeman's works by Jacob Meyer were published during the second half of the seventeenth century, accompanied by his own prolific Pietist writings. Guldin and his associates, however, claimed that their Pietist movement was inspired directly by God and was not the result of human influences. Nonetheless, they steeped themselves in Pietist literature and travelled broadly to extend their experiences, including a stay at the University in Halle. From 1692 to 1698 the movement in Bern flourished. In 1696 Guldin received an appointment to the promising and distinguished position of assistant at the Minster in Bern. Conventicles were established, literature published and distributed, and a large following attended the enthusiastic services of the popular young Pietists. Among the published works was a German translation of Brakel's *Steps of the Spiritual Life*.[40] Counteraction by the Orthodox followed. After long proceedings against the Pietists, Guldin and his friends were deposed. For a brief time he was allowed to return to the pastorate but his passionate preaching led to his dismissal again and his banishment as well. He published a defense of his position and a refutation of the charges against him. After a period in North Germany, he left for Pennsylvania, arriving in 1710.

Guldin lived for the next twenty-five years at Roxbury on the Wissahickon. There he came to know many of the radical Pietists who had preceded him to Pennsylvania. He served many of the settlers as pastor, though there was no established Reformed congregation at that time. In his first years as a churchly Pietist, Guldin had found himself in a dilemma. As an early biographer of Guldin expressed it: "[Churchly Pietists] stood between two fires, and were likely to be singed by both. Though their sole purpose was to revive the ancient churches in accordance with the spirit of the gospel, they were charged with heresy, and often unjustly persecuted and condemned. On the other hand, fanatics accused them of lacking courage to express their convictions."[41] Not having been able to accomplish his original purpose nor having succumbed to the lure of the radicals, Guldin became an independent Reformed minister.

One of the charges against Guldin in Switzerland had been his association in religious societies with members of other denominations. A tendency to disregard denominational labels and to emphasize unity of faith on such matters as rebirth was a mark of Pietists generally. (This was also one of the charges against Frelinghuysen, as it was to be against George Whitefield.) This longing for unity in faith was a mark of Guldin's continuing ministry, though his was no party posi-

40. Theodorus à Brakel, *Die Staffel dess Geistlichen Lebens,* Bern (1689). This translation passed through numerous editions and was reissued in Frankfurt am Main in 1733. Extensive prefatory material by the Pietist pastor of Offenbach, Wilhelm Conrad Baumann, accompanied the Frankfurt editions.

41. Joseph Henry Dubbs, "Samuel Guldin, Pietist and Pioneer" in *Reformed Quarterly Review,* vol. 39 (1892), p. 312.

tion. Another of his biographers described him as "no doubt a saint, but the treatment he had suffered from the organized Church had queered his outlook on life."[42] He at first participated in Count Zinzendorf's so-called Pennsylvania Synods, but in 1743 he published a critical analysis of the Synods and their misguided efforts to establish "A Congregation of God in the Spirit."

In Guldin's *Non-partisan Testimonial* he agreed that it was deplorable that so many different denominations existed. "But who is Christian?" he asked. There are in every denomination, he declared, those who are "neither true believers nor members of Christ's." Bringing them together under one roof would have no positive effect on their souls but would simply honor man—not God. It would in fact create a hindrance. "We must seek to become true Christians and united with Christ before we seek only to be united with one another."[43] If churchmen are truly united to Christ, denominational unity will automatically follow. He expressed the great need for 'earnestness, awakening and penitence" but devoted a large section to constructive judgment. This he entitled: "Balm in Gilead on the wounds and injuries of all religious sects and parties in Pennsylvania and in the whole of Christendom." In this section he appealed for a rising above sectarianism. Sects bring judging and divisions and more sects. He described his own position in stating, "If one does not wish to create sects, even as the Separatists made none nor wished to, and as the Pietists also made none" then one should follow their example.[44] Clearly, in Guldin's mind separatism and Pietism found their virtue in their emphasis on first principles rather than "on the doctrines which divide." The two groups were not synonymous, for Pietism according to Guldin existed in varying degrees in all denominations. His doctrine of separatism made it possible for him to function as a free spirit in Pennsylvania when no German [or Swiss] Reformed Church existed there, and yet to move equally freely among the Reformed when churches were established there. In addition to his pastoral ministrations, he also preached occasionally at the Re-

42. William J. Hinke, *Ministers of the German Reformed Congregations,* Lancaster (1951), p. 265.
43. Samuel Guldin, *Unpartheyisches Zeugnüss,* Germantown (1743), pp. 8–11. Guldin's booklet was reprinted with an altered title in 1744 (see Hinke, p. 263).
44. *Ibid.,* p. 35.

formed church in Germantown. His activities were welcomed by many but deprecated by others, and particularly by the orthodox pastor Johann Philip Boehm (1683–1749), who shared in the oversight and direction of the growing Reformed churches in the Middle Colonies. "Old Guldi" (as he was affectionately known in later years) fought hard for individual rebirth and against preoccupation with denominational growth. "No one can be born for another; everyone must go through the narrow gate for himself, one after another."[45]

Like many pastors who shared his Pietist judgments, Guldin spoke out clearly against unconverted clergy: "For those who have eyes to see it is an unspeakable calamity and affliction to see who Christ has for servants of his Word on earth."[46] He quoted Gilbert Tennent for support; and, at this early stage of James Davenport's ministry, Guldin defended Davenport's attacks on the unrepentant clergy as well. Though more mildly, the Boston Huguenot pastor, Andrew Le Mercier, had also pointed to the necessity of judgment, even as Paul had spoken against Peter (Galatians 2:11–12). "Now if he did not spare an Apostle when he went astray, how much less regard ought we to have to ordinary teachers or rather to false teachers, to walk in their wrong steps."[47] Clerical pride and denominational pride were alike anathema to Guldin. In concluding one passage on the subject, he summed up in parody his feelings: "Great is Diana of Ephesus, *or,* This is the best congregation in Pennsylvania."[48]

Another early Reformed Pietist pastor was Johann Peter Müller (later changed to Peter Miller), the son of a Reformed minister in the Palatinate. Miller (1709–1796) came to Pennsylvania in 1730, where he was ordained by Gilbert Tennent and two other Presbyterians. He had already received his education at the University of Heidelberg.

Through the earlier ordination and the continuing ministry of Boehm, the German Reformed in Pennsylvania had come under the oversight of the Classis of Amsterdam. The methodical and exacting Boehm had sought to persuade Miller to be ordained with Classis permission at the hands of the Dutch Reformed pastors in New York, as he had been. To this Miller replied that "he would like to know who had given

45. *Ibid.*, p. 52.
46. *Ibid.*, p. 110.
47. Le Mercier, pp. 190–191.
48. Guldin, p. 50.

authority to the Classis of Amsterdam to rule over the Church in [America]."[49] Miller was among the most learned and personable of the young pastors. He embarked upon an active ministry to the German Reformed of Philadelphia, Germantown, and still other congregations before settling in the Tulpehocken region and ministering in the upper end of the Conestoga Valley. One of his congregations was located just a little more than a mile from the radical Pietist community at Ephrata. There he came intimately to know Conrad Beissel (1691–1768), the Palatine leader of the community and a convert from the Reformed faith. Five years after his ordination Miller, attracted to the Ephrata doctrines, left the Reformed church, sought the solitary mystical life of a monk, and entered the Ephrata Cloister in November of 1735. A visiting Swedish pastor characterized him later as of "friendly face and friendly manners, on which account strangers always get introduced to him and seek his society. He is open-hearted toward those to whom he takes a liking, and is modest and genial."[50] Despite his membership in the Ephrata fellowship, however, he occasionally preached his Pietist message to the members of his old congregation as well—and this in the face of strong opposition from Boehm who had long worked against Miller and his doctrines. After Beissel's death Miller became the head of the order at Ephrata, a role which he filled until his own death at the age of eighty-six. In addition to his other services, Miller had been active in the publication of many of the Pietist works issued by the Ephrata press, a factor of great importance for the Germans in the Colonies.

Numerous other evidences exist of strong Pietist voices during the early years of the German Reformed of the Middle Colonies; but the most decisive period was marked by the arrival in 1746 of Michael Schlatter (1718–1790), another Swiss-born Pietist. He was born and raised in St Gall where Christof Stähelin (1665–1727) was his pastor. Stähelin, father of St Gall Pietism, had widely influenced Swiss Pietism through the publication of his brief catechism, *The Conjugal Yes,* based on the *Halleluja* of Theodor UnderEyck (1635–1693), and on his own extensive Pietist exposition of the Heidelberg Catechism.[51] Like Voetius, he was a mixture of orthodoxy and piety,

---

49. Hinke, p. 301.
50. Israel Acrelius, *A History of New Sweden,* Philadelphia (1874), p. 374.
51. Christof Stähelin, *Catechetischer Hausz-Schatz, oder Erklärung des Heidelbergischen Catechismi durch Frag und Antwort,* Basel (1724). The edition used for this work was the third, Basel (1737).

characterized as working "exactly in the manner of the Dutch Pietists."[52] Young Schlatter—restless, energetic, and adventuresome—early imbibed this churchly Pietism and went to the Netherlands to pursue further studies. After much travelling and a short settled period in a vicariate back in Switzerland, he returned to the Netherlands where he offered himself for active service in Pennsylvania. The Reverend Fathers "profoundly rejoiced that they had encountered so worthy and capable a subject."[53]

The Dutch church, and the German as well, had been alarmed by the activities of Zinzendorf and the dissension within the Pennsylvania churches which had been fomented by his attempts to create "A Congregation of God in the Spirit." Boehm had written a "Faithful letter of Warning" against the Moravians in 1742. This had been followed the next year by Guldin's book, as well as tracts by Presbyterians Tennent and Samuel Finley.[54] All of these works were indebted to the writings of the articulate Dutch spokesman against the Moravians, Amsterdam's Domine Gerardus Kulenkamp (1700–1775). Boehm's book was in substantial measure a translation and paraphrase of much of Kulenkamp.[55] (Schlatter came to know Kulenkamp very well and later named one of his sons in his honor.) The Dutch realized that the action of Zinzendorf in Pennsylvania had to be counteracted if the authority of the Classis was to be maintained. Various solutions for handling the problem were considered. The loosely scattered German Reformed congregations were served by only four regular pastors and various "independent Reformed ministers." With a supposed thirty thousand Reformed settlers in and around

52. Paul Wernle, *Der schweizerische Protestantismus im XVIII Jahrhundert,* Tübingen (1923), vol. 1, p. 136. Also useful for studying Swiss Pietism is Wilhelm Hadorn's *Geschichte des Pietismus in den Schweizerischen Reformierten Kirchen,* Konstanz (1902). This volume is filled with useful details but is lacking in perspective and analysis. Of use also is Ernst Stähelin's "Schweizer Theologen im Dienste der Reformierten Kirche in den Ver-einigten Staaten" in *Schweizerische Theologische Zeitschrift,* vol. 36 (1919), pp. 196–238.
53. Hinke, p. 38.
54. Gilbert Tennent, *Some Account of the Principles of the Moravians ... being an Appendix to a Treatise on The Necessity of Holding Fast the Truth,* Boston (1743). A London edition appeared in the same year. Samuel Finley, *Satan Strip'd of his Angelick Robe ... With an Application to the Moravians,* Philadelphia (1743).
55. Johann Philips Boehm, *Getreuer Warnungs Brief ... vor denen Leuthen, welche unter dem Nahmen von Herrn-Huther bekandt seyn,* Philadelphia (1742). This was followed the next year by a leaflet on the same subject.

Pennsylvania in 1743, the Classis of Amsterdam, on behalf of the Synods of North and South Holland, inquired of the Presbyterian Synod of Philadelphia about the possibility of union as a means of facing its problem. As this solution failed to materialize, attempts were made to find a pastor who could minister to the German colonists and communicate regularly with the church in the Netherlands. Deputies from the Synods of North and South Holland met with Schlatter. They felt "that through him they could organize the scattered Pennsylvanians."[56]

Schlatter then visited Domine Wilhelmius, formerly Frelinghuysen's Pietist teacher at Lingen but now in the last years of a lengthy pastorate in Rotterdam. Wilhelmius, as a member of the Classis of Rotterdam, was a member of the Synod of South Holland. He had long taken a particular interest in the Pennsylvania German Reformed, thousands of whom had passed through Rotterdam on their way from the Palatinate. Others, however, had departed for the New World through other ports and after having made other contacts. Some of the confusion among the Pennsylvania Reformed clergy resulted from the fact that lines of relationship to the Netherlands' classical and synodical bodies were not clear. This was not surprising in that most of the pastors had come from Germany or Switzerland and had ecclesiastical ties of various sorts with their home churches as well. When the Synods of both North and South Holland joined together in Schlatter's appointment, they were attempting to clarify the situation. Unfortunately, the Dutch Reformed Church in the Middle Colonies was under the direct authority of the Classis of Amsterdam. This posed difficulties for internal cooperation among the various colonial Reformed churches. These problems were never resolved or even adequately confronted.

By the summer of 1747, the end of Schlatter's first year in America, he had visited, surveyed, and analyzed the forty-six weak and disparate congregations. He had gained the confidence of the other four active pastors and was able to organize an annual Coetus for mutual examination, strengthening, and planning by the pastors and their elders. On the other hand, his attempt to create a joint Coetus with the Dutch churches was frustrated by their differing relationships with the Netherlands' mother bodies. He brought peace to

---

56. Hinke, p. 38.

churches long in dissent and restored to the Reformed fold the Pietist pastor Jacob Lischy (1719–1780), who had gone over to the Moravians. (His visits with Peter Miller, however, achieved no similar success.) In the first three years of ministry he was scarcely ever out of the saddle, travelling a distance of more than eight thousand miles. He preached well over six hundred times, though none of these sermons is known to remain to give explicit content to his message. The wide-flung work of the churches, however, was beyond the means of even so active and dedicated a man to fulfill. With the encouragement of the Coetus, he returned to Europe in 1751 to raise money for the support of the churches and their schools, and also to find six new recruits for the ministry in Pennsylvania. While there he published an extensive account of the churches, their problems, opportunities, and needs. It appeared first in Dutch, then in German and in English. Though convinced that God would "have mercy upon Zion in Pennsylvania," he was pleased beyond all expectation with the success which followed on his travels. An endowment of at least twelve thousand pounds was gathered, the income of which helped support the work of the churches of the Coetus for decades. In addition to his financial success, six young students from the University of Herborn accompanied him back to Philadelphia. Among these recruits was Philip Wilhelm Otterbein, later to become leader of the Pietist wing of the German Reformed Coetus.

Schlatter himself became increasingly involved in defining and meeting the educational needs of the children. "Yes, if the children are not instructed in the principles of divine worship, according to their capacity, will not their external devotional exercises, if any shall yet remain among them, degenerate into superstition, and," he added, "will they not, in time, corrupted into an entire neglect of God's service, in this respect also become like the blind heathen among whom they dwell?"[57] Through the response to the English edition of his tract and the efforts of sympathetic churchmen, a reported sum of twenty thousand pounds was raised—one thousand from King George himself. Trustees were chosen who constituted "A Society for Propagating Knowledge of God among the Germans." They appointed Schlatter as inspector of the free schools which they were to support. Many of the German

---

57. Henry Harbaugh, *The Life of Rev. Michael Schlatter,* Philadelphia (1857). The tract is printed on pp. 87–123.

settlers, however, angered by some of the deprecating remarks made by those raising the money and also fearing Anglicizing tendencies in the project, turned against the effort and became suspicious of Schlatter. These suspicions, aggravated by old antagonisms of a group of Philadelphia malcontents, were fanned again into open hostility by one of Schlatter's young recruits whom he had sternly censured for excessive drinking. The young man also sought to establish himself with the dissidents in Philadelphia rather than going to his assigned country parish. Schlatter handled these matters in an overly expeditious and too independent way. His actions were misunderstood by the Dutch church; and after much agony, he was relieved of his position. In 1757 he served as a chaplain to the German troops among the English forces which overthrew the French in Canada. Though he preached occasionally thereafter, and frequently served as pastor to numerous inquiring Colonists, he never again served as regular pastor of a congregation.

His labors had created a "Church" when there had been only "churches," yet his work was "rewarded with ingratitude."[58] Nonetheless, his Pietist spirit continued to motivate his deep personal desire for peace so that he accepted the Synods' action where others would have set the churches into turmoil. He continued many of his old friendships, including the close relationship which from the beginning had grown between him and the Lutheran pastor and superintendent, Henry Melchior Muhlenberg (1711–1787). Muhlenberg, sent by the Halle Pietists to counteract the movement of Zinzendorf, shared with Schlatter a similar spirit of piety and a disposition for peace. Their efforts were always of mutuality rather than competition or conflict, even often to the extent of sharing services together. In his journal Muhlenberg testifies to their "old unfeigned friendship and love."[59]

Reformed Pietism was not limited to the North, yet Pietism in the Southern Colonies is a separate chapter in American colonial history and one which cannot easily be written along denominational lines. The Reformed sought many times to attract men to America to serve in Virginia and other southern colonies where there were German-speaking communities. These appeals were heightened by the en-

58. Hinke, p. 46.
59. Henry Melchior Muhlenberg, *The Journals*, Philadelphia (1942), vol. 1, p. 342.

thusiasm created by Whitefield's itinerating activities. Chief among Reformed voices in the South was Johann Joachim Züblin (or John J. Zubly, 1724–1781). Like Schlatter, Zubly was a St Gall Pietist and his numerous publications in both North and South attest to his piety and his scholarship. Zubly shared intimately in the Georgia mission of Whitefield and at one time travelled to the North on behalf of Whitefield's Bethesda orphanage. He worked closely with Pietist pastors of various denominational persuasions; one of his first American publications was a 1747 funeral sermon preached for a departed Lutheran pastor. To responsive crowds he long served independent parishes in Charleston, South Carolina, and later in Savannah, Georgia. Typical among his numerous Pietist publications was a tract entitled *True and False Conversion and the Difference Between the Two.* [60] He regularly preached mornings in German, afternoons in French, and evenings in English. In 1770 Princeton testified to Zubly's scholarly eminence by awarding him the doctorate. Muhlenberg met frequently with Zubly during his trip to Georgia in the fall and winter of 1774 and 1775. They worshipped together, counseled together, studied together. One evening, Muhlenburg recorded in his diary, "We read the forty-seventh chapter of Ezekiel and made comments on it. We did not try to swim in it like elephants, but rather tried to wade through it like lambs. Closed with prayer in unison."[61] Among the independent Reformed, as well as among southern colonial churchmen generally, Zubly was one of the foremost pastors and one of the most influential writers.

Among Schlatter's Herborn recruits, Philip Wilhelm Otterbein was preeminent, contributing most importantly to the development of the Reformed churches. He also was Pietism's most eloquent and persuasive voice among the German Reformed, giving form to a Pietist program. Though the foundations of the Pietist position had been well laid before Otterbein's arrival in Pennsylvania, it was his work to articulate that position to a church confronted with growing complacency and religious formality. Early in the nineteenth century his efforts were to feed importantly the new movement known as the "United Brethren." In spite of this, his commitment to

---

60. Johann Joachim Züblin, *Die wahre und falsche Bekehrung, und den Unterscheid Zwischen Beyden,* Germantown (1747). Cited in Hinke, p. 350, where a list of Zubly's twenty publications appears.
61. Muhlenberg, vol. 2, p. 610.

the Reformed church of his fathers remained unbroken until his death at the age of eighty-seven. As circumstances allowed, he was faithful in his denominational responsibilities, in attending meetings of the Coetus and in maintaining contact with other Reformed pastors.

Otterbein brought to the colonial churches a Pietist tradition which supplemented those already represented. The contrast between Herborn Pietism and St Gall Pietism lay in its stress on covenant theology. St Gall Pietism had been more importantly influenced by the earlier structures of Dutch Pietism—those which found their culmination in the theology of Voetius and the piety of the Brakels. Herborn Pietism reflected those later developments which had incorporated much of the theology of Coccejus and was typified by the work of Friedrich Adolph Lampe. The difference was not one of kind but of emphasis.

Otterbein's first parish in Pennsylvania was the Lancaster church. It was there that Otterbein "in accordance with the temporal process of the 'order of salvation' " was brought by degrees "to the knowledge of the truth."[62] In 1757, when his five-year contract with the Lancaster congregation was completed, he sought to resign. He felt a deep dissatisfaction with the lack of spirituality that was combined with an equal absence of discipline. To enforce a more rigid discipline was seemingly impossible because of the independence of the congregations in America; the pastor was virtually at the mercy of his parishioners. So eager were the people to retain Otterbein that they agreed to subscribe to any rules which he would draw up for their spiritual guidance. Eighty members committed themselves to "obedience to their minister and officers in all things that are proper."[63] This included a personal conference with the pastor on their spiritual state before receiving the Lord's supper, a dear Pietist practice, though one seldom experienced in the Colonies.

In the years that followed, the pastoral ministrations of Otterbein were greatly sought after by numerous congregations. After Lancaster he served churches around Tulpehocken and then moved to the church of Frederick, Maryland. In both parishes he established informal worship gatherings, akin

---

62. J. Steven O'Malley, *Pilgrimage of Faith: The Legacy of the Otterbeins,* Metuchen, N.J. (1973), p. 172. Also important for material on Otterbein is Arthur C. Core's *Philip William Otterbein: Pastor, Ecumenist,* Dayton, Ohio (1968).
63. Hinke, p. 73.

to the earlier conventicles and an intermediary step to the "prayer meetings" of the nineteenth century. Later, during his long years as pastor in Baltimore, Otterbein continued and developed these Pietist meetings. In 1774, the same year that he moved to Baltimore, Otterbein joined in a Pietist circle with six of the other nineteen Reformed pastors then members of the Coetus. The minutes of these gatherings testify to an intense striving for personal piety in their own lives and for spiritual direction in their guidance of the churches.

Each of Otterbein's congregations was devoted to him and each appealed to him or to the Coetus for his continuing ministrations. After Otterbein's departure from Frederick, the Coetus testified to his evangelistic effectiveness by writing in its minutes that that congregation possessed "the greatest number of awakened and convicted souls."[64] In spite of successes, however, Otterbein was not totally exempt from conflicts with other pastors or with certain parishioners; nonetheless his wise handling of such problems generally led to amicable settlements and restored good feelings. In 1788 his orthodoxy was called into question, but a forthright letter from the Coetus testified that "Do. Otterbein has grown old and gray, and is almost disabled by the hard service of the Gospel in America. He has done much good, has zealously toiled for the salvation of many souls. The aim of his ministry, even if it did not agree in every respect with the opinions of all, is edification and blessing, for what else should it be?"[65] In his own defense, Otterbein wrote to the Deputies of the Synods including statements of his position on predestination. "To tell the truth, I cannot side with Calvin in this case. I believe that God is love and that he desires the welfare of all his creatures. . . . I believe in election, but cannot persuade myself that God has absolutely and without condition predestined some men to perdition."[66] For the most part, Pietists emphasized man's rejection of God in refusing Christ, rather than God's rejection of man according to foreordained decrees.

In the last years of his long life Otterbein was an active participant in the developing activities of the "United Brethren," initially an "unsectarian society" of Pietist clergyman. His Pietist doctrines and broad churchmanship led him to closer fellowship with like-minded men outside his own denomina-

---

64. German Reformed Church, *Minutes and Letters of the Coetus,* Philadelphia (1903), p. 240.
65. *Ibid.,* p. 425.
66. Hinke, p. 78.

tion than with narrowly conservative Reformed churchmen. For example, in 1784 he shared in the special ordination of the Methodist Francis Asbury and he retained a warm lifelong friendship with Asbury. In this respect he followed in the Pietist tradition of ecumenical fellowship already exemplified in the ministries of men like Guldin, Zubly, and Schlatter.

Pietism's cornerstone was the doctrine of rebirth. As Otterbein attested, this could be sudden and violent: "And did any greater enemy of Jesus Christ ever live on earth than Paul before his conversion? But how suddenly his heart was changed by grace! This is what Jesus still wants to do in us."[67] Yet Otterbein knew, as Pietists generally acknowledged, "There is a cost involved before one can come to peace with God. The new birth and its process does not happen without much pain. . . . Consequently, if these things are yet strange to you, then your Christianity is merely appearance, imagination, shadow tricks."[68] Otterbein's death in 1813, roughly a hundred years after Guldin's arrival, marked far more than simply a century of early American Reformed Pietism. It marked, too, the integration of Pietism's witness into the fabric of American theology. Pietism had established a new pattern of evangelism and a new form of revivalism; it had opened unforeseen and uncontrived avenues of ecumenism; and it had created America's own odd mixture of personal piety, moralism, and national faith. Each characteristic was one of a series of safeguards for a biblically oriented faith, and yet each was to nurture distortions which were to mark with equal force the future of Christianity in America.

SELECTED BIBLIOGRAPHY–CHAPTER TWO

Bemesderfer, James O., *Pietism and its Influence upon the Evangelical United Brethren Church* (1966)
Ecclesiastical Records [of the] State of New York (1901–1916)

---

67. Philip William Otterbein, "The Salvation-Bringing Incarnation and Glorious Victory of Jesus Christ over the Devil and Death," pp. 77–90 in Core; see esp. p. 89.
68. *Ibid.*, p. 88.

Frantz, John, "The Awakening of Religion among the German Settlers in the Middle Colonies" (unpublished paper)

German Reformed Church, *Minutes and Letters of the Coetus—1747–1792*, Reformed Church Publication Board (1903)

Harbough, Henry, *The Life of Rev. Michael Schlatter: with a Full Account of his Travels and Labors among the Germans—1716–1790* (1857)

Hinke, William J., *Ministers of the German Reformed Congregations in Pennsylvania and other Colonies in the Eighteenth Century* (1951)

Lodge, Martin, *The Great Awakening in the Middle Colonies* (a dissertation for the University of California, Berkeley, 1951)

Maxon, Charles H., *The Great Awakening in the Middle Colonies* (1920)

O'Malley, J. Steven, *Pilgrimage of Faith: The Legacy of the Otterbeins.* A.T.L.A. Monograph Series, No. 4 (1973)

Tanis, James, *Dutch Calvinistic Pietism in the Middle Colonies; A Study in the Life and Theology of Theodorus Jacobus Frelinghuysen* (1967)

CHAPTER THREE

THE IMPACT OF PIETISM UPON THE MENNONITES IN EARLY AMERICAN CHRISTIANITY

by Martin H. Schrag

MENNONITE HISTORIAN CORNELIUS KRAHN HAS WRITTEN, "NO other single religious movement has had such an impact on the Mennonites in all countries with the exception of the Netherlands as Pietism."[1] The impact of Pietism on Mennonites has been considerable, and this chapter will delineate the influence of Pietism upon Pennsylvania Mennonites during the eighteenth century. The center of attention will be developments in Lancaster and surrounding counties.

Pietism has been variously defined and historically manifested itself in a variety of ways. Some of the types of Pietism will be noted in the chapter. As the word is used in the title, it refers primarily to the awakening among the Pennsylvania Germans fostered by two Pietist leaders, Philip W. Otterbein and Martin Boehm.

The Mennonites of Eastern Pennsylvania reacted in three ways to Otterbein-Boehm Pietism. Some responded favorably, largely accepting this posture of Pietism, then became a part of the movement that issued in the United Brethren in Christ Church. On the other end of the spectrum there were the Mennonites who basically rejected Pietism. They remained Mennonites. Between these two extremes were those who sought to integrate what they considered to be the genius of both movements. These became part of the River Brethren

---

1. "Pietism," *The Mennonite Encyclopedia,* vol. 4 (1959), p. 176.

movement, a group which designated itself as Brethren in Christ since the time of the American Civil War.[2] Thus the three ways in which Mennonites reacted to Otterbein-Boehm Pietism were acceptance, rejection, and integration.

The chapter is divided into two parts. The first section is historical in nature dealing with the spiritual conditions of the Mennonites during colonial times, the emergence of the Otterbein-Boehm movement, and the rise of the River Brethren. Having secured the historical background in the first section, the second section will consist of an analysis of the original River Brethren Confession. It will be especially through the study of the Confession that the case will be made that the Mennonites reacted in the above-mentioned three ways to Pietism.

MENNONITE HISTORY

The Mennonite migration to Pennsylvania (and Maryland) was a part of the much larger movement of Germans to William Penn's experiment. Beginning to come in 1683, an estimated 100,000 Germans were residents in Pennsylvania by the time of the American Revolution. Among these pioneers there were not only large numbers of Lutherans and Reformed but also significant minorities of groups like the Dunkers and Mennonites. An estimated 3000 to 5000 Mennonites came to the New World. First settling in Germantown, the Mennonites soon found their way to the rich farming lands in what are now Montgomery, Bucks, and Lancaster counties of Pennsylvania.[3]

Anabaptist-Mennonite history had shaped a unique people. It was the barbaric persecution inflicted upon the Anabaptists in the sixteenth and seventeenth centuries that was so determinative for their subsequent history. In the choice between emphasizing the Great Commission, and thus possibly being exterminated, and living in isolation as the church of the remnant, the Mennonites chose the latter. Where the Mennonites survived, they did so by fleeing the centers of population and the immediate reach of social controls. In

2. The group referred to themselves simply as "brethren" in the first years of existence. Carlton O. Wittlinger, "The Origin of the Brethren in Christ," *The Mennonite Quarterly Review,* vol. 48, p. 68.

3. "Pennsylvania," *The Mennonite Encyclopedia,* vol. 4 (1959), p. 136. C. Henry Smith, *The Mennonite Immigration to Pennsylvania in the Eighteenth Century* (1929), pp. 75–176. Oscar Kuhns, *The German and Swiss Settlements in Colonial Pennsylvania* (1914), pp. 1–3.

Switzerland they maintained a precarious existence in solitary valleys and on mountain slopes, but in most instances persecution forced them into alien cultures where they settled on the frontiers to develop virgin land or on land devastated by war. Tolerated by governments because of their agricultural proficiency, most often Mennonites became cultural enclaves, living in agrarian simplicity, separated from neighbors by what sociologists refer to as spatial isolation and mechanical insulation.[4]

The Mennonite answer, then, to persecution and discrimination was the Mennonite agricultural community. The aim of the subculture was to be the true church. The shape of life, however, between sixteenth-century Anabaptism and eighteenth-century Mennonitism was considerably different. In contrast to the earlier mobility of itinerancy, family and community life became a permanent part of an ordered existence. With this went the stability of occupation. Farming became a sacred occupation involving a minimum of economic integration with the larger society. Language was identified with the faith of the fathers. Marriage was within the group. Certain cultural forms, in matters of dress, food, and social custom, were frozen and given religious connotation. Political life was avoided and higher education rejected. The cultural patterns of the larger community were not only resisted, but, in many instances, a sharp line of separation was drawn against possible worldly influences. The practices of other churches were seen as worldly. The effort was to build a Christian island in the sea of the world.

Persecution and the agricultural community altered aspects of the faith. The missionary surge was replaced by a people becoming *die Stillen im Lande*. The voluntary commitment and believer's baptism became a matter of keeping "Mennonite" children in the fold. Discipleship became a matter of following the accepted cultural patterns of the Mennonite community. The original creative quest for insight was

---

4. Roland Bainton, "The Anabaptist Contribution to History," *The Recovery of the Anabaptist Vision,* ed. Guy F. Hershberger (1957), p. 320. Leland David Harder, "The Quest for Equilibrium in an Established Sect, a Study of Social Change in the General Conference Mennonite Church" (Ph.D. diss., Garrett Theological Seminary, 1962), p. 21. Christian Neff, "The Mennonites of Germany, Including Danzig and Poland," *Mennonite Quarterly Review,* vol. 11, p. 34.

replaced by a strong accent on the faith of the fathers. There was a loss of eschatological expectancy, the remnant status being accepted as more or less permanent.[5]

There are Mennonite historians who see quietistic Pietism as giving the Mennonites a spiritual rationalization for the basic change of life. Radical discipleship involving missionary outreach and the willingness to suffer for Christ in the process of building brotherhood communities were replaced by subjectively experiencing the Christ of comfort, peace, and forgiveness. Christianity had become an inner heart condition issuing in a life of high personal morality. The conflict with the world was minimized, the Mennonites merely asking for the right of a quiet existence.[6]

The pattern just outlined was basically true of the Mennonites who migrated to Pennsylvania. As the first generation of immigrants passed, communications with European Mennonites became virtually nonexistent. Also with the passing of the first generation went the better trained leadership that had come from Europe. There was virtually no creative writing. Mennonite historian S. F. Pannabecker has indicated that the Mennonites, in an effort to perpetuate their own point of view, placed themselves on the unpopular side of three issues of the day. They supported in government the Quakers who were forced out by those wanting a stronger military posture. This ended the limited political activities of the Mennonites (such as voting for Quakers). Secondly, they opposed the schools sponsored by the "Society for the Propagation of Christian Knowledge Among the Germans in Pennsylvania." These schools appeared to them as a return to the state-controlled institutions of the Old World and threatened the dangers of Anglicization. Thirdly, the Mennonites refrained from supporting the Revolutionary War. Discontinuing relations with European Mennonites, neglecting the training of leaders, and separating themselves from the dynamic forces of American society, the Pennsylvania Mennonites turned their back on the

---

5. J. Lawrence Burkholder, "The Problem of Social Responsibility from the Perspective of the Mennonite Church" (Ph.D. diss., Princeton Theological Seminary, 1962), pp. 190ff. H. S. Bender, "Farming and Settlement," *The Mennonite Encyclopedia*, vol. 2, (1956), p. 303. Robert Kreider, "Vocations of Swiss and South German Anabaptists," *Mennonite Life*, vol. 8, p. 42.

6. Robert Friedmann, *Mennonite Piety Through the Centuries* (1949), pp. 3–268.

"American experiment" and were thrown back increasingly on the "faith of the fathers."[7]

Adhering to the traditional faith meant maintaining the status quo. No evangelistic or missionary work was undertaken. The patterns of worship were frozen. Throughout the eighteenth century "no significant changes were made and no one intended to make any. The Bible had not changed; why should anyone introduce any innovations."[8]

Mennonites at this time were not only maintaining the status quo, they were moving toward greater isolation. A further example of this was the Mennonite reaction to the attempt of the Moravian leader Zinzendorf to bring the German Christians in America together in his "Pennsylvania Congregation of God in the Spirit." This ecumenical effort paradoxically strengthened denominational consciousness. Mennonites rebounded from the series of meetings exploring cooperation with a concerted program of publication aimed at nurturing Mennonites on the sixteenth-century Anabaptist vision.[9]

The important point is that this mood of withdrawal prevailed during the time Otterbein and Boehm (the co-founders of the United Brethren) sought to spark an awakening.

Traditionalism was not the only force affecting the Pennsylvania Mennonites. There also was Pietism (pre-Otterbein-Boehm varieties). In fact, many Protestant groups were influenced by Pietism prior to their arrival in America. Lutherans and Reformed felt the yeast of Pietism. The Moravians were given a new direction by the movement. The Dunkers (see footnote for description) owe their inception to a considerable degree to Pietism.[10] The Pietist influence was also felt among the Mennonites in Europe. As Pietism spread over

---

7. "The Development of the General Conference of the Mennonite Church of North America in the American Environment" (Ph.D. diss., Yale University, 1940), pp. 101–108.

8. John C. Wenger, "The Mennonites Establish Themselves in Pennsylvania," *Mennonite Life*, vol. 2, p. 28.

9. John Joseph Stoudt, "Count Zinzendorf and the Pennsylvania Congregation of God in the Spirit," *Church History*, vol. 9, p. 376.

10. The Dunkers were that body of Christians who originated at Schwarzenau, county of Wittgenstein, Germany, in 1708. Known by a variety of names, the group in 1836 adopted the name, "Fraternity of German Baptists." In 1871 the name was changed to "German Baptist Brethren." The present society known as the Church of the Brethren is the largest of

Germany, many Mennonites in the Palatinate (area which most Mennonites came to Pennsylvania) "recogni. some kinship with the movement and opened hearts and homes to this new message."[11] It was especially Württemberg Pietism that was influential in South Germany. The Pietist influence among Mennonites continued in America, for it appears Mennonites read more Pietist literature (e.g., John Arndt) than Anabaptist literature. Apparently the Pietism that was absorbed was non-emotional, moralistic, and quietistic. Thus Pennsylvania Mennonitism was shaped not only by traditional Mennonitism but also to at least a small degree by Pietism.

The Mennonites were not the only religious society that suffered a spiritual decline in the New World. The pioneers of other denominations, when confronted with the task of taming a wilderness, suffered a great decline in religious ardor and vitality. In the new land, cut off from their mother churches, often without religious leadership and needing all their energies to carve out a new civilization, the pioneers experienced an ebbing of religious commitment.

It was the clergymen of Pietist orientation on both sides of the Atlantic who were especially concerned to keep the colonists from lapsing into paganism. Numerous individuals responded to the challenge. The two that we are concerned about sparked an awakening among the Germans living in Pennsylvania, Maryland, and Virginia. They were the already mentioned Philip Otterbein and Martin Boehm.

THE OTTERBEIN-BOEHM MOVEMENT

Before delineating the history of the Otterbein-Boehm movement, it is well to indicate that some Pietists sought to reform the church by working within the existing ecclesiastical structures and in the context of traditional theology. Although critical of the church, these Pietists, often characterized as "church-related," sought to be the yeast transforming the whole body. In contrast to the latter there were others who felt the existing denominations were beyond hope. They worked outside the existing churches in various ways to realize

---

the groups descending from the Dunkers. Donald F. Durnbaugh, ed., *The Church of the Brethren Past and Present* (1971), pp. 9–10.
11. Friedmann, *Mennonite Piety*, p. 65.

true Christianity. Since the majority of them separated themselves from existing churches, they have been tagged as separatists. It should, however, be noted that separatism was part
of a larger posture labelled by historians as radical Pietism.
This posture must be defined in greater detail.

Radical Pietism was a complex phenomenon; it assumed
many forms. It emerged, in Germany, during the last decade
of the seventeenth century. One authority has defined it as
"that branch of the Pietistic movement in Germany which
emphasized separatistic, sectarian and mystical elements,
particularly those originating in Boehmism."[12] Boehmism, the
work of the German thinker, Jacob Boehme, is not to be confused with the Martin Boehm already mentioned in this chapter. Further insight into radical Pietism will be given as the
chapter is developed. Enough has been stated to proceed to
delineate the history of the Otterbein-Boehm movement. We
start with the spiritual pilgrimages of the two leaders.

Philip W. Otterbein was born in Germany (Dillenberg,
Hesse-Nassau province) in 1726 and in home, church, and
school he was exposed to Pietist teaching. Two of his brothers
were pietistically oriented theologians. Philip received his
theological education at Herborn, an institution which had on
its faculty apostles of *Thaetiges Christenthum,* i.e., active or Pietist Christianity. Herborn, a strong center of Reformed
Pietism, vigorously opposed radical Pietism. It prepared men
to work in the Reformed church. Thus church-related Pietism
was the heritage of Otterbein.

When a call was given for qualified missionaries to work
in colonial America, Otterbein responded and arrived in
America by 1752 as a Reformed clergyman. In a series of
Reformed pastorates in Pennsylvania and Maryland, he
sought to move his hearers from "cold formality" to the "life
and power of faith." In his first pastorate (Lancaster, Pennsylvania), toward the end of religious vitality and discipline, he
began the practice of examining members prior to the Lord's

---

12. Chauncey David Ensign, "Radical German Pietism" (Ph.D. diss., Boston
    University, 1955), p. 1. Dr. F. Ernest Stoeffler suggests that three streams
    of mystical piety converged to form the background of radical Pietism.
    These were the piety of Johann Arndt, the theosophy of Jacob Boehme,
    and the quietism of men like Miguel de Molinos. *German Pietism During the
    Eighteenth Century* (1973), pp. 168–171.

supper. More important, it was at Lancaster that he profound religious experience which some have identifie conversion experience. Others have seen it as a gift of the Holy Spirit, or the subjective awareness of assurance. Whatever the explanation, the experience influenced the rest of his ministry. He began to preach extemporaneously. The message was aimed at the heart.

In his second charge at Tulpehocken, Pennsylvania, Otterbein introduced the weekly private meeting and entered fully into pastoral visitation. The weekly meeting polarized the people, some being distressed at people mourning and weeping over their lost condition. In subsequent pastorates, Otterbein became deeply burdened for the spirituality of the German people of Pennsylvania and Maryland (especially rural people) causing him to go into the "highways and hedges" to proclaim the message of salvation.[13] Staying within the denominational structure, Otterbein yet sought to awaken people of various backgrounds.

The second leader of the awakening was Martin Boehm. He was born (1725) to Mennonite parents living in Lancaster County, Pennsylvania. According to tradition, one of his grandfathers had been a Pietist in Switzerland. In due time Martin became a member of the Mennonite church, but the religious crisis of his life was precipitated by his being chosen a minister by lot. Although "blameless" in life, Boehm was deeply disturbed, for despite his best efforts, he had no message. In deep distress, he continued in prayer. While praying for a message to preach, the thought dawned upon him that his basic problem was his own salvation. He became alarmed.

> I felt and saw myself a poor sinner. I was LOST. My agony became great. I was ploughing in the field, and kneeled down at each end of the furrow, to pray. The word *lost, lost (velohren)* went every round with me. Midway in the field I could go no further but sank behind the plough, crying, Lord save, I am lost!... In a moment a stream of joy was poured over me. I

---

13. A. W. Drury, *The Life of Rev. Phillip William Otterbein, Founder of the United Brethren* (1890), pp. 24–30, 39. Paul Himmel Eller, *These Evangelical United Brethren* (1957), p. 25. Arthur Core, *Philip William Otterbein* (1968), pp. 13–61. John Steven O'Malley, *Pilgrimage of Faith: The Legacy of the Otterbeins* (1973).

praised the Lord and left the field, and told my companion what joy I felt.[14]

The date of the experience was 1758. This crisis newbirth experience gave Boehm the needed motivation.

Converted, Boehm had a message. Hardly able to wait for Sunday, he used the first Sunday's opportunity to speak of his experience. While he spoke of his lost estate and agony of mind, some began to weep. This encouraged Boehm and he told of the Fall, man's lost condition, and the need of repentance. He continued Sunday after Sunday, preaching to his Mennonite audience. Boehm recounted that all this new life, new faith, new love, and strong praising of God was new to the Mennonites. (He did admit that his mother's sister had the experience before he did.) Mennonites knew about the Fall, man's sinfulness, the need of repentance, and the new birth. It was the style and form that was new.

Boehm soon discovered that preaching made different impressions on different persons. Some were repelled. It was at this juncture that Boehm was sent to Virginia to evaluate reports of an awakening among Mennonites there. To the surprise of many, Boehm endorsed the awakening because it was the same kind of thing he had experienced. Based on the Virginia experience and his own preaching, Boehm became more and more convinced that men everywhere must repent "and this repentance must be accompanied by a godly sorrow, deeply felt, and that there can be no rest, no peace, no hope and no faith without it."[15]

Boehm moved cautiously, or his enlarging vision developed slowly. A year after his conversion experience, he was made a bishop in the Mennonite church. As such, the possibility of influence increased. We do not know precisely the nature of the ongoing relationship between Boehm and the Mennonites, but we do know that lay evangelists traveling through Lancaster County would often stop at Boehm's home. Such visits would lead to awakening preaching in Boehm's home.

---

14. Henry G. Spayth, *History of the Church of the United Brethren in Christ* (1851), pp. 28–31.
15. F. Hollingsworth, "Biography," *The Methodist Magazine*, vol. 6 (1823), pp. 210–211. J. B. Wakely, ed., *The Patriarch of One Hundred Years: Being the Reminiscences, Historical and Biographical of Rev. Henry Boehm* (1875), p. 12. Abraham Hershey, "Lieber Bruder Erb," *Die Geschäftige Martha*, vol. 1, p. 105.

One of the techniques Boehm adopted for the spreading of the good news was the big meeting (to be described below). It was at such an occasion that Otterbein and Boehm met. Boehm was conducting a big meeting held in Isaac Long's barn (Lancaster County). Otterbein was there and the two sensed their spiritual kinship. They embraced and are reported to have exclaimed, *"Wir sind Brüder* (We are brothers)."

The two, although from varying backgrounds, one Reformed and one Mennonite, were of one heart regarding the centrality of the crisis new birth and the need of a subsequent life of verbal witness and personal holiness. It was this message which transcended denominational values or structures. It was at the meeting under discussion that the two in effect joined forces to foster the awakening. Historians in retrospect see the meeting of the two men as the informal beginning of the United Brethren in Christ Church. Denominationally oriented people did not look upon this joining of forces with favor.[16]

Boehm's ministry apparently became more far-reaching. He preached in homes, churches, and at large meetings. Not limiting his proclaiming to Sunday, he at times also held meetings on week nights. He spoke to large crowds in Pennsylvania, Maryland, and Virginia with the center of his ministry being Pennsylvania. The big meeting, *Grosse Versammlung*, was effectively used. It usually lasted for two to three days with meetings held in big barns to accommodate the large crowds. Sometimes groves or orchards were used. People from many denominational backgrounds would come to these meetings: Reformed, Mennonite, Lutheran, Dunker, Moravian, Amish, etc. Many were awakened.[17]

It must be remembered that the work of Otterbein and Boehm was a new phenomenon. Dr. John Nevin, the famed Reformed theologian, not a friend of revivals, nevertheless wrote in 1842 about conditions of the time of Otterbein and Boehm:

---

16. A. W. Drury, *History of the Church of the United Brethren in Christ* (1924), pp. 88–89. Hollingsworth, "Biography," p. 153.

17. Drury, *United Brethren in Christ*, p. 101. John Denig, *Autobiography of the Rev. Samuel Huber* (1858), pp. 212–215. A. Bearss, "Origin of the Dunkers in Canada," *Evangelical Visitor*, vol. 1, p. 154. The *Evangelical Visitor* was and is the official publication of the Brethren in Christ. Abram A. Cassel, "Origin of the River Brethren" (handwritten copy in the Cassel Collection, Juniata College Historical Library, July 1, 1882).

To be confirmed, and then to take the sacrament occasionally, was counted by the multitude all that was necessary to make one a good Christian, if only a tolerable decency of outward life was maintained besides, without any regard at all to the religion of the heart. . . . True, serious piety was indeed often treated with marked scorn. In the bosom of the church itself, it was stigmatized as *Schwaermerei, Kopfhaengerei* or miserable, drivelling Methodism. The idea of the new birth was treated as pietistic whimery. Experimental religion in all its forms was eschewed as a new-fangled invention of cunning imposters, brought in to turn the heads of the weak and lead captive silly women. Prayer-meetings were held to be a spiritual abomination. Family worship was a species of saintly affection, barely tolerable in the cases of ministers (though many of them gloried in having no altar in their houses), but absolutely disgraceful for common Christians. To show an awakened concern on the subject of religion, or a disposition to call on God in daily secret prayer, was to incur certain reproach. . . . The picture, it must be acknowledged, is dark, but not more so than the truth of history would seem to require.[18]

Boehm did his most effective work among the Mennonites, especially in Lancaster County. At the same time, the strongest opposition to him also centered in that denomination. The more Boehm moved away from his Mennonitism toward Pietism, the stronger was the opposition against him. Some Mennonite churches were closed to Boehm, foreshadowing his excommunication from that body. Put out of the church, Boehm could not work as a yeast in his home denomination.

Less consideration will be given to the work of Philip Otterbein because he worked among Mennonites only in a limited way. It was in his York, Pennsylvania, pastorate that Otterbein became something of an itinerant. He still had his charge, but he freely used his energies to preach and proclaim the work at other points. He continued this work when he moved to his last pastorate, serving a church in Baltimore. The congregation was an independent Reformed body. Otterbein then had a dual relationship in the sense that he remained in the German Reformed Coetus and yet gave leadership to the societies formed as a result of the awakening.

---

18. Quoted in D. Berger, "History of the Church of the United Brethren in Christ," *A History of the Disciples of Christ, The Society of Friends, the United Brethren in Christ and the Evangelical Association,* The American Church History Series, vol. 12, p. 331.

If any of the converts gained by the movement joined the established churches, it is not known. The major development, we do know, was the gathering together in classes or societies of the converts. Otterbein and Boehm gave leadership to the movement. The following quote gives a picture of the gathering together of the awakened in Lancaster County, Pennsylvania:

> Among the several German denominations, especially among the Mennonites, being the most numerous society in Lancaster county, awakenings were more common. Between sixty and seventy years ago [written in 1848], awakened persons of Mennonites, Lutherans, German Reformed, Brethren or Taeufer, "whose hearts were closely joined together—had a common interest, not only in regard to the general cause of religion, but in each other's individual edification," and they met in the capacity of a social devout band, from house to house, to make prayer and supplication for the continued influence of God's Spirit.[19]

The quote notes that it was especially among the Mennonites in Lancaster County that awakenings occurred. The prominence of Mennonites in the Otterbein-Boehm movement is further reinforced by the statistic that at a conference of fourteen leaders held in 1789, nine were Reformed and five were Mennonites.[20]

When Otterbein and Boehm began their work, they had no intention of starting a new denomination. They sought to transform individuals and thus revitalize the church, not actualize a new church. Yet gradually an organization took shape. At least as early as 1774 the "united ministers," preachers working under the direction of Otterbein, met for edification and planning. A meeting which included all the ministers of the emerging United Brethren (both those working with Otterbein and Boehm) was held in 1789. This was the first general council of ministers. The organization was completed in 1800 when the first regular annual conference was held. The name adopted was the United Brethren in Christ.[21] A denomination came into being not primarily to actualize the New Testament church, but rather for the need of a corporate

19. A Familiar Friend, "History of the River Brethren," *History of All Religious Denominations in the United States* (1848), p. 553.
20. Berger, "United Brethren in Christ," p. 347.
21. John Lawrence, *The History of the Church of the United Brethren in Christ*, vol. 1 (1868), pp. 263–299.

existence to realize personal edification and a base for evangelism.

Having traced the Otterbein-Boehm awakening, we need to answer the question as to whether the movement represented church-related Pietism or radical Pietism. Mention has already been made that Otterbein began his work in the former tradition. Throughout his days in America he served Reformed churches working within the Reformed structure. Even during the latter part of his ministry when he gave leadership to the societies emerging out of the awakening he maintained his membership in the regular Reformed Coetus, although it should be mentioned he was not very active in the Coetus as he gave his energies to the new societies. The new societies in time became organized congregations. In a basic sense Otterbein was a church-related Pietist. As for Martin Boehm, he began his work within an existing church, in this instance the Mennonite church. He sought to awaken the members of the Mennonite brotherhood. He did not leave his denomination and there is no evidence that he condemned it as "Babel" or "Babylon"—practices of some of the radical German Pietists. He soon preached to crowds including people from many denominational backgrounds but apparently he continued to work out of the Mennonite church. He gave leadership to societies that came into being because of the awakening. The giving of such leadership probably began before he was excommunicated (about 1775) from the Mennonite church. After his excommunication, Boehm's connections consisted of giving leadership to the newly formed societies. As already stated, these moved toward organization in the 1770s and 1780s with full organization by 1800. Boehm, as was true of Otterbein, was one of the first overseers in the United Brethren in Christ. There is evidence he enrolled in a Methodist society in his last days. Thus Boehm also was a church-related Pietist although the evidence is not as uniform as with Otterbein. The commitment to church-related Pietism is seen in the fact that the two men organized their societies as the United Brethren in Christ.

Having examined the evidence of church-related Pietism, it is yet necessary to note some tendencies toward radical Pietism. It is not, as far as we know, that any of the awakened were theologically or ideologically radical Pietists. There is no sign of Boehmist theosophy, no indication of belief in the ultimate salvation of all men, no acceptance of celibacy as the ideal, no belief that the immediate guidance of the Spirit transcends the Scriptures, and no harsh condemnation of the existing churches. At the same time Otterbein and Boehm put the new birth, holiness, and evangelism above denominational lines and beliefs. The awakened left the existing churches for what at first were very loosely organized societies, something akin to the conventicle meetings of the radical German Pietists. For a time they were without fully organized churches. There is a reference to working "untrammeled by any sect or church," implying the emerging United Brethren were not one of the existing sects or churches, but essentially a part of the universal church. At one point the ministers of the group are referred to as *unparteiische,* which is translated as unsectarian and in the context[22] of radical German Pietism was often used to indicate those who had connections with no church body but were in full liberty, living the full Christian life individualistically and in informal groups.

The evidence for radical or separatist Pietism is limited. It appears the Otterbein-Boehm movement did not self-consciously think of itself as radically pietistic, although individual members may have. Yet there do seem to be some separatist tendencies in the years between leaving the existing churches and the formal organization of the United Brethren in Christ.

The important point for the development of the story of the chapter is that some Mennonites became a party of the Otterbein-Boehm movement. Of the three responses to Pietism suggested at the beginning of the chapter, these Mennonites accepted Otterbein-Boehm Pietism. There are no statistics as to how many Mennonites became a part of this movement, but we do know the number was not small. At the least they were a significant minority in the United Brethren Church.

THE RIVER BRETHREN

Having explained the spiritual condition of eighteenth-century Pennsylvania Mennonites and sketched briefly the emergence of the United Brethren in Christ Church, our next task is to trace the rise of the River Brethren, i.e., the Brethren living near the Susquehanna River. A study of the beginnings

---

22. Drury, *United Brethren in Christ,* pp. 184–185.

of the River Brethren is necessary for us to understand the relationship among and between the Mennonites, Dunkers, United Brethren, and River Brethren and as a background for the analysis of the River Brethren Confession.

The River Brethren attempted to integrate some Anabaptist ideas and practices mediated by the Mennonites and Dunkers with certain aspects of Pietism, of the Otterbein-Boehm and possibly Dunker vintages. Attention will first be focussed on the relationship between the River Brethren and the Anabaptist side of the heritage.

First, what was the relationship of the River Brethren to the Mennonites? Many sources attest to connections with Mennonites. A Lutheran magazine of 1814 stated that some of the first River Brethren had earlier been Mennonites. An able account (1848), written by one who knew the River Brethren well, footnoted that the Brethren were occasionally called River Mennonites because some of their first ministers had been Mennonites. The first account of River Brethren beginnings written by one within the Brethren brotherhood mentioned that the ancestors of the River Brethren had been Mennonites. Ulrich Engle, father of Jacob and John Engle, both instrumental in the formation of the River Brethren, was known to have been a Mennonite. Jacob and John themselves may have joined the Mennonite church. There is a strong tradition that John (Hansley) Winger, an early Brethren leader, had a Mennonite background. Another early leader, John Greider, had been a Mennonite.[23]

The evidence does not indicate that the River Brethren were the result of a Mennonite schism, as affirmed by some historians, but rather that some of the first Brethren had a Mennonite background. Probably not all the first Brethren were Mennonites, but the Mennonite connection is adequate for the transmission of Anabaptist ideas and practices.

No mention has been made to this point of the relationship of the Dunkers to the River Brethren. That the Dunkers had some influence on the River Brethren cannot be doubted.

---

23. "Gestalt des Reiches Gottes unter den Deutschen in Amerika," *Evangelisches Magazin,* vol. 3, p. 135. A Familiar Friend, "History of the River Brethren." H. S. Bender, "A Swiss Mennonite Document of 1754 Bearing on the Background of the Origin of the Brethren in Christ Church," *Mennonite Quarterly Review,* vol. 34, pp. 308–309. Norman W. Nauman, Wenger Genealogist, Route 1, Manheim, Pennsylvania, "Notebook No. 1."

The closeness of the two is shown by the fact that when the River Brethren determined to begin as a church, they turned to two Dunker elders for baptism. (The two, each for his own reason, did not baptize the first River Brethren.) Influence on the River Brethren is seen in the fact that the River Brethren, following the Dunkers, "stressed the wearing of the beard, selected church officials by election rather than by lot, held love feasts in connection with the communion services, conducted deacon visitations of congregational membership, and practiced trine immersion." (In each of these instances the River Brethren followed the Dunkers rather than the Mennonites, who had other practices.)[24] The relationship between the Dunkers and River Brethren is difficult to trace because of the lack of documents. Yet an attempt to gain fuller understanding must be made.

The known relationship between the Dunkers and the River Brethren is worthy of exploration because the Dunkers, like the River Brethren, were indebted to both Pietism and Anabaptism. To understand fully how the River Brethren brought Pietism and Anabaptism together we need to give attention to the Dunker synthesis.

The Dunkers began their corporate existence in Schwarzenau, Wittgenstein, Germany, when, in 1708, eight persons decided to reconstitute the New Testament church. Mostly coming out of the Reformed tradition, the first members-to-be were attracted to radical Pietism. After a few years as radical Pietists, the eight were strongly influenced by the Anabaptist-Mennonite tradition. It was at the point of the impact of Anabaptism that they organized themselves into a *Gemeinde*. The result of this spiritual pilgrimage was that the Dunker orientation is indebted to both radical Pietism and Anabaptism. Dunker historians have been trying to decipher the synthesis for some years.

During their days as radical Pietists, two of their leaders especially left their imprint on the Dunkers-to-be. It was the evangelist Ernst Christoph Hochmann von Hochenau who spread the "gospel" of radical Pietism in the southern and western parts of Germany. He awakened many of those who later became Dunkers and was the spiritual mentor of many early Dunkers. A close personal relationship was established between Hochmann and the first Dunker leader, Alexander

---

24. Wittlinger, "Brethren in Christ," pp. 59–60.

The second radical Pietist of considerable influence
...storian Gottfried Arnold. His influence was through
...ngs, rather than personal contact, for Arnold re-
...ie history of the Christian church, presenting the
...estament church as the ideal model and stating the
precise practices of the church of the first two or three centuries. Through these two men and others, the Dunkers accepted certain tenets of radical Pietism. Such tenets, as they
relate to the River Brethren point of view, will be discussed as
the original River Brethren Confession is analyzed.

As already indicated, the Dunkers were also related to,
and influenced by, the Anabaptist-Mennonite tradition. The
basis of this influence was, first of all, through the many contacts between the emerging Dunkers and the Mennonites.
Space will not allow the enumeration of all such contacts, but
mention should be made of the visits of the first Dunker
leader, Alexander Mack, Sr., to Mennonite congregations in
"heartfelt love." When the Dunkers first organized, many ob-
servers saw the similarity between the Dunkers and the Anabaptist-Mennonites. This is proven by the fact that many called
the Dunkers *Neu-Täufer* in contrast to the old Baptists or
Anabaptist-Mennonites. The strongest evidence of indebtedness to the Anabaptist tradition is found in the writings of
Mack, Sr. He specifically quotes the *Martyrs Mirror* on several
occasions. In his first major writing, Mack stated that the Dunkers were in complete agreement with Anabaptist thought and
that the Anabaptists taught nothing contrary to the Gospel. He
further stated that the Mennonites had turned out much better
than all other groups such as the Lutherans or Calvinists.
Lastly, Mack indicated that the Dunkers had moved beyond
their radical Pietist days.[25]

Church of the Brethren (Dunker) historian Donald
Durnbaugh has shown that the two unifying Dunker concepts
were their "view of the church (restitutionism) and their emphasis on obedience (discipleship)." These were the two controlling concepts of Anabaptism, and Durnbaugh attributes
their presence in Dunker thought to their "conscious adoption

---

25. Donald F. Durnbaugh, "The Genius of the Brethren," *Brethren Life and
Thought*, vol. 4, pp. 4–33. William George Willoughby, "The Beliefs of the
Early Brethren" (Ph.D. diss., 1951), pp. 62–63. Durnbaugh fully outlines
the Dunker-Anabaptist-Mennonite relationship.

from Anabaptist thought."[26] Other authorities agree that the Dunker concept of the church was rooted in the Anabaptist vision. More attention will be given to Dunker thought in the analysis of the River Brethren Confession.

It is significant that when the Dunkers instituted their Anabaptist-style church, there was a break between Mack and Hochmann. Hochmann did not object to participating in Dunker ordinances such as baptism or communion, if these were for personal edification. His objection was in making such practices mandatory. Hochmann became more and more critical of sectarianism.

The second tradition, in contrast to Anabaptism, that shaped the vision of the founding fathers of the River Brethren was Pietism as developed in the Otterbein-Boehm movement. In our study of the Otterbein-Boehm movement, we noted the gathering together of awakened people for the sake of edification. The quote used above to make the point, stated this was common among the religious people in Lancaster County. It pointed out that the awakened "met in the capacity of a social devout band, from house to house, to make prayer and supplication for the continued influence of God's Spirit." The quote then continues by affirming that "out of these social circles was organized the Religious Association, now commonly known as the RIVER BRETHREN."[27]

The details of the rise of the River Brethren are not clear and various theories have been proposed. It has been mentioned above that Martin Boehm awakened many people in Lancaster County who informally met for personal edification. These groups were in the style of the Pietist conventicles. One of these groups was the River Brethren. Just what relationship Boehm had with the emergence of this group is not certain. It is known that Boehm preached in Donegal Township, the location of the River Brethren. Were these people awakened one by one and did they then form their own group apart from Boehm, or was the group organized by the well-known evangelist? It does appear that the River Brethren, individually and/or collectively, had some relationship with Boehm. He apparently was the one who awakened them and may have

---

26. Donald F. Durnbaugh, "Brethren Beginnings: The Origins of the Church of the Brethren in the Early Eighteenth Century" (Ph.D. diss., 1960), pp. 168–173.

27. A Familiar Friend, "History of the River Brethren," p. 553.

by example or word the worth of meeting informally
...al enrichment.

...he important point is that in contrast to other
...d groups, the River Brethren, because of Mennonite-
influence and background, realized that there is not
only aɪɪ individual normativeness to Christianity (personal piety), but also a corporate normativeness to the faith, namely,
the church. As has already been indicated, the Otterbein-
Boehm awakening was built on the idea that there was only one
essential, namely, personal piety (i.e., conversion and a holy
life). The River Brethren, in contrast, stated there was a second
essential, the church. To make the point in another way,
people in the Otterbein-Boehm movement met corporately,
basically for the sake of building up the inner man and for a
base for evangelism. In contrast, the River Brethren met not
only for personal edification but also to constitute the people of
God. They were the new society of the New Testament,
edified, empowered, and led by the Spirit, not only individually but also corporately. The River Brethren organized themselves for theological reasons.[28]

Much is made of the traditions regarding the River
Brethren that have come down to us about the importance of
correct baptism. The point of this concern was not only with
the act itself. The Brethren realized that the shape of baptism
was integral to the nature of the church. The Brethren went
beyond the idea that the church consisted of all the converted
in all the denominations, to the concept that the converted will
be empowered and guided to actualize the visible, gathered,
and convenanted people of God. The earliest in-group description of the founding of the River Brethren is as follows:

> While he [Jacob Engle] and his co-laborers met together in
> council, and after deep meditation, and discarding all human
> creeds, and taking the unadulterated Word of God as a guide,
> and seeking to follow the primitive teachings of Christ and His
> apostles, and adopting the New Testament as their rule of

---

28. Jacob Erb, "Fortsetzung Meiner Gedanken über unsere Gesellschaft,"
Die Geschäftige Martha, vol. 1, p. 93. John Stehman, "Origin of the River
Brethren," *Christian Family Companion*, vol. 3, p. 147. Cassel, "Origin of the
River Brethren."

faith and practice, founded the church in the United States of America.[29]

This quote indicates that under the leadership of Jacob Engle, the River Brethren made the corporate decision to fashion a corporate life according to the New Testament. The precise year this event transpired is not known. It was between the years 1775 and 1788.[30]

In the historical portion of the chapter we have documented the low spiritual state of the Mennonites during colonial times. Secondly, we have sketched the awakening led by Otterbein and Boehm among the Germans in Pennsylvania, Maryland, and Virginia. People from many denominations were awakened. Among such people were many Mennonites who cast their lot with the Otterbein-Boehm kind of Pietism at the expense of their Mennonite connections. Lastly, attention was given to the rise of the River Brethren. Two traditions were involved in the formation of the River Brethren: Pietism and Anabaptism.

We now embark on the analysis of the original River Brethren Confession of faith. The immediate consideration will be to identify the Pietist- and Anabaptist-rooted components of the Confession. This will help to clarify the original vision of the River Brethren. The more basic purpose of the analysis will be to note the impact of Pietism on the Mennonites in early American Christianity.

A detailed history of the original River Brethren Confession is not required for the analysis to be undertaken. At the same time some data is in order. There are six extant copies of the text, three in English translation and three in the original German. A study has been made as to the time and place of writing, and it can be affirmed on the basis of the evidence that the Confession was written in about 1780 in Lancaster County. The date and place are those of the beginnings of the River Brethren. Whether the Confession was ever officially adopted by the Brethren cannot be answered with absolute certainty. There is evidence in both directions. Mention must be made that three of the extant texts are signed by the same group of

29. Levi Lukenbach, "Brethren in Christ," *A Book for the Use and Benefit of the Church in the Dayton District* (1879). Written manuscript in the Brethren in Christ Archives, Messiah College, Grantham, Pa.

30. Wittlinger, "Brethren in Christ," pp. 55–58.

eight men. Several of these men, like Jacob Engle, were known to have been the founding fathers of the River Brethren church. The signatures plus a study of the content of the text are adequate bases for affirming that the Confession does represent the views of the River Brethren church at its beginning.

When the six texts are compared it is obvious some editing took place in the history of the text. At this point it is difficult to know which of the texts is most primitive. This may vary from section to section in the Confession. The author or authors of the text cannot be determined, although there is some evidence it may have been John Engle, the brother of the first leader of the Brethren, Jacob Engle.[31]

The Confession theologically breaks down into three sections: the conversion experience, the nature of the church, and the relationship to the world.

THE CONVERSION EXPERIENCE

The Confession begins with the doctrine of God. The development of the first two sentences is very significant. With a minimal consideration of the character and attributes of God, the nature and economy of the Trinity, and no mention of God's role as Creator and Sustainer nor any rejection of heterodox views, the first sentence immediately relates the eternal God with the eternal Savior.

> We believe and confess a triune, everlasting and almighty Being, and that a holy almighty God has been from eternity, and is, and will remain, and has provided Jesus Christ as Saviour of mankind before the foundation of the world.

The important consideration about God was not a careful systematic definition of his nature and work, as in Protestant Scholasticism, but rather his provision of experiential salvation.[32] Theological exactitude or rational comprehen-

---

31. Copies of all six texts are located in the Brethren in Christ Archives, Messiah College, Grantham, Pennsylvania. For additional information on the texts, see Martin H. Schrag, "The Brethren in Christ Attitude Toward the World" (Ph.D. diss., Temple University, 1967), pp. 305–322. Five of the texts are printed in Martin H. Schrag, *The First Brethren in Christ Confession of Faith* (1974).

32. The contrast is seen immediately by examining such confessions as the Westminster Confession, the Augsburg Confession, or the Dordrecht Confession.

siveness were not the aim, but rather the point was to experience God existentially.

The second sentence of the Confession states the first major point of the Confession, namely, the centrality of personally and subjectively knowing this Savior, how this is done, and what are the results. The sentence reads:

> To learn to know or to find this Redeemer we must obtain and receive forgiveness of sins by means of true repentance, be reconciled to God by the blood of Christ, and being reconciled we obtain the living faith in Jesus.

The rest of the section on the conversion experience is an elaboration of this second sentence.

The statement of faith found to resemble the Confession under consideration most closely in intent at this point is that of Hochmann von Hochenau, the radical Pietist. After a brief statement about the nature of God, Hochmann stated he did not consider it necessary to dispute about the nature of God. The important thing was to submit oneself to God and "to experience his inner workings."[33] Thus the River Brethren Confession is in line with the generally held Pietist view that the important thing was not concern over fine points of theology but rather entering into a conscious relationship with God and living a life of piety.[34]

After an ambiguous statement regarding authority, the Confession continues by elaborating on the nature of faith. In the second sentence of the Confession, quoted above, it is affirmed that this living faith is received through reconciliation with God. The text continues by stating that man does not have this faith by nature, and, therefore, it is necessary to ascertain from whence this faith comes.

To understand the concern with the obtaining of true faith, it is necessary to return to the origins of German Pietism. Many nominal Lutherans assumed they had faith by observing the formalities of the church. The Word and sacraments were considered to be objectively efficacious (*ex opere operato*). The Pietists argued, however, that faith is not produced by outer conformity. It is not only assent to propositions. There is no

33. Hochmann quoted in John S. Flory, *Literary Activity of the German Baptist Brethren* (1908), p. 5.
34. Carl Mirbt, "Pietism," *The New Schaff-Herzog Encyclopedia of Religious Knowledge*, ed. Samuel Macauley Jackson, vol. 9 (1911), p. 57. Philip Jakob Spener, *Pia desideria*, tr. Theodore G. Tappert (1964), pp. 49ff.

faith apart from depth repentance, *fiducia,* and the amendment of life.[35] The Brethren Confession subsequently relates these factors to "living faith" and thus the influence of Pietism is again apparent in determining the content of the Confession.

To identify the starting point of faith, the Confession in simple fashion states that Adam and all his seed lost the divine image, that is, "faith, love and trust." These three were replaced by "fear, unrest and doubt." This inner condition has been passed on from generation to generation. It must be noted that the image of God and the inner condition or state resulting from its loss are largely defined in terms of subjective states experienced by man. The accent is not on rebellion, disobedience, or moral states. Thus the Fall is defined in terms of subjective states to set the stage for the description of salvation as a conscious, subjective experience. The accent on feeling was prominent in much of Pietism, as will be documented later.

After noting the coming of the serpent-destroying Messiah, the Confession takes up the actual conversion experience. The new birth is a deeply felt crisis event. The description of the conversion experience begins with an elaboration of the penitential struggle, "true repentance," the *Busskampf* of some forms of Pietism.[36] As stated in the Confession, the work of Christ has transpired outside of us, but that we might "know and experience this in our hearts," the healing grace of God appeared to convict and teach us that by nature we have a "heart averse from God, devious and sinful." The light reveals to man the depth of the fall of Adam and his children.

The background of this sense of conviction was the strong Pietist belief in human depravity. The penitential struggle was precipitated by the recognition of depth depravity. Many Pietists stressed this depravity, among them Otterbein and Boehm. It was the impact and realization of this dire

---

35. Henry Ernest Ferdinand Guerike, *The Life of Augustus Herman Franke* (1837), p. 40. J. A. Dorner, *History of Protestant Theology,* tr. George Robson and Sophia Taylor, vol. 2 (1871), p. 209.

36. Dale Brown, "The Problem of Subjectivism in Pietism: A Redefinition with Special Reference to the Theology of Philip Jakob Spener and August Herman Francke" (Ph.D. diss., Northwestern University, 1962), p. 263. William H. Nauman, "Theology and German-American Evangelicalism: The Role of Theology in the United Brethren and the Evangelical Association" (Ph.D. diss., Yale University, 1966), p. 13.

inner state that so sharply focussed the conviction of sin. As it is put in the Confession, if this state is felt, "it works a regret and sorrow and inner soul-pains." "It causes a longing, praying, a weeping and a calling to the promised Saviour." It was this concept of conversion involving a strong feeling of lostness that was one of the characteristics of certain types of Pietism and that informed the River Brethren Confession at this point.

The Confession continues by stating that if, in the penitential struggle, the "poor sinner" will open his heart, the Lord Jesus will come and "enter and hold the communion meal" (*Abendmahl*). Another translation (for which we do not have the original German) puts it this way: "In such a poor sinner's opened heart the Lord Jesus will then enter in and sup with him and he with Him." This intimate person to person relationship was found within Pietism.[37]

This spiritual inner communion issues in the receiving of "comfort, peace, love and trust" within. The record of sins as well as the guilt of the sin of Adam is erased. When this happens, the one experiencing the new birth "receives comfort and forgiveness of sins and eternal life." Lest anyone mistake the intent, the point is made that all this is felt and experienced. A conscious crisis experience is described.

The experiencing of pleasurable emotion at the receiving of saving grace was a Pietist emphasis. Salvation was "present salvation."[38]

An aspect of this pleasurable emotion, the Confession indicates, is that of an inner assurance of salvation. Experiencing the grace of God has given the poor sinner "positive confidence." The doctrine of assurance was a characteristic of Pietism and informed the United Brethren.[39]

---

37. John Arndt, *True Christianity or the Whole Economy of God Towards Man and the Whole Duty of Man Towards God*, tr. William Jaques, vol. 1 (1815), pp. 60–61. Guerike, *Augustus Herman Francke*, p. 20. Spener, *Pia desideria*, p. 63. George Conner, "The Influence of German Pietism on American Religious Thought and Practice" (Th.M. thesis, McCormick Theological Seminary, 1947), p. 74. F. Ernest Stoeffler, *The Rise of Evangelical Pietism* (1965), p. 13. Koppel S. Pinson, *Pietism as a Factor in the Rise of German Nationalism* (1934), p. 66.

38. Arndt, *True Christianity*, p. 68. Guerike, *Augustus Herman Francke*, pp. 18, 23. Brown, "The Problem of Subjectivism in Pietism," p. 260. Wilford Nagler, *Pietism and Methodism or the Significance of German Pietism in the Origin and Early Development of Methodism* (1918), p. 36. H. E. Goven, *The Life of Gerhard Tersteegen with Selections from His Writings* (1898), p. 38.

39. Stoeffler, *Evangelical Pietism*, p. 14. Nauman, "German American Evangelicalism," p. 13.

The understanding of the conversion experience as a deeply felt crisis event, beginning with a profound sense of lostness and ending with streams of joy, was not found in all of Pietism but was accentuated in certain manifestations of the movement. Martin Boehm's experience has been recounted above. The Otterbein brothers, including Philip, were committed to the conscious crisis experience. Halle Pietism, church related in form and centering at the University of Halle, also recognized this pattern of *Wiedergeburt*. Many radical Pietists insisted on a "violent break-through," a "painful birth" and a "thorough cleansing of the heart."[40] It is impossible to determine fully through which channel the crisis experience was mediated to the River Brethren, but the evidence suggests the primary, if not only, source was the Otterbein-Boehm movement.

Also a part of the new birth experience was a commitment to a life of discipleship and obedience. According to the Confession, the person involved fully submits himself to the Lord Jesus. That is to say, obedience is not some second step the converted take after they have been saved by faith. Commitment to obedience is a part of the conversion experience. This concept of discipleship in terms of *Nachfolge Christi* was prominent both in certain circles of Pietism and throughout Anabaptism.[41] In radical Pietism, this was often interpreted individualistically so that the believer as an individual followed Christ. Spiritualistic adherents of radical Pietism, such as Hochmann, tended to stress the inner attitude rather than outward conformity to the commands of Jesus Christ found in Scripture. Hochmann would follow the historic Jesus if and when the living Christ validated the commandment within. The Anabaptist emphasis on discipleship was stronger than was generally found among Pietists and, possibly, more important. Discipleship involved the formation of the gathered fellowship of believers. Thus it appears that the concern with obedience came to the River Brethren via both Pietism and Anabaptism. But it will be noted that in the remaining portions of the Confession, discipleship is especially related to fashioning the New Testament church (Anabaptism).

Throughout this first section on the new birth experience, the Confession tends toward a concept of regeneration

---

40. Stoeffler, *German Pietism,* p. 179. O'Malley, "The Otterbeins," p. 458.
41. "Anabaptism and Pietism: Theological Definitions in Historical Perspective," *The Covenant Quarterly,* vol. 28, p. 122.

rather than one of forensic justification. The implication is that an ontological change has transpired in the human heart. Because of the regeneration of man's nature, a life of discipleship and holiness was possible in the power of the Spirit. The centrality of regeneration as compared to justification was important to the Pietists.[42]

Having covered the new birth experience section of the Confession text, attention must be given to a few overall characteristics of the same. First, it is apparent in this section that only those doctrines considered "essential" to personal salvation and personal piety were given consideration. In typical Pietist fashion, the other doctrines were, by implication, non-essential or secondary. Secondly, those essential doctrines were stated with "apostolic simplicity," as was characteristic of Pietism. Lastly, the point of the Confession was not to define the faith rationally, but to lead one to a personal relationship with Jesus Christ.

This concludes the analysis of the first section of the Confession, namely, the one dealing with the new birth. What are the conclusions and observations that can be made in the light of the section?

1. The evidence suggests that the River Brethren gained their understanding of the new birth from Pietism as shaped by the Otterbein-Boehm movement with some possible Dunker influence.[43] Additional confirmation of this conclusion is given in the first history of River Brethren beginnings

---

42. Stoeffler, *Evangelical Pietism,* p. 241.

43. The early Dunker view of the new birth is difficult to discern. The early leaders wrote very little about the new birth. The Dunkers, in contrast to the Mennonites, were basically not attracted to and did not become a part of the Otterbein-Boehm movement. Minutes of the Dunker annual meetings during the first years of the nineteenth century condemn the loud, revivalistic understanding of conversion. Dunker historians have made very little of the new birth. One Dunker historian has suggested the Dunkers were the "dry-eyed" moralistic kind of Pietists. It appears Dunker conversion was not so much a matter of much emotion but rather a deeply felt commitment of the will to discipleship. Yet there is at least one description of the new birth by a Dunker that sounds very much like what was going on in the Otterbein-Boehm movement. *Minutes of the Annual Meetings of the Church of the Brethren, 1788–1909* (1908), pp. 38–40, 44. Personal letters from Floyd E. Mollat December 9, 1960, and May 19, 1965. Christian Longenecker, "On the True Conversion and New Birth," tr. Vernard Eller, *Brethren Life and Thought,* vol. 7, pp. 23–32. Donald F. Durnbaugh, ed., *The Brethren in Colonial America* (1967), pp. 431–433, 445.

written by one who was himself of the River Brethren. He wrote:

> Although they were raised up among a peaceable, law-abiding and order-loving people, yet true evangelical religion was but very little known among them. But God's grace and His convicting spirit was at work and finally those two persons, John and Jacob Engle, with others, were led to see themselves as sinners and sought and obtained pardon of their sins and their acceptance with Christ. . . .[44]

2. The crisis newbirth experience was really central to the United Brethren movement. The early leaders of the United Brethren, Otterbein, Boehm, Newcomer, Geeting, Huber, and others, testify to the centrality of personally experienced salvation. The heart of the faith was rebirth; no single experience was more essential. Sacraments, ethics, church order, or theology were quite secondary to personal experience. The term "brother" was reserved for those who had been converted. Thus the United Brethren were the uniting of all who had been converted. It was not that all had to have identical experiences, only similar ones. Historian A. W. Drury argues that in the early years of the United Brethren, evangelism was almost the sole function of the church.[45] What separated men like Otterbein and Boehm from the other clergy was not a new doctrine but the message of personal salvation. One present-day author has summed it up in this manner.

> The core of religion is held to be God-in-the-heart, cleansing, conforming, empowering to which the religious consciousness gives decisive testimony. These men, in revolt from the concept of religion as doctrine or conduct placed major emphasis upon Christian experience.[46]

Several examples will illustrate the point. We have already described the experience of Martin Boehm. Chosen for the ministry, he began to pray for a message. Rather than receiving a message he felt a sense of lostness. He was deeply

---

44. Lukenbach, "Brethren in Christ."
45. Drury, *United Brethren in Christ*, pp. 552, 155–162. John Denig, ed., *The Autobiography of the Rev. Samuel Huber* (1858), pp. 13–22. Nauman, "Theology and German-American Evangelism," p. 9. James O. Bemesderfer, *Pietism and its Influence Upon the Evangelical United Brethren Church* (1966), p. 80.
46. Eller, *United Brethren*, p. 31.

convicted of sin until in a crisis point he was flooded with joy. A second illustration is that of John Neidig. A member of the Mennonite church, he found spiritual life through a religious experience. In time, he was put out of the Mennonite church.[47]

Another significant case is that of Christian Newcomer. Reared in a Mennonite home, Christian at an early age sought religious peace. He consulted with two Mennonite ministers. One told him to be baptized, join the Mennonite church, and take the sacrament. This counsel was of no avail for Newcomer's heart condition. The second minister suggested to Newcomer that he was too firmly convinced of a religion of experience. Christian became acquainted with the preaching of William Otterbein and George Geeting, the latter also a preacher of the awakening. He was impressed because these men "insisted on the necessity of genuine repentance, pardon of sin and in consequence thereof a change of heart and renovation of the spirit."[48] Because these men preached the same doctrine that he had experienced, Newcomer left the Mennonite church and became a member of one of Otterbein's societies. Of his experience he wrote,

> Henceforth my peace flowed again like a river. With confidence I could now draw up to the throne of grace, crying Abba Father. My whole soul was swallowed up in love to God.[49]

That the Otterbein-Boehm movement centered in the personal aspect of Christianity is shown by the manner in which the leaders dealt with church structure. The ministers saw themselves as nonsectarian, having no theology of the visibility of the church that was essential. Church organization developed functionally.

3. As has already been mentioned, some Mennonites accepted the Otterbein-Boehm form of Pietism. They were among the awakened. The evidence suggests these Mennonites did not discern the continuities between Mennonitism and Pietism. They might have noted that Mennonitism also stressed the need of a conscious conversion experience including repentance, confession, and faith. They could have perceived that Mennonitism and Pietism both accentuate personal sanctification and discipleship. If so inclined, they would have

---

47. Drury, *United Brethren in Christ*, p. 160.
48. Samuel S. Hough, ed., *Christian Newcomer: His Life, Journal and Achievements* (1941), p. 13.
49. Quoted in Drury, *United Brethren in Christ*, p. 151. See also Hildt, pp. 6–7.

seen that both movements are practically and existentially oriented.

Another area of commonality is that both movements were concerned with fellowship, the one in the gathered church, the other in the conventicle. A bit of study would have revealed that the Anabaptists originally were very missionary minded. The continuities, however, were not discerned; the possibility of synthesis was not realized. Mennonitism was seen as dead, cold, and institutionalized. Christian Newcomer, reared in a Mennonite home and an early bishop of the United Brethren, states that after his awakening he attended a Mennonite church in his home community. He affirms that the Mennonites "continued in the same inexperience of religion as when I left them."[50] Thus, some Mennonites felt that to truly embrace the awakening it was necessary to say "no" to their Anabaptist rootage.

4. The Mennonites, however, on the whole rejected the Pietism of Otterbein and Boehm. Most Mennonite historians accept the fact that the Mennonites were influenced by Pietism both in Germany before migrating, and in America. It must be remembered that Pietism took many forms and its influence varied. That some Mennonites were influenced by Pietism would give a basis for their being attracted to the Otterbein-Boehm movement. On the other hand, the influence of Pietism was not of such a nature as to move the whole of the Mennonite brotherhood into the Otterbein-Boehm camp.

The Mennonite rejection of the Otterbein-Boehm movement is illustrated by three men cited in the last portion dealing with the United Brethren and the new birth. All three, Martin Boehm, Christian Newcomer, and John Neidig, had been related to the Mennonite church. All three were awakened and either left or were forced out of the Mennonite church.

There are two happenings that particularly highlight the Mennonite rejection of Otterbein-Boehm Pietism. The one is the expulsion of Boehm from the Mennonite church and the other is the publication of a writing of the Mennonite bishop Christian Burkholder.

Martin Boehm was excommunicated from the Mennonite church in about the year 1775. In an extant copy of the Mennonite defense for excommunicating Martin Boehm, we

---

50. Hough, *Christian Newcomer*, p. 12.

learn of the charges made against him. In the first place, Martin denied the doctrine of Christ by having "a great deal to do with forming a union and associating with men (professors) which allow themselves to walk on the broad way, practicing warfare and the swearing of oaths." The latter two, warfare and oaths, were explicitly in opposition to the teachings of Christ. Secondly, he fellowshipped with those under church censure, rather than admonishing them to seek reconciliation with the church. Martin, it was affirmed, stated that "Scripture might be burned" and that the Mennonites placed too much emphasis on rules and ordinances. He was further quoted as having said that "Satan was a benefit to man" and that "faith cometh from unbelief, life out of death and light out of darkness." On the basis of these charges, Boehm was excommunicated from the Mennonite church.[51]

Unfortunately we do not have a statement from Boehm or someone from the Otterbein movement. Boehm's son stated that the reason Martin Boehm was expelled was because he was "too evangelical." United Brethren historian A. W. Drury affirms that the real causes of Boehm's expulsion were that he promoted revivals and associated with those who belonged to other churches. Another historian suggests the Mennonites were irked because Boehm promoted revivals and used the English language.[52] Mennonite historians tend to agree the issue was revivalistic beliefs and practices.

The precise content of the conflict cannot be fully discerned. It does appear, from the defense and from the facts gathered from other sources, that Boehm saw the essence of the faith in terms of personal experiential piety. He was willing to enter into spiritual fellowship with anyone who had been born again. Ethical norms, sacramental practices, "nonessential" doctrine, governmental structures, and denominational lines were all secondary. The implication of this posture is that the church is conceived primarily as invisible. It consists of all the truly converted in all the denominations. The concept of conversion shaped the definition of the church.

The Mennonites, on the other hand, judged Boehm from their two major concepts, discipleship and the Mennonite view of the church. Boehm was not true to the faith as shown by the fact that he was not obeying all the commandments of

---

51. John F. Funk, *The Mennonite Church and Her Accusers* (1878), pp. 41–59.
52. Wakeley, *The Patriarch of One Hundred Years*, p. 12. Drury, *United Brethren in Christ*, p. 106. Eller, *Evangelical United Brethren*, p. 27.

Christ. This dealt not only with practicing warfare and swearing of the oath but also involved fashioning a corporate body under the direction of Christ. Boehm was putting his individual interpretation above the light given the church by the historic and living Christ.

To the Mennonites the church was to be made visible on earth and it consisted of all the truly converted (Mennonite style) and baptized who in convenant under God and with one another perceived themselves as the new people of God. This meant separation from all who walked the broad way. When Christ is accepted he is accepted not only as Lord personally but also as the head of the church. Thus when people enter, they accept Christ's authority as mediated through the church. It is the corporate body that discerns the will of God, not, as with Boehm, the individual. The main body of Mennonites decided against Pietist awakenings.

The second item that highlights the Mennonite response to the Otterbein-Boehm movement is a book written by Mennonite bishop Christian Burkholder. Penned in 1792, it was not printed until 1804, at which time it was endorsed by twenty-seven ministers and deacons of the Mennonite church. The number probably constituted the entire official ministry of the Lancaster Conference. The work, therefore, was something of an official publication of the Lancaster County Mennonites.[53]

The book is written to deal with the issues of the times. Thus there is a discussion on baptism in which immersion is refuted (against the Dunkers). It would appear that one of the major purposes of writing the book was to meet the challenge of the awakening fostered by Boehm and Otterbein. The book reflects the influence of Pietism, sometimes in terms of accepting Pietist ideas and at other times by rejecting these ideas. The subjects discussed reflect Pietist influence; they are "true repentance," "saving faith," "pure love to God and neighbor," "obedience," and "full surrender."

The bishop develops some continuities with Pietism but his real intent was to instruct Mennonite youth on the genius of their heritage, and to move them away from Pietism. The

---

53. Christian Burkholder, *Nützliche und Erbauliche Anrede an die Jugend von der Wahren Busse, von dem Seligmachenden Glauben an Jesu Christo* (1804), pp. 1–90. Many editions in English have been published; *Conversations on Saving Faith for the Young in Questions and Answers* (1941), pp. 175–246.

Mennonite concerns on which he focussed included non-resistance, a strong sense of separation from the world, a strong emphasis on self-denial, and an overwhelming accent relating discipleship to conversion. Conversion does not center in an emotional experience; rather it is basically an ethical matter of commitment to the Lordship of Christ.

As for the motifs and accents of the awakening, the bishop makes his position clear. He affirms none should "dictate to God how he [God] is to go to work to effect the same [new birth] in you." The thrust is against the tendency of some Pietists to set up a rigid pattern of the conversion experience. Bishop Burkholder continues by stating, "My experience can help you nothing; [and] your experience can help me nothing."

In any case, "boasting much of ourselves is the work of the 'old man.'" Surely the bishop is speaking against the Pietist testimonies and meetings which center in discussing one's inner condition. He defends the private meeting of instruction held for Mennonite youth. The point is that some youth are too bashful to express themselves in public. The mood of the bishop's answer is in opposition to the spirit of Pietism. For the bishop, conversion is focussed in the will and in ethical results. "Christ identified the new birth with the following of him." Indeed the fruit of the Christian life (obedience) "is the only sign whereby the children of God can be known." The sign of conversion is not the emotional, subjective experience but the walk of discipleship.

Burkholder continues by affirming that the new birth can come without emotional demonstration and there is need of growth in the new birth. The author also speaks against individualism and condemns those who cause church divisions. There can be little doubt that Bishop Burkholder sees some serious weaknesses in the Otterbein-Boehm movement. These weaknesses are not peripheral issues, but cut to the heart of the faith. The bishop does not want to lose his Mennonites to revivalistic Pietism.

It should be mentioned that Mennonites were vitally concerned about such matters as repentance, faith, grace, the new birth, and discipleship. Just *how* these aspects of Christianity were handled by Mennonites at this time is not fully known. There may have been more continuity between Mennonite views and the views of the Confession than has been suggested. Conversion, almost certainly routinized in practice, was a non-emotional commitment of the will to discipleship. When the River Brethren Confession is compared with the writings of Christian Burkholder, the difference between the two is apparent. The one is Pietist oriented, the other is Anabaptist oriented.

The Mennonite attitude to the Otterbein-Boehm awakening being expounded is in keeping with the evaluation of some Mennonite historians. Dr. Pannabecker states that the Mennonites on the whole "were opposed to both the new evangelistic movement grounded in Pietistic thought and methods, and in its expression in active work." He continues by stating that Mennonites had been trained in the "suppression of feeling, not only in religion but also in everyday life. Practical virtues and stability in the face of difficulty were to them the traditional tests of true religion."[54] Historian J. C. Wenger has suggested that in colonial times Mennonites did not stress experience and a vital new birth but rather obedience. With Mennonite piety went a commendable "modesty which frowned on 'testimony meetings' and tended to regard them as an evidence of spiritual pride."[55]

The conclusion is that the majority of Mennonites in Eastern Pennsylvania could not accept the Otterbein-Boehm understanding of Pietism. Of the three responses mentioned at the beginning of this chapter, they chose the way of rejecting Pietism.

The Mennonite rejection of Pietism, as just outlined, is to be viewed in the light of the spiritual orientation of colonial Mennonites as described in the first pages of this chapter. There it was suggested that faith was institutionalized and the status quo was to be maintained. The mood was one of withdrawal. If the Mennonites who accepted the Otterbein-Boehm type of Pietism and became United Brethren are to be faulted, so should the Mennonites who rejected the Otterbein-Boehm possibilities. They also had the possibility of discerning continuities and working for synthesis. The challenge confronting the Mennonites was not that of accepting Otterbein-Boehm

---

54. Samuel Floyd Pannabecker, "The Development of the General Conference of the Mennonite Church of North America in the American Environment" (Ph.D. diss., Yale University, 1944), p. 114.
55. *Glimpses of Mennonite History* (1940), p. 60. Wenger continues, "the emphasis (among Mennonites) was placed on the deeper life with God, rather than noisy emotionalism."

Pietism in its totality, but they should have evaluated the new movement in the light of the Anabaptist vision.

5. The Otterbein-Boehm movement was essentially of a church-related type of Pietism. Yet there were some evidences of radical Pietism. It is not possible to identify what aspects of the River Brethren concept of the new birth were due to church-related Pietism and what motifs were rooted in radical Pietism.

THE CONCEPT OF THE CHURCH

The second section of the River Brethren Confession, dealing with the concept of the church, begins with a short definition of the church. The starting point is discipleship, and the thought is that as Christ has become our redeemer, so he will also be our pattern (*Vorbild*) in the erecting of the church. Thus discipleship was not only an individual pursuit but was also a corporate assignment. The Confession indicates that those drawn to Christ through the new birth are drawn to one another through love. Those drawn together in love constitute the "believing community" (*Gläubige Gemeinschaft*). The new corporate unity is the work of the Holy Spirit.

The church is here defined as the converted, gathered fellowship of believers. The implication (also confirmed by the rest of the text) is that God in his grace, and as a means of mediating grace, has revealed in Jesus Christ a blueprint for the ordering of brotherhood life. Under the guidance of the head of the body, Jesus Christ, the people of God are under biblical obligation to actualize such a fellowship of believers. The quality of life in the visible company of believers is to be determined by love, and the oneness and unity are to be the result of the work of the Holy Spirit.

The church as just defined was precisely the concept of the church held by the colonial Mennonites and Dunkers because of their Anabaptist heritage.[56] The group is to be the new gathered people of God, living in love and actualizing the new society made possible by God's grace.

Some have argued that the Dunkers gained their concept of the church not only from the Anabaptists but also from

---

56. Burkholder, *Conversations on Saving Faith,* p. 234. Peter Bowman, *A Testimony on Baptism as Practiced by the Primitive Christians* (1831), tr. not given.

some of the views of radical Pietism. Included among the latter
are the following: the radical Pietists rejected the state
churches (but also such sectarian groups as Mennonites). Some
of them favored adult baptism. Hochmann in his confession
(written in 1702) stated that the Lord's supper should be limited to the truly converted. Gottfried Arnold had projected the
New Testament church as the ideal. In addition there were
some loosely organized groups among the radical Pietists who
had made the attempt at some kind of corporate living. On the
basis of such evidence and the implications involved, the Dunkers were merely developing to its logical and theological conclusions the radical Pietist view.[57]

There were some radical Pietist views that militated
against such reasoning. Radical Pietists tended to be individualistic and spiritualistic. Sometimes the authority of inner
spiritual guidance was more important than biblical command.
The radical Pietists as a whole, when they left the established
churches, believed to organize a new body would be but to add
another established church. As one asserted, "the true
separatists form no new sects."[58] The radical Pietists tended to
follow their Lord individualistically. They felt they were a part
of the invisible universal church and were committed to the
philadelphic concept of the church. God would in due time
institute the true and perfect church. It is not to be set up by
man and it will come with "mighty evidence of apostolic spirit
and power." Lastly, as will be pointed out below, the radical
Pietists had no love for church discipline and regular church
order. The conclusion is that the basis for the Dunker concept
of the church is Anabaptism. At the same time, as will be shown
below, radical Pietism did contribute to the Dunker view of the
church.

As for the church-related Pietists of Europe, they were
given to the territorial concept of the church. To such the
basic emphasis tended toward the invisible church.

The United Brethren in their first decades relegated
matters of church form to a secondary place and generally
assumed Scripture did not impose on them the necessity of
fashioning a church according to the pattern laid down by
Jesus and the Apostles. For years they had no intention of
organizing a church; their corporate forms were concerned

---

57. Ensign, "Radical German Pietism," pp. 276–291. Martin Grove Brum-
    baugh, *A History of the German Baptist Brethren in Europe and America*
    (1899), pp. 16–28.
58. Ensign, "Radical German Pietism," p. 401.

with fostering personal piety, not actualizing the new community of the people of God. The real church was the invisible one consisting of all truly born again.[59] The River Brethren were indebted to the Anabaptist tradition for their concept of the church.

Continuing its development of the concept of the church, the Confession next outlines three ordinances: baptism, the Lord's supper, and feetwashing.

After rejecting any thought of baptismal regeneration, the statement on baptism strongly emphasizes that in baptism one is to follow Jesus Christ. In addition to the authority of Jesus Christ, four other authorities were amassed for the action of baptism, namely, "the written word," the "illumination of the Good Spirit," the example of the Apostles, and the practice of the New Testament churches. Baptism is for believers only. The mode prescribed is trine immersion. Those baptized renounce the devil, the world, and all sinful life. Baptism is a "sign of the burial" of the old life. Through baptism one is related to the church.

Both the Mennonites and Dunkers made a great deal in colonial times of the necessity of following Christ in baptism. Both groups baptized only believers. Both put emphasis on the importance of baptism in relating one to the gathered fellowship of believers. The Dunkers practiced trine immersion, whereas the Mennonites believed in sprinkling or pouring.[60] In contrast to these clearly defined views on baptism, the United Brethren believed that whether baptism should be administered to infants or believers, by pouring or immersion, was a matter for each individual to decide. The manner of baptism was to be left up to the individual, according to the first United Brethren Confession. If the heart was correct, the baptism would be correct regardless of form, in the opinion of one writer.[61]

The Dunker view of baptism may have been in part due

---

59. Drury, *Phillip William Otterbein*, p. 95. "United Brethren—Baptism—Reception of New Members," *Religious Telescope*, vol. 8, p. 156.

60. Henry Funk, *A Mirror of Baptism with the Spirit, with Water and with Blood* (1890), tr. not given. This was first published in 1744 under the title of *Ein Spiegel der Taufe mit Geist, mit Wasser und mit Blut.* Bowman, *A Testimony on Baptism*, pp. 16, 23. Benjamin Rush, *An Account of the Manners of the German Inhabitants of Pennsylvania*, The Pennsylvania German Society, vol. 19 (1910). The work by Rush was first printed in 1789.

61. *Doctrine and Discipline of the United Brethren in Christ* (1819). Heinrich Kumler, "Verschiedne Taufen und Doch nur Eine," *Die Geschäftige Martha*, vol. 2, p. 84.

to radical Pietist views. As already mentioned, some radical Pietists were committed to adult baptism in contrast to infant baptism. Hochmann was such a one. But Hochmann and many other radical Pietists believed that outer acts such as baptism are to be engaged in only if there are inner promptings by the Spirit. Outer practice must never be made mandatory by the group for the individual. The baptism most dear to the heart of Hochmann was invisible "Spirit" baptism.[62]

It is apparent that the River Brethren basically followed the Mennonites and Dunkers in the centrality of following Jesus and the Apostles in baptism, in the assumption that baptism is for believers only and in the belief that the form of baptism is prescribed in Scripture. The River Brethren followed the Dunkers in the practice of trine immersion. They held with the Dunkers and Mennonites (Anabaptist family of churches) that a given concept and form of baptism is commanded in Scripture.[63]

In what appears to be a postscript to the section in the Confession on the doctrine of the church, it is stated in regard to the other fundamentals, such as infant and unregenerate baptism, "we leave it to those who can satisfy themselves with them." Then follows the surprising statement that "where the teachings of the Lord Jesus are silent, there we will also be silent." These quotes reject infant baptism as far as the River Brethren are concerned but leave the way open for others to practice infant baptism.

This view definitely is not Anabaptistic. It seems to reflect the Otterbein-Boehm awakening movement in which it was decided that the mode of baptism be left to the desire of people involved. This is the only known instance in River Brethren history that indicates tolerance toward infant baptism. It would appear that the Confession is not fully consistent on the point of baptism. The River Brethren historically have practiced and strongly defended believer's baptism.

The Confession moves on to consider the Lord's supper. It is to be celebrated, for in so doing one will be following the pattern of Jesus Christ and the Apostles. Thus one remains

---

62. Brumbaugh, *German Baptist Brethren,* p. 84. Martin Schrag, "The Early Brethren Concept of Authority," *Brethren Life and Thought,* vol. 9, pp. 109–115.

63. The last sentence of the River Brethren Confession indicates that all who are truly baptized, not only the River Brethren, are a part of the universal church.

steadfast in the Apostles' doctrine. The Lord's supper is interpreted as a memorial and as the actualization of fellowship.

The thought of the statement on the Lord's supper is very close to that of the Mennonite Dordrecht Confession (widely used conservative Mennonite confession of faith written in 1632 in Dordrecht, Holland), although there is no evidence of copying.[64] That the Lord's supper is an act of obedience, for disciples only, a memorial, and an actualization of fellowship are all in keeping with Mennonite and Dunker thought.

The Dunker view of the Lord's supper may have been in part gained from the radical Pietists. Hochmann believed that only the regenerate should take part in communion. Once again, however, the Lord's supper should be practiced only if there is a direct inspiration from God. The written word by itself was not normative. The Dunkers went beyond Hochmann in their insistence that the Lord's supper was limited to Dunker baptized members.[65]

Turning to the emerging United Brethren, we see that they viewed the sacrament in a more individualistic light. Newcomer's journal indicates that the United Brethren frequently celebrated the Lord's supper, but it appears that the central concern was the individual personal relationship to God. The constitution adopted by Otterbein in his pastorate in Baltimore (1774) projected no theology of the sacrament, but it did suggest people may come to the Lord's table even if not members of the local congregation. It also stated that those may be admitted who are "seeking their salvation." The first United Brethren Confession of Faith stated that the manner of celebrating the Lord's supper is left to the discretion of those involved. The lighter attitude toward the ordinances may also have been exemplified in the charge made against Boehm by the Mennonites, that Boehm felt the Mennonites were putting too much emphasis on such things as baptism and communion.[66]

The River Brethren understanding of the Lord's sup-

---

64. The Dordrecht Confession was formally accepted by the Pennsylvania Mennonites. It is printed in full in John C. Wenger, *The Doctrine of the Mennonites* (1950), p. 80. Brumbaugh, *German Baptist Brethren,* p. 80.

65. Ensign, "Radical German Pietism," p. 200. Willoughby, "Early Brethren," p. 124.

66. *Doctrine and Discipline of the United Brethren in Christ,* p. 21. Funk, *The Mennonite Church,* p. 49.

per is in keeping with the Mennonite-Dunker (Anabaptist) view. The Anabaptist family of churches would have found it impossible to serve one at the Lord's table who was still seeking his salvation, nor would they have accepted the idea that the manner of celebration was to be left to the discretion of those involved. To them, the pattern and meaning of the Lord's supper was laid down in Scripture.

The ordinance of feetwashing is discussed next in the Confession. The starting point again is Jesus Christ, his teaching and practice. "Jesus Christ established, practiced and ordered it to be practiced." It is to be practiced as a sign of true humility, love, lowliness, self-denial, and obedience to Jesus Christ, our *Vorbild*. Through feetwashing the church members "become inheritors of grace, shoots on the vine, and members of the body of Christ."

In the United Brethren tradition, feetwashing was either ignored or seen as optional, depending on individual judgment. Newcomer does not mention the practice in his journal, nor does Otterbein mention it in his 1774 Baltimore constitution.[67] The first United Brethren Confession stated the practice "must remain free to the judgment of everyone."[68] Historian John Lawrence, writing in 1861, indicated some of the early United Brethren believed that feet should be literally washed, whereas others did not.[69] The United Brethren did not see feetwashing as a scriptural requirement in obedience to Christ.

Both the Mennonites and Dunkers practiced feetwashing. The River Brethren statement on feetwashing is very similar to the views expressed in the Mennonite Dordrecht Confession. The Dunker sources all agree that they washed feet.[70] For the Anabaptist family of churches, feetwashing was a matter of being true in discipleship, of realizing the equality of believers, and of actualizing true fellowship. It was the realization of the new community of the New Testament. The River Brethren were one with the Anabaptist family of churches in the matter of feetwashing.

The study of the three ordinances has shown that the River Brethren took their understanding of ordinances from

---

67. Hough, *Christian Newcomer*. Lawrence, *The History of the Church of the United Brethren in Christ*, pp. 234–245.
68. *Doctrine and Discipline of the United Brethren in Christ*, p. 21.
69. *Church of the United Brethren*, p. 48.
70. "Feetwashing," *The Brethrens' Encyclopedia*, ed. Henry Kurtz (1867).

the Mennonites and Dunkers (Anabaptist tradition) wi
possible radical Pietist influence via the Dunkers.

The next subject developed in the Confession is that of
growth in grace, individually and corporately. It is significant
that this subject is developed in the section dealing with the
concept of the church. According to the Confession, for
growth in grace both public and private meetings are necessary. The public meetings are to be times of presenting the
Word and exhorting the people to repent. The private meetings are for the purpose of sharing religious experiences
toward the end that the craftiness of the devil would be uncovered and the body of Christ renewed.

> Private ones [meetings] where such children may often gather
> to reveal themselves childlike to each other, by which means
> love is increased and faith and trust are strengthened and
> when such children are exposed to temptation for instance,
> the cunning of Satan is discovered by this childlike revealing
> and one may counsel the other edifying the body of Christ. . . .

The private meeting is closely related to Pietist history.
It was used early in the Reformed tradition, and the Pietists
seem to have copied the form. Congregations begun as the
work of Otterbein were divided into classes.[71] In contrast
neither the Mennonites or Dunkers used the private meeting,
although that which transpired there was very much a part of
the Anabaptist concept of the church, namely, the sharing of
burdens and the exercising of responsibility for the spiritual
state of the brother.

As the Confession continues, the sense of responsibility
for the brother is extended to cover the economic and social
aspects of life. It is stated that since members of the fellowship
are bound through love to watch out for one another, it is
necessary that no important matters such as marriage, change
of address, or the buying of real estate should be engaged in
without brotherly advice. The quality of the inner life of the
brotherhood is to be that of love and this meant assuming
responsibility for the brother and the body as a whole. This
mutuality was not limited to spiritual well-being; it also included social and economic well-being.

There is here a commitment to assist the brother at
every level of life. Manifested here is a very strong sense of
group identity. The corporate body was to seek the mind of

---

71. Drury, *History of the Church of the United Brethren*, p. 137.

Christ and mediate it to the individual. All of life was to be lived in the context of the church and under the umbrella of its guidance. The brotherhood was to be a total community.

The United Brethren sources have nothing to say about brotherly counsel in regard to economic and social matters. Church-related Pietists do not have the gathered concept of the church as the context of brotherly mutuality. Radical Pietists were sporadic in their emphasis on mutuality.

In contrast we find the concern with social and economic mutuality in the Mennonite and Dunker sources. Mennonite historian Harold S. Bender suggests Mennonite disciplines have at times covered conduct, dress, marriage, occupations, food, and the relationship to the world. The Anabaptist (Strassburg) discipline of 1568 provided that there was to be no buying, building, or large business dealings without the counsel, knowledge, and consent of the church. The Amish church discipline of 1779 states members are not to enter into major business transactions or marriage without the advice, knowledge, and consent of the church.[72] Brotherly consultation in all areas of life is but an implication of the Anabaptist concept of the church.

The Confession next takes up the matter of church discipline. In the consideration, two classes of offenders and two levels of discipline are developed.

The first class of offenders are those who trespassed in "small matters." Such persons are to be dealt with according to the steps of Matthew 18. First one brother is to admonish the offender privately in love. If the offender does not accept the admonition of one, then two or three are to approach him. Should the small party not be heard, then the matter is to be presented to the congregation. If the offender refuses to hear the church, then the guilty party is to be considered as a heathen and publican. When this lesser ban is applied one may eat and drink with the banned but not have religious intercourse with him.

The second class of sinners are those who have fallen into outright and open sin (as outlined in I Corinthians 5:11). In such instances, brotherly investigation according to Mat-

---

72. "Discipline, Concept, Idea and Practice of," *The Mennonite Encyclopedia*, vol. 2 (1956), p. 69. Harold S. Bender, "The Discipline Adopted by the Strasburg Conference of 1568," *Mennonite Quarterly Review*, vol. 1, p. 66. *Idem*, "An Amish Church Discipline of 1779," *Mennonite Quarterly Review*, vol. 11, p. 166.

thew 18 is not necessary for, as stated in II Thessalonians 3:6 and 14, one is not to have company with such persons. This means one is not to eat with such persons, to say nothing of religious intercourse. A greater degree of separation is required in the case of the gross sinner.

Yet the banning and separation were toward the end of winning back the offender. He was not to be treated as an enemy but was to be warned so that he might repent and once again become a member of the brotherhood community. The aim was that the offender might once again experience God's love directly and through the brotherhood.

The concern regarding discipline varied with the different kinds of Pietism. Two of the leaders of church-related German Pietism, Philipp J. Spener and August H. Francke, felt the church was not doing enough in the area of discipline. The problem, however, is that the territorial concept of the church makes discipline difficult. The radical Pietists were strenuously opposed to excommunication (the *Bann*) and shunning (*Meidung*). This kind of externalism was anathema to them.[73]

In the United Brethren literature, little is said about discipline. They believed transgressors were to be dealt with according to Matthew 18, but the meaning of this was not developed. It has already been indicated that the United Brethren accepted as basic the concept of the invisible church in terms of all the converted in all bodies. They did not see as a divinely given responsibility the necessity of actualizing the pure church. They referred to themselves as "untrammeled by sect." In their first years the ministers referred to themselves as the *unparteiische* preachers.[74]

In contrast to the views of the Pietists and the United Brethren, the Mennonites and Dunkers did believe in the maintaining of a pure church. The wheat and tares were not to grow together, but rather the tares were to be pulled out. The gathered church was to be without "spot or wrinkle" and the "spots and blemishes," mentioned in the Dordrecht Con-

---

73. Allen C. Deeter, "An Historical and Theological Introduction to Philip Jakob Spener's *Pia desideria:* A Study in Early German Pietism" (Ph.D. diss., Princeton University, 1963). *Idem,* "Membership in the Body of Christ as Interpreted by Classical Pietism," *Brethren Life and Thought,* vol. 9. Guerike, *Augustus Herman Francke,* pp. 74–75. Stoeffler, *German Pietism,* p. 29.

74. Lawrence, *Church of the United Brethren,* pp. 236–238, 244. Drury, *United Brethren in Christ,* p. 185.

fession, were to be removed by excommunication. A sharp distinction was to be maintained between the church and the world, and excommunication was to be the means of keeping the church pure and undefiled. Two levels of excommunication were used among some Mennonites.[75] The Dunkers favored the maintaining of the pure church. Thus Dunker Michael Frantz stated that if a member becomes impure he must be *abgehauen* (separated) from the body. The River Brethren from the beginning sought a pure church.[76]

Mennonite and Dunker literature contains very similar discussions on the details of banning and the extent of intercourse with the banned as is found in the River Brethren Confession.

It is abundantly clear that the River Brethren concept of discipline and avoidance was virtually identical with that of the Dunkers and Mennonites. All three bodies were concerned with maintaining the purity of the gathered, sharing, and disciplined people of God. They felt it was the plan of God not only to save individuals but to have his gathered people constitute a society that was an actualization of the New Testament blueprint for the church. All this meant a sharp sense of separation from the world in a corporate sense. The saints were to keep themselves unspotted by the world.

THE RELATIONSHIP TO THE WORLD

The first subject discussed in the third section of the Confession is that of marriage. Several concerns are registered in the section on marriage, the first appearing to be (the text is not clear) that engaged persons, both being believing persons, can be married before being baptized. The second belief was that children of Brethren may be married and considered a part of the Brethren community even if they are not yet awakened persons. The marriage of Brethren children was possible only if there was proper consultation, i.e., children stand under their parents, the parents under the congregation, and the congregation under Christ. Lastly, the ideal is expressed that young people should be converted before they are married.

Church-related Pietism and the United Brethren man-

---

75. Wenger, *Doctrines of the Mennonites*, p. 82. Christian Neff, "Ban," *The Mennonite Encyclopedia*, vol. 1, p. 219.
76. *Einfältige Lehr-Betrachtungen, und kurtzgefasztes Glauben-Bekantnisz des gottseligen Lehrers* (1770), p. 37. "Writings of Michael Frantz," *Schwarzenau*, vol. 2 (1941), pp. 78–82.

ifested no interest in the control of marriage or the setting down of guidelines for marriage. On the other hand, the ideal among some radical Pietists was celibacy. Hochmann distinguished five types of marriage from the completely beastly to the soul married to the Lamb (celibacy). The River Brethren were not given to celibacy but they did seek to guide their members in matters of marriage.[77]

Both the Mennonites and Dunkers legislated that the church was to guide its people in marriage. For both groups, marriage was to be within their respective brotherhoods, and those who did not follow these guidelines were excommunicated. The church was to be kept pure, and the line of separation from the world clearly defined.[78] The River Brethren basically accepted the Mennonite and Dunker point of view on marriage in terms of its being under the jurisdiction of the brotherhood and within the people of God.

The next issue in the Confession is that of the nonswearing of the oath. It is stated that the teachings of Jesus (Matthew 5:34) forbid the swearing of the oath. This is another illustration of the effort to follow the commandments of Jesus Christ. The nonswearing of the oath also reflects an attitude toward government, for it was the government that asked the swearing of the oath as a pledge of total loyalty. The nonswearing of the oath implied that the authority of Jesus Christ transcended that of government and that the Christian was not to be a part of government.

Church-related Pietism as a whole and the United Brethren were silent on the oath. Many radical Pietists did not swear the oath and this may have been a factor in the shaping of the Dunker view. The Anabaptists from the beginning did not swear the oath, so that Mennonites and Dunkers were of one mind on the oath. The Dunkers in their yearly meetings (1785 and 1790) rejected the oath as contrary to the work of Christ, and Mennonite leaders stated (1773) that the Mennonites in Pennsylvania do not swear the oath.[79]

Closely related to the swearing of the oath in the River Brethren Confession is the rejection of Christian participation

77. Ensign, "Radical German Pietism," pp. 174–177.
78. Burkholder, *Conversation on Saving Faith,* pp. 237–238. Wenger, *Doctrines of the Mennonites,* pp. 80, 81. Kurtz, *Brethrens' Encyclopedia,* p. 142.
79. *Minutes of the Annual Meetings of the Church of the Brethren* (1908), pp. 10, 14. John C. Wenger, *History of the Mennonites of Franconia Conference* (1937), pp. 395–402. Ensign, "Radical German Pietism," p. 418.

in warfare. Once again the authority cited is the teaching of Jesus Christ (Matthew 5:39–40). Implied in the rejection of military activity was that the loyalty of Christ transcends loyalty to the state.

There is no evidence that the United Brethren took a pacifist stance in colonial times. Church-related Pietists were not pacifists but some of the radical Pietists did reject warfare. Apparently the radical Pietist pacifism combined with the Anabaptist pacifism to make the Dunkers pacifist. Both the Dunkers and Mennonites were absolute biblical pacifists. The annual meeting of the Dunkers declared against war in 1781, 1785, 1790. The Mennonites and Dunkers together petitioned the Pennsylvania House of Representatives in 1775 stating their opposition to war and appealing for freedom of conscience in regard to war.[80] The River Brethren were at one with the Dunkers and Mennonites in the rejection of war on the basis of the teachings of Jesus Christ.

The last doctrine discussed in the River Brethren Confession is that of the relationship of the Christian to the government. According to the teachings of the Lord Jesus and his Apostles, no follower of Christ is permitted to occupy magisterial office (*obrigkeitliche Ämter*). Government, however, is not to be opposed; rather one is to be obedient in all that is good, praying for the rulers and paying taxes. According to Paul, government is the servant of God, it being God's method of ruling the world. It is also for the benefit of the children of God; otherwise the world would be still a more difficult place in which to live. Christians were to pray for the rulers so that the children of God may live a quiet and blessed life pleasing to God.

The United Brethren in their early literature at no point developed a Christian posture to political life. Some of the radical Pietists, however, developed views similar to the River Brethren. Hochmann believed that government was ordained of God and is to be obeyed in all civil matters. Should the government, however, ask one to do something contrary to the Word of God, the Christian must obey God rather than man. Although allowing for the possibility that a ruler could be a true Christian, Hochmann on the whole considered rulers as

---

80. Brown, "The Problem of Subjectivism," pp. 100, 291. *Minutes of the Annual Meetings of the Church of the Brethren,* pp. 6, 9, 14. Rufus Jones, *The Church of the Brethren and War* (1944), pp. 79–81. Ensign, "Radical German Pietism," p. 418.

heathen powers. The end of governments is in sight as they will cease to exist with the second coming of Christ. One's concern thus should be in spiritual not governmental matters.[81]

Here again radical Pietism may have interacted with Anabaptism. In this instance it probably contributed to the state.

The views of the Dunkers and Mennonites relative to government were virtually identical with those of the River Brethren. In the late eighteenth century both the Dunkers and the Mennonites believed Christians should not serve in government nor take an active role in politics. Government was ordained of God to keep in check the evil tendencies of man. Christians were to be obedient to government as long as its demands were not contrary to that of God. Christians were to pray for rulers and pay taxes. Dunker and Mennonite withdrawal from political life was conditioned, in part, by the loss of the control of the Pennsylvania government by the Quakers and by the persecution felt by the groups during the Revolutionary War.[82] It is apparent, then, that the River Brethren took their clues in regard to government from the Mennonite-Dunker tradition.

Having analyzed the concept of the church and the relationship of the church to the world, we need to delineate the conclusions and implications of the two sections.

1. It is apparent the River Brethren gained their concept of the church and their attitude toward the world from the Anabaptist tradition. At several points the radical Pietist understanding was similar to that of the Anabaptists (some historians believe Anabaptism was one of the sources of radical Pietism) so that both traditions probably had a part in shaping the Dunker views. Yet it should be mentioned that the River Brethren accepted those aspects of radical Pietism mediated through the Dunkers that were in keeping with the Anabaptist posture. There were certain Dunker views gained from the radical Pietists that the River Brethren rejected. The most distinctive doctrine was the ultimate salvation of all people. Other radical Pietist ideas that may have been held by some Dunkers and which came to fruition in the Ephrata Society

---

81. Brumbaugh, *German Baptist Brethren*, pp. 85–87.
82. Frantz, *Einfältige*, p. 21. Bowman, *Church of the Brethren and War*, pp. 98–99. Wenger, *Franconia Conference*, p. 400. Harold S. Bender, "State, Anabaptist-Mennonite Attitude Toward," *The Mennonite Encyclopedia*, vol. 4, p. 615.

were rejected by the River Brethren. The evidence indicates the River Brethren gained their church-world attitude basically from the Anabaptist point of view. The Mennonite influence was also a factor in the River Brethren acceptance of Anabaptist ideas.

In our conclusions listed after the analysis of the new-birth part of the Confession, we indicated the River Brethren gained their understanding of the new birth from the Otterbein-Boehm Pietism with some possible assists from the Dunkers. Thus the River Brethren sought to combine or integrate what they considered the best aspects of both the Pietist and Anabaptist traditions.

This was the third reaction to Pietism on the part of the Mennonites: they discerned the continuities between Pietism and Anabaptism. The number of Mennonites who became River Brethren was not great but some did take the third option.

In the River Brethren orientation the Pietist influence was especially apparent in the emphasis on the crisis conversion experience, in the provision for private meetings, and in the attitude taken toward infant baptism. The Anabaptist influence was pronounced in the concept of the church and the relationship of the church to the world. In greater detail this involved discipleship, the understanding of the ordinances, the concept of brotherhood, the concept of discipline, views toward marriage, the nonswearing of the oath, nonresistance, and the attitude toward government.

Because the River Brethren accepted the crisis newbirth experience as normative, they could not merge with or relate to the Mennonites. Because they accepted the Anabaptist-rooted view of the church and its relation to the world they could not be a part of the United Brethren development. Seeing reality as they did, their choice was to become a new church grouping.

2. The study of the last two sections of the Confession makes clear that those Mennonites who became a part of the United Brethren turned their backs on much that was central to the Anabaptist understanding of the faith. The gathered brotherhood community, the need of a pure church, the nonswearing of the oath, nonresistance, and nonparticipation in government were all basic to historic Mennonitism. These Mennonites accepted Pietism at the expense of their Mennonitism.

3. The analysis of the last two sections has also under-

scored why most Mennonites remained Mennonites. To them the corporate understanding of the faith as forged in Anabaptist-Mennonite history was essential.

The Mennonites of Eastern Pennsylvania in the eighteenth century reacted in three ways to Pietism. Some accepted it fully at the expense of Mennonitism; others rejected Pietism to maintain traditional Mennonitism, and still others sought to integrate the two traditions.[83]

SELECTED BIBLIOGRAPHY–CHAPTER THREE

Bemesderfer, James O., *Pietism and its Influence upon the Evangelical United Brethren* (1966)
Boehm, Henry, *The Patriarch of One Hundred Years: Being the*

---

83. Additional research since writing this chapter has brought me to some further conclusions. In the chapter I state that the Otterbein-Boehm type of Pietism was essentially church related as over against radical Pietism. That statement needs to be modified. Actually Otterbein attempted to plant his feet in both movements. Some of the charges against Boehm may have been rooted in some of his radical Pietist views. Actually it appears to me that the attempt to accurately portray the movement by staying within the polarity of churchly Pietism and radical Pietism is not to understand fully the developments. In the struggle between the two types of Pietism, there emerged a third type. It was theologically orthodox, i.e., did not accept the Boehmist views, was increasingly indifferent to denominationalism (as compared to the hostility of radical Pietism to institutional churches) and focused the faith in personal conversion and personal piety. This was the direction of Otterbein and Boehm.

A few of the phrases in the River Brethren Confession may reflect radical Pietist influence. I am referring as one example to the rather unusual reference in the statement of authority to the Word and the Truth as over against the typical Protestant statement of the authority of Scripture. Secondly, some of the texts in relation to baptism refer to "the dew of the morning glow." Personal letter, C. David Ensign to Martin Schrag, September 25, 1973.

I have stated above that some of the charges against Boehm, as "Satan was a benefit to man," and "faith cometh from unbelief, life out of death and light out of darkness," may reflect radical Pietist influence. It has also been suggested that these views may be rooted in the views of Samuel Hopkins, a disciple of Jonathan Edwards.

Reminiscences, History and Biography of Rev. Henry Boehm. Ed. J.B. Wakely (1875)

Burkholder, Christian, *Nützliche und Erbauliche Anrede an die Jugend von der Wahren Busse, von dem Seligmachenden Glauben an Jesu Christo und der reinen Liebe zu Gott und Seinen Nächsten* (1804)

Climenhaga, A. W., *History of the Brethren in Christ Church* (1942)

Drury, A. W., *History of the Church of the United Brethren in Christ* (1949)

Eller, Paul Himmel, *These Evangelical United Brethren* (1957)

Friedmann, Robert, *Mennonite Piety Through the Centuries* (1949)

Funk, John F., *The Mennonite Church and Her Accusers* (1878)

Newcomer, Christian, *Christian Newcomer: His Life, Journal and Achievements* (1941)

Smith, C. Henry, *The Mennonite Immigration to Pennsylvania in the Eighteenth Century* (1929)

Spayth, Henry G., *History of the Church of the United Brethren in Christ* (1851)

Stoeffler, F. Ernest, *The Rise of Evangelical Pietism* (1965)

———, *German Pietism During the Eighteenth Century* (1973)

Wenger, John C., *History of the Mennonites of Franconia Conference* (1937)

CHAPTER FOUR

MORAVIANISM IN THE AMERICAN COLONIES

by John R. Weinlick

THE MORAVIAN CHURCH TODAY, DESPITE ITS NUMERICAL SMALL-ness, finds itself in the mainstream of American Christianity. If Moravians are still referred to as a sect, sometimes even in authentic reference volumes, it is because of size rather than of character. It has long been an active participant in the various ecumenical ventures of the twentieth century.

COLONIAL STATUS

Though always ecumenically minded, its acceptance by other denominations was quite different in colonial America. The story is that of a tiny minority seeking to establish itself in an unfriendly church environment. Moravians came to America relatively late, their first settlement being made in Georgia in 1735, three years after the chartering of that colony, which was the last of the thirteen. Of the some fifteen colonial churches still existing today, only the Methodists appeared on the American scene after the Moravians. Episcopalians, Congregationalists, Presbyterians, Baptists, Lutherans, Reformed (both Dutch and German), Roman Catholics, Friends, Mennonites, and Schwenkfelders were all here when the Moravians arrived. Furthermore, most of these churches were well established in the Old World before they were transplanted to America. The Moravian church, though its roots were in the

Hussite, pre-Reformation movement,[1] was still in the process of formation.

Following the Thirty Years' war the Unity of Brethren (Unitas Fratrum), as the church was first known and which still is its official designation under the Peace of Westphalia, was forced underground, becoming a refugee group. The process of renewal, through German Pietism, shaped by Count Nicholas Ludwig von Zinzendorf, had not yet been completed when a chain of events brought them to America. As the Renewed Unitas Fratrum, henceforth to be known in the English-speaking world as Moravian, it had the imprint of Pietism much more than that of the early brethren. The theology of the Renewed Church was predominantly Lutheran, while the latter days of the old Unitas Fratrum had been characterized by Calvinism.[2] Zinzendorf's effort to unite these two traditions in the Pennsylvania Synods created both confusion and resentment.

Moravian ties with Europe were much stronger during the colonial era than was the case with most other denominations. Furthermore, because of the organizational structure of the Moravian church, the process of Americanization took much longer. Not until the mid-nineteenth century did the church really achieve its independence of European control. Therefore it is essential that we first understand the formation of the Renewed Church under Zinzendorf before speaking of Moravianism in the colonies.

ZINZENDORF, PIETISM, AND REFUGEES

Count Zinzendorf, born in Dresden in the year 1700, was of a long line of German and Austrian nobility. The Reformation had split the Zinzendorf family in its native Austria, and in the seventeenth century a branch established itself in Protestant Saxony. This accounts for the father's being a member of the Saxon court at the time of the son's birth. That the young count should have become a Pietist is quite understandable, since

1. Remnants of the Hussites organized themselves under the name of Unitas Fratrum in 1457 at Lititz, Bohemia. When Luther began his reform in 1517 they numbered 200,000 members in 400 churches in Bohemia and adjoining Moravia.
2. The Unitas Fratrum had fraternal relations with both Luther and Calvin, but as time passed they moved closer to Calvinism, preferring his stricter congregational discipline.

nents

Prof. John Buchner

AZUZA street

Origin of Pentecostal

Pietism

both his parents were among the many members of the nobility deeply influenced by the movement. Pastor Spener himself was close enough to the family to be a godfather at the count's baptism. Six weeks after the birth of his son the father died, and mother and child went to live with her parents, also in Dresden. Two years later the maternal godfather died and the two widows moved to the elder woman's country estate, some sixty miles from the capital. When the count was four his mother remarried and took up residence with her husband in Berlin, leaving her son in the care of his grandmother at Hennersdorf. In the household was an unmarried aunt, Henrietta, fifteen years his senior. These two women were to have a profound influence upon the precocious child who almost from infancy had a deep piety which was to mark his life of sixty years. Grandmother Gersdorf was a gifted person, well known in Pietist circles for her character, her competence in religious discussion, her poetic gifts and gracious hospitality. She was able to read the Scriptures in the original Hebrew and Greek.

Between the ages of ten and sixteen Zinzendorf attended Francke's preparatory school at Halle, where despite great difficulties of adjustment, his faith was deepened. Here he established friendships which were to last a lifetime and which were to aid him in his life work. Here he also made enemies who were to oppose him when Moravian Pietism diverged from that of Halle.

Next he unwillingly enrolled for the study of law at Wittenberg at the insistence of his guardian uncle who was not in sympathy with Pietism. His desire was to become a clergyman, but his social status as one of the nobility did not permit this. Even his grandmother objected. However, while formally studying law he actually spent more time studying theology and moral philosophy.

Upon completing his studies, the count took the customary grand tour of cultural centers, especially Paris, where he spent several months. This experience, which young men of his rank traditionally turned to advantage in pursuit of a secular career, convinced the count that he was destined for something else. Indicative of his frame of mind was his experience in an art gallery in Düsseldorf. What impressed him most was a thorn-crowned *ecce homo* by Domenico Feti, with the Latin inscription "This I have done for you, but what have you done for me?" He felt that he had done little and prayed "that he might be drawn into the fellowship of his suffering." Such orientation at the outset of his tour was hardly calculated to round him off as a man of the world.

Reluctantly in the latter part of the year 1721 he became a counselor at the court of the king of Saxony in Dresden. In the meantime, upon receiving a considerable inheritance, he bought a country estate from his grandmother, near her own in Upper Lusatia, a part of Saxony. Thwarted in his desire to enter the ministry, he felt that such a place would provide an opportunity for him to maintain a program of religious activities for his tenants and those on neighboring manors. Included in the property was the village of Berthelsdorf with a Lutheran church. Though residing in Dresden, he promptly began the erection of a manor house for himself at Berthelsdorf. The following year he married Erdmunthe Dorothea von Reuss, who from the start actively shared in her husband's religious activities. The young couple's apartment home in Dresden became the center of extra-church services led by the count. For five years they divided their periods of residence between Dresden and Berthelsdorf.

In the meantime something entirely unexpected entered the picture. By this time the Pietist awakening had spread to the German-speaking evangelicals of Bohemia and Moravia, nominally Roman Catholics by virtue of the law of the land, but at heart Protestants. Among them were families aware of their spiritual descent from the Unitas Fratrum. John Amos Comenius, one of the Unity's latter bishops, had long before spoken of them as the "Hidden Seed." Defying the law, those near the border stealthily worshipped in nearby Protestant churches in Silesia. Others left their homeland permanently.

By chance, through a converted carpenter from Moravia, Christian David, Zinzendorf in May of 1722 heard of these people and promised to help them find a home in Germany. At this point he was not quite prepared to offer his own manor, still in process of development under his new ownership. He hoped for some place in central Germany, on the domain of his brother-in-law who was already sheltering exiles. Christian David, however, moved so rapidly that the die was cast without Zinzendorf's knowledge.

THE FOUNDING OF HERRNHUT

The impulsive carpenter returned at once to Moravia where he found two families who were prepared to emigrate immediately. It was but a few days' journey by foot to Berthelsdorf, and by mid-June a refugee band of eleven souls, aided en route by friendly pastors, had reached their destination. The count was in Dresden, but through the cooperation of his grandmother Gersdorf and his steward, John George Heitz, a Swiss of the Reformed faith, accommodations were found for them in a vacant home. Heitz, a shrewd manager, envisioned more than just a religious enterprise, but a thriving settlement as a means of restoring a rather run-down manor. He picked a strategic site on the highway between Lübau and Zittau. Christian David was there on June 17, 1722, to fell the first tree used in the building of what was to be called Herrnhut,[3] the mother community of the Renewed Unitas Fratrum.

Upon hearing of what had happened Zinzendorf approved, but he could hardly have known the full import of it. His plans for Berthelsdorf, while ambitious, did not include the revival of an old church. His first contact with the refugees was in late December when he and his bride came to Berthelsdorf for a brief stay in their new home. Seeing the recently erected cottage beside the road, he stopped to welcome the newcomers and before leaving knelt in prayer with them. Knowing little or nothing of the Bohemian Brethren, he regarded the newcomers simply as earnest Christians to whom he was pleased to give asylum.

Other refugees joined the first contingent in rapid order. Herrnhut, a mile from Berthelsdorf, began to grow into a village. With its Lutheran parish, Berthelsdorf was, of course, the center of worship and where the sacraments were administered. Yet Herrnhut, with its extra-church services in homes, was developing a religious life of its own. Encouraged by what he saw, the count conceived of Berthelsdorf-Herrnhut as performing a service somewhat along the lines of what he so admired at Halle.

In 1723 he entered into a covenant with three friends: Frederick deWatteville, a school friend at Halle; his own pastor, John Rothe of Berthelsdorf; and Pastor Melchior Schaeffer of neighboring Görlitz. Calling themselves the Order of the Four Brethren, they pledged themselves to the cultivation of holiness, to carry on personal correspondence to influence others, to enlist pulpits in the preaching of revival, to publish Christian literature, to work for the improvement of pastoral

---

3. *Herrnhut* may be translated either "on watch for the Lord," or "watched over by the Lord."

methods and the inner life of the churches, and to promote Christian schools. Dresden, Görlitz, and Berthelsdorf were to be the first three centers of this program. Enlisting the help of friends, they lost little time in implementing their plans and were successful enough to arouse both enthusiasm and opposition. Clergymen, professors, and members of the nobility in large numbers gave them support. Zinzendorf's and deWatteville's social status gave them entrée to the upper circles, but it also helped focus the attention of the opposition.

There were serious growing pains. Herrnhut attracted a steady stream of exiles, creating both religious and political complications. Austrian authorities were annoyed by the emigration of their citizens and complained to the Saxon government. The Moravians and Bohemians, having left their own country for the sake of religious freedom, were none too happy at being obliged to worship as Lutherans at Berthelsdorf. Others besides refugees, religious seekers from all over Germany, among them some of Calvinistic leanings, had come to Herrnhut. A completely separatist group was a contingent of Schwenkfelders who came to Berthelsdorf in 1726.

For a while the very existence of the community was threatened. To add to Zinzendorf's difficulties was the displeasure of his friends at Halle over what was taking place. The estrangement deepened following the death in 1726 of the elder Francke whose son and successor, August Gotthilf, remained a lifelong opponent of the count. The opposition from the men at Halle arose partly from their disapproval of sectarian tendencies which they felt were arising, and partly because they had not been consulted in the establishment of activities duplicating their own.

The years between 1725 and 1727 were especially crucial and in the latter year the count left his position at Dresden to devote full time to what was happening on his Lusatian estate. Besides the above-mentioned problems there was the relationship between Herrnhut and Berthelsdorf. Herrnhuters had their own extra-church services, but were not organized as a parish. After getting to know them better, he realized that he would have to allow them to retain their identity as a continuation of the old Unitas Fratrum. To do this without violating the church laws of Saxony was a delicate matter. It would have to be done within the framework of the establishment. Accordingly, in consultation with his legal advisor and pastor Rothe, he drafted a set of rules for Herrnhut, providing for its life both as a civic community and as a sub-organization within an established parish. The more legal part of the document set forth the relationship of the residents to Zinzendorf as their feudal lord, in a form common to such communities. The other part was entitled *Brotherly Agreement of the Brethren from Bohemia and Moravia and Others, Binding Them to Walk According to the Apostolic Rule.*

The agreement, formally ratified at a public ceremony on May 12, 1727, initiated a summer-long period of revival, during which harmony was restored to the community. A decisive factor of the summer also was Zinzendorf's becoming acquainted, at the library in Zittau, with the church discipline of the Bohemian Brethren as written in their official *Ratio Disciplinae.* A memorable communion service in the Berthelsdorf church on August 13[4] is regarded as the real birthday of the Renewed Unitas Fratrum, the present-day Moravian church. Thereafter Herrnhut was a dynamic community of committed Christians with an outthrust soon to be felt around the world. The Moravian Brethren were happy in having retained their identity. Being officially classed as Lutherans did not distress them as long as they could have their own services and discipline in addition to the regular church services.

DENOMINATION OR DIASPORA?

Temporarily this was a solution for Herrnhut, but for the future Moravian church it was only the beginning of a process of adjustment barely completed during the lifetime of Zinzendorf. Through the years the relationship between these two lines of development was to be a troublesome question. The refugees from Bohemia and Moravia had injected into Zinzendorf's plans for fostering Pietism within the established churches something he had not reckoned with, namely, a denomination older than his beloved Lutheranism. He much preferred, even then, to keep the Herrnhuters from developing into a denomination, but eventually he had to yield. Had he not done so, the refugees would quite likely have left and gone elsewhere. They might simply have merged into the population of Germany, as did thousands of other evangelical refu-

---

4. August 13, 1727, is looked upon by Moravians as a pentecostal experience and is observed as an important church anniversary.

gees who had not come to Herrnhut, or they might have gone to some other country and tried to revive the church of their fathers without Zinzendorf's aid.

Though the refugees belonged to a previously existing denomination, their continuance as such was not any more welcome to German authorities than if they had been a sectarian split from the state church. Under the restricted freedom of his day, it was only by keeping the Moravians close to the state church that he won toleration for them. This he did by convincing the theologians that Moravians, despite their distinctive ways of worship and life style, were loyal to the all-important Augsburg Confession. Had Zinzendorf allowed the refugees to become a denomination immediately, they would have been promptly outlawed. Without his restraining hand there would have been no renewal of the Bohemian Brethren.

This dilemma during the formative years left its permanent stamp upon Moravianism on the Continent. It became both a denomination and an inter-church society, the latter known as the Diaspora.[5] As a denomination the Moravian church continued in the tradition of the Unitas Fratrum. Part of this was the transfer of the episcopal succession of the latter through consecration of bishops in the Renewed Church. This was done by surviving bishops who had maintained the succession in Poland where they also served as pastors of the Reformed church. One such bishop was Daniel Ernest Jablonsky, grandson of John Amos Comenius, Court preacher in Berlin. In 1735 he consecrated David Nitschmann, the first bishop of the Renewed Church. Later the traditional orders of bishop, presbyter, and deacon became part of the polity of the Moravian church.

Within the first decade Herrnhut grew into the kind of community that was to serve as a model for the twenty or more Moravian "settlement congregations" founded during the next fifty years. About half of these were in Germany and the others in Holland, England, Ireland, Denmark, Russia, and the United States. They were small towns in which church, civic, and economic life were an integrated unit. Handicraft industries, small businesses, and farming not only supplied local needs, but also gave rise to a considerable trade with the

---

5. The term "Diaspora" is from the Greek of I Peter 1:1 where it is translated "scattered."

outside world, providing support for the Moravian church's far-flung mission, evangelistic, and educational programs. For the first generation at least these settlements were composed of spiritually elite, experiential Christians with a sense of mission not unlike members of orders within Roman Catholicism dedicated to specific tasks for the church.

The first decade saw the development of those emphases which were to characterize Moravianism wherever it went: the cultivation of an intense community religious life by frequent daily services; the division of the community into choir groups based upon sex, marital status and age, namely, children, single brothers, single sisters, married couples, widowers and widows, each choir with its own spiritual supervisor; a school program closely related to the church; the use of music, both choral and instrumental; an active program of Diaspora evangelism; an overriding concern for missions to the heathen world, particularly the oppressed negro slaves in the West Indies and to peoples of preliterate cultures.

There were, of course, widely scattered Moravians not living in the settlements, members of the Diaspora and those attached to congregations outside of the settlements. But all looked to the settlements as points of reference. While the piety cultivated had much in common with that of Halle, it had much more of the element of joy and less emphasis upon the struggle with sin and subsequent conscious conversion. One of the accusations Hallensian Pietists made against Zinzendorf was that he never had had a conversion experience.

FAILURE IN GEORGIA

It was this group, partly denomination and partly intra-church society, which first came to Georgia in 1735. It was the first Moravian venture in the thirteen colonies, though not the first in the new world. Three years earlier they had begun their work among plantation black slaves on St. Thomas in the West Indies.

An unusual chain of events had led the Moravians to a colony set up by the English to keep the Spaniards in Florida and the French on the Mississippi from encroaching on the English colonies. To speed colonization free passage and land were promised to prospective settlers. Many Protestant Salzburgers took advantage of the offer. Other Germans began settling there also. As previously noted, Zinzendorf in 1726 had sheltered a contingent of Schwenkfelders at Berthelsdorf. In 1733 Saxon law caught up with them and they were ordered to leave. Thereupon Zinzendorf negotiated with the Georgia trustees to find a haven for them. In May of 1734 forty families, numbering 180 persons, left Berthelsdorf under their leader Christopher Wiegner, but also accompanied, at their request, by the Moravian evangelist, George Boehnisch. It was planned that another Moravian, Augustus Gottlieb Spangenberg, follow later to serve as their pastor in Georgia. However, traveling via Denmark and Holland, the Schwenkfelders encountered friends who persuaded them to go to Pennsylvania instead.

Uneasy with the political climate of Saxony, Zinzendorf foresaw the possibility of his own Herrnhuters being exiled also and looked to Georgia as a place to settle as insurance against that eventuality. In November of 1734 Spangenberg went to London to make arrangements for this venture. German enemies of the count, particularly court preacher Ziegenhagen from Halle and Count Stollberg Wernigerode, almost succeeded in blocking Moravian plans. A direct appeal to General Oglethorpe, governor of the colony, thwarted the opposition, and Spangenberg succeeded not only in securing a grant of land, but also the immunities of freedom of worship and exemption from bearing arms. In February of 1735 ten Moravian men, led by Spangenberg, sailed to Georgia where they landed at Savannah on April 8. At the request of the trustees Spangenberg had also superintended a company of Swiss emigrants en route to South Carolina. The Moravians built a cabin, planted crops, and projected a mission to neighboring Indians on the island Irene in the Savannah River, all in preparation for a second colony which arrived in February of the following year.

Little need be said further of this settlement in Georgia, for it was short-lived. As pacifists the Moravians became unpopular when hostilities broke out between the English and Spaniards. This, added to malarial illness and internal dissensions, eroded colony morale to the extent that some returned to Europe while others moved to Pennsylvania. By 1740 the settlement had dwindled from thirty to twelve persons. A related Moravian effort to evangelize among Germans and black slaves at Purysburg, South Carolina, also was unsuccessful.

JOHN AND CHARLES WESLEY

Yet through this Georgia venture there emerged something destined to have a far-reaching effect upon English Protestantism. It was on the second ship carrying Moravians to Georgia that John and Charles Wesley first met these German Pietists. The former was en route to his assignment as Anglican rector in Savannah and the latter as secretary to General Oglethorpe. John Wesley's account in his journal about the storm at sea and his favorable impression of the Moravians' calm faith, in contrast to his own and that of the other passengers, is too familiar to be retold here. Suffice it to say that it was the beginning of two and a half years of Moravian influence upon the Wesleys, leading to the Aldersgate experience back in London on May 24, 1738.

In Georgia John Wesley had lived for a few weeks with Spangenberg, Bishop David Nitschmann, and other Moravians. It was Spangenberg who seems to have helped him most. A Methodist writer says: "But for Georgia there would have been no Aldersgate. But for Spangenberg it is doubtful whether Peter Boehler would have found so fertile a soil."[6] Following his attendance at the ordination by Nitschmann of Anthony Seiffert as a Moravian minister, Wesley described the solemn simplicity of the service as carrying him back to the days of the Apostles. He was also sufficiently impressed by the Indian mission of the Brethren to consider seriously learning the Indian language and cooperating in the effort. Moravian influence in Georgia upon Charles Wesley is less certain, but he too had a deep religious experience through them in London a few days before John's Aldersgate experience.

Spangenberg's influence upon the young Anglican cleric was cut short by Spangenberg's departure in mid-March for Pennsylvania where he was to continue Boehnisch's ministry to the Schwenkfelders and to investigate Moravian prospects among the Germans and Indians in that state. It was here that the Moravians in 1740 were to establish themselves permanently in colonial America. Spangenberg's stay after his arrival from Georgia in 1736 stretched out to three years, during which time foundations were laid for the future Moravian church in America. Spangenberg was admirably suited to his role. Born in northern Germany, in 1704, the son of a Lutheran minister, he received an early classical education

---

6. C. W. Towlson, *Moravian and Methodist* (1959), p. 45.

and went on to study theology at Jena, a Pietist center second only to Halle. After obtaining his master's degree he stayed on as a popular lecturer between 1726 and 1732. He also spent much time in pastoral activity among spiritually awakened students. Beginning in 1728 many of these students and Spangenberg himself had active associations with Herrnhut. Eventually most of these were to become ministers of the Moravian church, among them Peter Boehler who was to play such an important part in the Moravian church both in America and England. It was he who counseled the troubled Wesley brothers after their return from Georgia.

At Jena Spangenberg adopted from Johann Franz Buddeus the two maxims that "children of God are to be found in all denominations and that the true Christian Church consists of those who live in intimate communion with the Savior."[7] From Jena he went to assist the younger Francke in the orphanage at Halle. It was an unfortunate assignment, for he clashed with Francke from the start over his continuing in touch with separatists and above all over his connection with Zinzendorf. In May of 1733 Spangenberg was dismissed from Halle and went to Herrnhut to throw in his lot with the Moravians. From this time on he was second only to the count as a leader. Long outliving Zinzendorf, he guided the church through various crises, serving faithfully until his death in 1792.

Spangenberg was more than an academic theologian. He was a man with a pastoral instinct, one who knew how to get along with people, and one with a high talent for organization. His three years among German farmers on the Pennsylvania frontier were in a real sense a post-graduate course in practical theology in preparation for his future role among the Moravians.

ASSOCIATED BRETHREN OF SKIPPACK

Organized church life in Pennsylvania was at this time in a sorry state. German migration, beginning in 1683, was continuing in flood proportions. Most immigrants had left their church associations on the other side of the Atlantic. There were few pastors to serve them, and only a handful of churches

---

7. Levin T. Reichel, *Early History of the Church of the United Brethren* (1888), p. 69.

among the Lutherans and Reformed had been organized before 1740. A few minority groups like Schwenkfelders, Mennonites, and Dunkers had come for the sake of religious freedom, but even these were losing much of their zeal. Poverty and toil had lowered the general cultural level and the absence of churches was matched by the absence of schools. Conditions were somewhat better among English-speaking peoples with their Anglican, Quaker, and Presbyterian churches.

In this fertile soil for sectarianism splinter groups were forming. About the time of Spangenberg's arrival a handful of devout and thoughtful persons of different denominations, but generally of separatist leanings, began meeting together to attempt improvement in religious life. The advent of a man of Spangenberg's caliber greatly encouraged them. Living mostly in the Skippack area of present-day Montgomery County, they began calling themselves the Associated Brethren of Skippack, a name they used for about three years. Prominent as a leader among them was Henry Antes, a lay preacher of the Reformed faith, whose homestead and mill were widely known in the area. Another of the leaders was the Schwenkfelder Christopher Wiegner who had headed the forced migration from Berthelsdorf. His farm became a place where the group met monthly to map strategy in evangelizing the Germans. There was also George Boehnisch, the Moravian who had accompanied the Schwenkfelders to Pennsylvania. Some twenty persons from areas as widely scattered as Germantown, Fredericktown, Oley, and Skippack comprised the core of the fellowship.

The Skippack Brethren turned out to be a distinct forerunner of the Moravian church in Pennsylvania. It was through them that Spangenberg, living at the Wiegner farm, was able to carry on a program of personal evangelization. At the farm the former professor of theology learned much about plowing, threshing, and other agricultural labor, which stood him in good stead when he later became manager of the Bethlehem-Nazareth community. He himself reported to a friend in 1738: "As regards my personal occupation, it is at present farm work; but it is as much blessed to my soul as formerly my studying and writing." But he did not neglect his primary mission to preach the Gospel, which he often did, especially at Oley and Tulpehocken. He made many friends among the Mennonites and Dunkers. Later Moravian settlers in Pennsylvania found that Spangenberg had made himself well known.

GEORGE WHITEFIELD AND THE MORAVIANS

Before the Moravians actually began their organized work in Pennsylvania, the demise of the Georgia colony played a part in the venture. By this time George Whitefield had appeared on the American scene as an itinerant evangelist of the Great Awakening. Early 1740 found him in Savannah when the last of the Moravians were preparing to leave. Under Peter Boehler, who had been in Georgia for the preceding two years, they booked passage for Philadelphia on Whitefield's own ship. They arrived on April 25 and found themselves at a loss what to do. They were expecting Bishop David Nitschmann with a contingent from Germany, who in the event did not arrive until late December.

They did, however, establish contact with the Skippack group while residing temporarily in Germantown. Early in May an unexpected opportunity opened up for them. Whitefield had bought 5000 acres of land in the Forks of the Delaware in present-day Northampton County with the purpose of erecting an orphanage and school for blacks. He conferred with Peter Boehler about his plans at Wiegner's farm where Boehler and his colleague Anton Seiffert were visiting. Since some of the Brethren had building skills he offered to employ them and asked Boehler to superintend the erection of such a school.

While these negotiations were in progress Whitefield preached to a great crowd at both the Wiegner and Antes farms; Boehler assisted by preaching in German. This helped to draw the two closer to each other. Boehler accepted the proposal with reference to the school and in late May some of the Moravians, seven men, two women and two boys moved to Whitefield's property which he had named Nazareth.

June of 1740 was a month of continuous rain, and building operations got off to a slow start. Difficulty in finding additional laborers also was an acute problem. Before winter set in all that had been accomplished was the completion of the stone foundation and cellar walls and the erection of two log cabins as shelters for those engaged in the work.

Then came the theological disagreement with Whitefield. Wishing to retain the influence they had gained in Georgia, the Moravians had responded to a request from the evangelist for an assistant there, by sending John Hagen. In close association with Whitefield, Hagen found himself in disagreement with his doctrine of election and reprobation. Later in the year, Whitefield met Peter Boehler again in Philadelphia and continued the argument which had begun in Georgia. A further source of the evangelist's displeasure were reports of troubles between the Moravians and their Scotch-Irish neighbors near Nazareth. The result was that the Moravians were ordered to leave the Nazareth tract at the outset of winter, though there was not much likelihood of it being enforced.

At this juncture Bishop Nitschmann and his group from Germany arrived on the scene with instructions to find another location for Moravian settlement. These had been given in Europe before the rift with Whitefield had developed. Within a matter of days Nitschmann selected as a place for settlement 500 acres of land, nine miles to the south where the Monocacy Creek flows into the Lehigh River. It was to be the site of Bethlehem. The agent was Nathaniel Irish, miller and justice of the peace, acting as land agent for William Allen of Philadelphia. Meanwhile Irish, as mediator in the quarrel with Whitefield, made it possible for the Moravians to remain at Nazareth for the winter while details of the purchase were being completed. At this time also Nitschmann replaced Boehler as leader, the latter being recalled for service in Europe.

Even before the property was legally theirs, the Moravians began clearing ground and building a log house on it. Half dwelling and half stable, it was completed by early spring and fully occupied in June. Meanwhile Whitefield had found himself in difficulties because of the death of his financial agent, forcing him to abandon the Nazareth project. Moravian representatives in England purchased the tract and, just about the time the brethren in America had vacated it, word came that their church was now the owner of it. However, for the next two years the smaller tract on the Lehigh received first attention and the development of Nazareth had to wait.

ZINZENDORF'S PLANS FOR PENNSYLVANIA

The man behind this thrust of Moravian Pietism onto American soil still had not set foot in the colonies, though he had made a brief visit to the West Indies in early 1739. He had plenty to occupy him in directing the work of Diaspora evangelism in Europe and mission efforts overseas. The latter by this time already embraced Greenland, Surinam, and South Africa in addition to the above-mentioned West Indies. It would not have been necessary for Count Zinzendorf to come to America simply to plant another Moravian colony. He could have delegated that to competent men like Spangenberg, Nitschmann, and Boehler, which of course he did. But he had something special in mind for Pennsylvania, something greater than the Moravian church. He was to call it a "Congregation of God in the Spirit." Spangenberg's association with the Skippack Brethren helped him to arrive at such a conception.

The whole Pietist movement, as a fellowship of experiential Christians, could in a sense be called that. Zinzendorf conceived of the Moravian Diaspora in this way. To him Pennsylvania seemed an ideal place for a full implementation of this idea. He did not believe that Pennsylvania needed another denomination to add to the already sectarian state of affairs. The fact that neither the Lutherans nor the Reformed had yet formed ecclesiastical organizations and that the other German bodies were but small minorities, raised in him the hope that something new might be effected, a union of Christians. He looked upon the Moravian church as an instrument through which this could be accomplished. Such were the dreams of the count who came to America in late November of 1741, where he was to stay for the next fourteen months.

He first spent a week in New York where hostility, originating from the Classis of Amsterdam in Holland, was strong among the Reformed clergy. This hostility was to plague Moravian missions among the Indians of the state for the next decade. It was nullified in 1749 when the English Parliament granted the Moravians recognition as an "ancient Protestant Episcopal Church." Parliament's action, in addition, accorded them exemption from bearing arms and taking oaths in court. In New York Zinzendorf was the guest of Thomas Noble, a member of the society organized by Boehler before his return to Europe a year before. This society was the beginning of a later Moravian congregation in the city. On Staten Island the count visited Captain Nicholas Garrison whom he had met in the West Indies and who was later to be skipper of the Moravian-owned vessel, the Irene, used to transport future colonies of the Brethren to America. This contact was likewise a forerunner of a congregation on the island.

On December 6 he left for Philadelphia, traveling overland via New Brunswick where he had an unfriendly encounter with Gilbert Tennent, one of his bitter opponents.

Bishop Nitschmann was on hand to welcome the count in Philadelphia and to see him received as a guest of the well-known Huguenot, John Stephen Benezet. Later he rented quarters on Second Street near Race. His arrival stirred excitement, as it had in New York, though he had reason to believe he would receive a fairer hearing. He announced his presence to Governor Thomas, not as Count Zinzendorf, but as the Reverend Mr. Thurnstein, one of his family names. He hoped, rather naively, that he could hide his identity by renouncing his nobility in a colony where such titles were unpopular. His associates addressed him simply as Brother Ludwig or Johanan. The Quakers addressed him as Friend Louis.

After a week in Philadelphia he went to join his brethren in the Forks of the Delaware. His itinerary reveals the key background role of the Associated Brethren of Skippack. He spent the first night at Germantown in the home of a licensed Reformed preacher and a member of the association. There he attracted a large crowd of visitors. The next two days were spent at the Wiegner and Antes homesteads. Antes and Zinzendorf discussed plans for the forthcoming "conference of religion," or what came to be known as the Pennsylvania Synods. The fourth day brought him to the still unnamed settlement on the north bank of the Lehigh.

BETHLEHEM COMES INTO BEING

Two hastily prepared rooms in a community house, still under construction, were to be his accommodations during his stay. Perhaps some thirty persons were on hand during this time, the handful of settlers, the group who accompanied the count from Europe, among them his sixteen-year-old Benigna, and friends who had joined him on the way from Philadelphia. Sunday, December 24, stands out, for on that day Bethlehem formally received its name. It was Christmas Eve, not for the colony as a whole, which was still observing the old calendar, but for the Moravians who were using the new calendar as followed by their Brethren in Germany. Holy Communion at nine in the evening climaxed a day of religious services in the sanctuary, separated only by a partition from the stable. The count's impulsive imagination seized the occasion and he led the group into the stable where all sang a familiar Epiphany hymn, the second verse of which says:

> Not Jerusalem
> Rather Bethlehem
> Gave us that which
> Maketh life rich;
> Not Jerusalem. [8]

No extant record describes exactly what happened next, but the hymn and the occasion are credited with a unanimous decision to call the settlement Bethlehem. More recently uncovered evidence than this tradition suggests that Zinzendorf had the name in mind for some time, but reserved announcement of it for this dramatic occasion.

He lost no time in getting on with his mission in Pennsylvania and left the next morning for the home of Jean Bertholet, one of the Skippack members at Oley, near present-day Reading. That night in Bertholet's home he preached his first sermon in Pennsylvania. Then he went on to Ephrata before beginning his return to Germantown, though without accomplishing his intention of meeting with Conrad Beissel, leader of the Ephrata community. Ten days after leaving Philadelphia Zinzendorf had completed his exploratory tour among the Germans and was back in Germantown at the Bechtel home.

His reception during this tour left him disappointed, as he revealed in an open letter in February to the Germans, in which he said:

> I expected to be received with love and confidence, but I encountered a great deal of mistrust and opposition. Is it to be wondered at, that I felt dejected, and that the lukewarmness of my countrymen in Philadelphia depressed me? But I thought: I will keep silent and not open my mouth. The Lord will help.
>
> I traveled through Pennsylvania, but could not speak anywhere except in Oley. Therefore, I can tell you, my countrymen, in a few words, what I have done these two months: I traveled and prayed and wept and bore witness, and sought for peace, and seek it still. [9]

Undiscouraged, he went about laying the groundwork for the future program of the Moravians in America. Generally speaking, Zinzendorf's activities in Pennsylvania fall into four phases: his pastoral work in Philadelphia and German-

---

8. J. M. Levering, *History of Bethlehem, Pa.* (1903), p. 78.
9. Reichel, pp. 96–97.

town; his participation in the Pennsylvania Synods; his organization of the Bethlehem-Nazareth communities; and his mapping strategy for missions among the Indians.

ZINZENDORF AS PASTOR

The first of these included both Lutheran and Reformed churches, the count's justification for this being that the history of the Unitas Fratrum, both of the old Unity and of the Renewed Church, combined both traditions. Following the practice of what he had been doing for many years in Europe, he held services in his quarters in Philadelphia. Many Lutherans attended and were favorably impressed with his sermons to the point of asking him to be their pastor, since they were still without one. He began his ministry to them on January 21 in their rented quarters on Race Street, though he was not duly installed as pastor until May 19. On the latter date also, John Christopher Pyrlaeus, fresh out of the University of Jena, became his assistant. Though the count's other interests took him frequently out of the city, he had an effective ministry.

Unfortunately, however, the Lutherans were sharing their place of worship with a Reformed congregation under Johann Philip Boehm, an adherent of the faction under the influence of the Classis of Amsterdam. He succeeded in stirring up dissent among the Lutherans against Zinzendorf, which before year's end moved the count to sever his pastoral relations with the congregation. Out of this came the beginning of a Moravian congregation in the city. Zinzendorf at his own expense built a place of worship for those of the Lutherans who remained loyal to him. Supplemented by later Moravian arrivals, the group became the first Moravian church in Philadelphia.

The situation was different in Germantown where the Reformed congregation belonged to a different wing of the church than the one in Philadelphia. The Germantown church followed the canons of the Synod of Berne of 1532. Zinzendorf preached to them on Sunday afternoons. His services were no longer needed after he had Bishop Nitschmann ordain Bechtel to the post and to be superintendent of other churches to be organized. At the same time he helped Bechtel prepare a catechism based on the articles of the Synod of Berne, which Bechtel had published under his own name. Zinzendorf also published a collection of hymns entitled *Hirten Lieder von*

Bethlehem (Pastoral Hymns of Bethlehem). Christopher Sauer, well-known German printer in Philadelphia, was engaged to print the collection. Sauer later was strongly anti-Zinzendorf. His *Pennsylvania Geschicht Schreiber* was a forum for the count's enemies.

THE PENNSYLVANIA SYNODS

Meanwhile the Pennsylvania Synods had gotten underway. They began as genuinely interdenominational gatherings. Lutherans, Reformed, Moravians, Quakers, Mennonites, Dunkers, Ephrata monks, the Inspired, and separatists were all there. The place and time of the seven which Zinzendorf attended were: (1) at Germantown in the vacant house of Theobold Endt, January 12–13; (2) at Falkner Swamp in the home of George Huebener, January 25–26; (3) at Oley in the home of John deTurck, February 21–23; (4) at Germantown in the home of John Ashmead, where Zinzendorf had his headquarters for a time, March 21–23; (5) in the Reformed Church of Germantown, April 21–23; (6) in the home of Lawrence Sweitzer at Germantown; (7) in the home of Edward Evans at Philadelphia, June 13–14.

The attendance at the first four gatherings averaged about a hundred. Actually the Moravians were not represented as an organized church until the seventh one. Shortly before, the first "Sea Congregation"[10] of fifty-six members under Peter Boehler had arrived in Philadelphia and were admitted as members, the first recognition by the Synods of the Moravians as an independent body. Prior to that some of the Moravians were present simply as individuals, and others registered as members of the church in which they had been reared. Zinzendorf himself registered as a Lutheran.

After the fourth meeting practically all but Lutherans, Reformed, and Moravians had deserted the venture. But even after the seventh and final one of the series, the members voted to continue the union by holding quarterly gatherings. They continued a show of being interchurch gatherings until 1745, but were actually Moravian meetings. The minutes of 1745, for instance, show Lutherans, Reformed, and even Anglicans, Presbyterians, Baptists, and separatists present. But a study of

---

10. The Moravians had their own ship on which it was customary to organize themselves into a congregation, hence the term "Sea Congregation."

names and places reveals the delegates to have been persons in active fellowship with the Moravians, people who in Europe would have been known as members of the Diaspora. The records also reveal that the matters discussed dealt largely with Moravian preaching places, missions, and schools. By 1747 the pretense of being union meetings was abandoned and they were referred to as Synods of the Brethren. In the meantime the other churches had launched a more denominationally minded strategy.

The obstacles to unity were evident from the first, when efforts were concentrated on defining a Christian position irrespective of creed. A strong Christocentric statement was arrived at. In print it was a fine document, but little did it reveal the underlying tensions. Just before leaving Philadelphia for New York on his return voyage to Europe, the count delivered an address at the home of Stephen Benezet on January 9, 1743. Known as the *Pennsylvania Testament*,[11] it reveals his thought with reference to the place of the Moravians in Pennsylvania. He cites Brethren adherence to the Consensus of Sendomir of 1570 and to the Bohemian Confession of 1575, both of them union efforts involving Bohemian Brethren, Lutherans, and Reformed. In his opinion the union character of the Moravian church, which now possessed the episcopal succession of the Old Unitas Fratrum, put it in a position to serve both Lutheran and Reformed churches by ordaining their clergy while allowing them to retain their church identity. He felt that the Moravians, composed of gathered, experiential Christians, could give the transplanted state churches vitality without disturbing their traditional creeds and organization. Obviously this was a bit too idealistic, not to say confusing, to be accepted at the Synods.

Zinzendorf was even more reluctant to have the Renewed Unitas Fratrum develop into a denomination in America than he had been to see such development in Europe where it was already an accomplished fact. He felt that there were already enough free churches in America and that if the Moravians became another such, they would soon become just like the others. In Europe, on the other hand, because of the restrictions within the state churches, there was justification for a body like the Moravians. His own words in the *Pennsylvania Testament* with reference to Europe are:

11. The *Pennsylvania Testament* is printed in full in *Büdingische Sammlungen, Einiger in die Kirchen-Historie,* etc., vol. 3 (1744), pp. 188–225.

> In Europe the house where the Lord Jesus and his people live, and where matters pertaining to his affairs and leading are sovereign ... is the Moravian Church. The reason the Moravian Church must be such a house is that in many places in Europe there remains suppression of conscience. There is prevailing sentiment against the Congregation of God in the Spirit.[12]

With reference to America he says:

> Here the Congregation of God in the Spirit is the *factotum* and not the Moravian Church. Here we live in an invisible house.... I see no reason (if the Savior does not specifically so direct) to introduce the Moravian orders and church discipline into this country. One thing prevents me from entirely abandoning her organization and moves me to permit her to exist as another church. It is that in the Moravian Church the Lutheran and the Reformed Churches are united.[13]

Obviously his concept was not that of an organic union, but rather that of a federal union. Under the circumstances it was difficult to understand and well-nigh impossible to implement. Yet that is how the Moravians tried to work for seven or eight years in Pennsylvania, still looking to the Synods for their directives. Some Moravian evangelists called themselves Lutheran, some Reformed, and others simply Brethren. When Spangenberg returned from Europe in 1744 to superintend the Bethlehem-Nazareth communities and their far-flung enterprises, he came as a bishop authorized by the Moravian governing authorities to ordain not only ministers of the Moravians, but also of the Lutherans and the Reformed who desired such ordination. It was a losing battle. As Hamilton states:

> They could not forever hold out against the logic of events. They might gather representatives of all sorts of faiths for common deliberation in behalf of unchurched colonists and heathen Indians, twelve denominations for example, amongst the members of the "Pennsylvania Synods" convened in the courthouse in Lancaster in 1745. They might record resolutions that Bethlehem was to be regarded not as a denominational settlement, but as the home of a missionary society; and that the congregations which were organized and supplied with ministers and schoolmasters as a result of the

---

12. *Ibid.*, pp. 204–205.
13. *Ibid.*, p. 217.

"Pennsylvania Synods" were to be considered attached to no denomination. As a point of fact, however, in spite of their purposes they could not prevent the synods from assuming a distinctly Moravian cast. These so-called undenominational congregations inevitably became Moravian, even though contrary to the intentions of the leaders of the Moravian Church.[14]

As union efforts the Synods were failures, increasing rather than decreasing rivalries. But negatively they ushered in revived church life by moving denominations to action. It was Zinzendorf's threat to the Lutherans which hastened the sending of Henry Melchior Muhlenberg to Pennsylvania in late 1742. The two had a brief, unpleasant encounter in Philadelphia during the count's last weeks in America. Likewise the Reformed lost little time in organizing behind the efforts of Michael Schlatter. Dunkers, Schwenkfelders, Mennonites, and even the Ephrata cloisters were galvanized into new life.

BETHLEHEM ORGANIZED

The organization of Bethlehem came next on the count's agenda, and it took much of his time after mid 1742. Up to this point only a handful of settlers under "Father" Nitschmann (David Nitschmann, uncle of the bishop with the same name) remained at the settlement to finish work on the large community house and lesser buildings. The community house was a combination dwelling, administrative headquarters, and place of worship. With the arrival of the First Sea Congregation under Peter Boehler, after the last of the seven Synods in June, Bethlehem's development was accelerated. The first step was official organization.

Saturday, June 23, was the beginning of a three-day series of worship services and conferences for some eighty persons now comprising Bethlehem. Highlights were the dedication of the completed upper room chapel of the community house, addresses of the count on the purposes for which Bethlehem was founded, and the reading of letters and reports from missionaries. The last was a practice which had developed at Herrnhut, Saturdays being set aside for it. Following Sunday morning services the congregation met as a council

---

14. J. T. and K. G. Hamilton, *A History of the Moravian Church* (1967), p. 168.

at which basic policies were arrived at. Though on the surface it all seemed quite democratic, historians who know both the Moravians of that time and the personality of Zinzendorf are generally agreed that the decisions were for the most part announcements of what the count had worked out beforehand. The final day of the proceedings, June 25, eventually was set aside as the official anniversary of the Bethlehem congregation.

The church was divided into two parts, a house congregation and a pilgrim congregation, the one to man the home base, the other the mission outposts. There were by this time about 120 Moravians in America and all of these were included in the plans laid down, not just the eighty who were present. Some had the opportunity to choose their assignments. For others the decision was made by use of the lot. The scheme allowed for flexibility and there was constant interchange between their choir system, that is, the division of each community into groups based upon sex, age, and marital status, as previously mentioned in connection with the growth of Herrnhut. In addition, to better foster spiritual cultivation there were small bands or classes.

A striking decision of that first organizational council was to set Saturday aside as a day of rest and worship, not to replace Sunday, but to supplement it. There were a number of reasons behind this action. There was, of course, the creation story according to which God rested on the seventh day. It was prompted too by the strong Christocentric emphasis of the Moravians who wished to acknowledge Christ's rest in the grave on the Sabbath. They remembered also that the first Christians continued to observe the Jewish Sabbath for some time after they had set the first day of the week aside as the Lord's day. But there were two local reasons which appealed to Zinzendorf. One was to seek closer relations with the Sabbatarians in the colony, particularly the Seventh-day Baptists at Ephrata. He felt that he could take away their monopoly on something they were emphasizing so strongly. The other reason, long discarded as fanciful, was that if the Indians were in truth descendants of the Lost Ten Tribes of Israel, restoring the Sabbath of their forefathers might be a step leading them back to the true God. This double holy interlude of Saturday-Sunday was for practical reasons discarded after a few years.

To other settlers in the area Bethlehem was indeed a

strange place, for many years misunderstood because of its peculiar life style. Though Protestant, it had a monastic character traditionally associated with Catholicism. One Moravian historian has called it "an economy of pilgrims, a missionary family on a grand scale." While the house congregation was engaged in building, setting up handicraft industries, and clearing fields, the pilgrim congregation was coming and going.

During Zinzendorf's stay the first meeting on Sunday morning, after the day's prayers, was generally a church council at which both internal and external affairs were discussed. Preaching was shared between him, Boehler, Nitschmann, Seiffert, and other clergymen. In the afternoon there were English services, Bible lectures, or private meetings for the different choirs and classes. Members of the itinerant portion of the congregation, of whom some were invariably present, participated in these. Bethlehem, as stated, was shaped after European settlements, but the freedom of the new world gave abundant room for experimentation. Zinzendorf's creative imagination took full advantage of this freedom and there was no fixed pattern of procedure.

A short-lived experiment deserves special attention. Among the First Sea Congregation were some English-speaking members who had stayed in Philadelphia. Following the organization of Bethlehem they too came to the Forks of the Delaware as the nucleus for a congregation to be located at Nazareth, under the leadership of a Scot named David Bruce. It was hoped that Nazareth would become the center for an evangelistic thrust among English settlers as Bethlehem was among the Germans. For reasons unclear, but probably because of the relatively small number of English-speaking people in the area, and the theological differences between the Lutheran oriented Moravians and the Calvinistically oriented Scotch Irish nearby, the venture lasted only a few months. Most of the group returned to Philadelphia, though a few later did itinerant work among English-speaking colonists in other areas. Nazareth was incorporated into the Bethlehem organization and the following year, 1743, the Whitefield House was completed and occupied. The Nazareth tract was subsequently subdivided into large farms, while in Bethlehem the emphasis was upon industrial development. This plan was implemented when Spangenberg came on the scene the following year.

EVANGELIZING THE INDIANS

With Bethlehem-Nazareth organized, Zinzendorf devoted much of his attention to laying ground work for further evangelization of the Indians, which in the North had been launched among the Mohicans in present-day Duchess County, New York, already in 1740. There at a station called Shekomeko Christian Henry Rauch had succeeded in gathering a small congregation. The count made three exploratory tours among the Indians, covering a total of seven weeks between July 9 and November 9, 1742. Accompanying him on each of the trips were about a dozen persons.

The first trip took only two weeks and was only partly in Indian country. Zinzendorf first visited the village of Meniolagameka, just north of the Blue Mountains, only a day's travel from Bethlehem. He remained in the area for five days and then rather spontaneously, without previous plan, decided to go to Tulpehocken, not far from present-day Reading, to talk with Conrad Weiser, the renowned German immigrant who had become fluent in several Indian tongues. Zinzendorf had come to know Weiser through the Synods. At Weiser's he was pleased to find deputies of the Iroquois Six Nations who were returning from Philadelphia where they had conferred with Governor Thomas on the delay of the Delawares in leaving the Forks of the Delaware. The count concluded a pact with these deputies, giving to the Moravians freedom to travel among the Six Nations. After a brief visit to Philadelphia he returned to Bethlehem on August 7.

Three days later he set out for Rauch's mission at Shekomeko. This involved a week's travel each way, over the Blue Mountains, through the New Jersey Minisink region and across the Hudson. During his eight-day stay at the mission he baptized converts, organized the first Moravian Indian congregation in the colonies, and made plans for extension of the work into Connecticut and evangelization among neighboring whites. The latter, however, never materialized.

His third expedition into the Wyoming Valley region of the upper Susquehanna was the longest and most strenuous, lasting six weeks, between September 21 and November 9. En route they were joined by Conrad Weiser at Tulpehocken. Then they moved up the Susquehanna to the Indian town of Shamokin, now the site of Sunbury. Here he met the chief Skikellimy, who was later to prove invaluable in aiding the

Moravians. He fared less well in his meeting with the notorious Madam Montour at Ostonwakin, and she became an obstacle to mission work. It was obvious that the count was not adept at this kind of enterprise. His background was ill preparation for rough frontier tavel and life among the Indians. Had it not been for the help of Weiser, who loved both the Indians and the count, he might have fared badly and little would have resulted from the trip. However, he did not lose his zeal for Indian missions. Before leaving America he had nominated twenty brethren for this branch of service. He had the vision, but it remained for lesser, more practical souls to give it reality.

Zinzendorf was eager to return to Europe, because news of what was happening there displeased him. According to his thinking, his followers appeared to be moving too much in the direction of denominationalism. But he still had much to do in Pennsylvania where he stayed two months longer, most of the time in Bethlehem. Between December 2 and 10 he preached seventeen times on a final tour among the Germans, mostly in barns and homes, because churches were scarce. He sailed from New York on January 20, assured that the Unitas Fratrum had been firmly planted in America. He never returned, but the strategy he had initiated, and which he would continue to direct from Germany for almost two decades more, determined the course of Moravian development to the end of the eighteenth century and beyond.

AMERICAN MORAVIANS UNDER SPANGENBERG

Spangenberg, consecrated a bishop just before leaving Europe, arrived in the fall of 1744 to be in charge of American affairs. He brought with him a plan, worked out by church leaders, relative to Bethlehem-Nazareth as the center of Moravian activities in the colonies. Called the "General Plan," it provided directives concerning community organization, Moravians' conceptions of themselves, relations with other churches, the Pennsylvania Synods, and Indian missions. The following excerpts are a clue to the tenor of the document:

> 2. The itinerants are to have their rendezvous ordinarily at Bethlehem, but are to move about "as a cloud before the wind of the Lord to fructify all places."

8. The Brethren in America should not call themselves Protestant or Lutheran or Moravian, but simply Evangelical Brethren and the Brethren's Church.

9. It shall not be the purpose to make things Moravian in carrying on the general evangelistic work; but if church settlement comes into existence at Nazareth, it could be formed as a Moravian congregation *ceteris paribus*.

10. The work among the Indians is to be prosecuted on apostolic principles without regard to denominationism.

12. The synod shall remain a general one, open to all servants of Christ who desire benefit from it for their denominations, or the salvation of their fellowmen. It shall be regarded as a Church of God in the Spirit with a general direction extending among people of all denominations. [15]

Under this plan the twin communities became thriving enterprises, though not growing beyond small towns for the next century. Economic organization during the eighteen years following 1744 was communal, with all enterprises owned and operated by the church. Residents worked with housing, food, and clothing as their reward. This was not so much a matter of religious conviction as one of expediency. It was the most practical way of establishing a community on the frontier, dedicated to missionary purposes. Recognized from the start as a temporary arrangement, the communal economy was abandoned in 1762 and in its place industries and commercial enterprises were leased to individuals by the church. It is to be noted that Bethlehem was the only one of all the Moravian settlements throughout the world where such a communal system was in effect for a time, though in all of them there was tight control over economic life.

By 1748 the Moravians had some thirty localities, served from Bethlehem-Nazareth, where religious ministrations were carried on. They were as follows: Germantown, Philadelphia, Lancaster, York, Donegal, Heidelberg, Quitopehilla (later Hebron and eventually Lebanon), Warwick (Lititz), Oley, Allemaengel, Maguntschi (Emmaus), Salisbury, Falckner's Swamp, the Trappe, Mahanatawny, Neshaminy, and Dansbury, all in Pennsylvania; Monocacy (Graceham) in Maryland; Maurice River, Racoon, Penn's Neck, Oldman's Creek, Paulin's Kill, Walpeck, and Brunswick in New Jersey; Staten

---

15. Levering, pp. 178–179.

Island, Long Island, and Canajoharies in New York; and Broadbay, Maine. There were other tenuous efforts. Two brethren itinerated west of the Susquehanna during the winter of 1747. Evangelists visited and attempted religious work among both whites and negro slaves.

Of these places three developed into settlements on the Herrnhut model, Bethlehem, Nazareth, and Lititz. A fourth such settlement was founded at Hope, New Jersey, in 1774. This was sold and evacuated in 1808. Emmaus in Pennsylvania and Graceham in Maryland were planned for such development, but did not materialize in this fashion and continued as ordinary congregations.

NORTH CAROLINA

The purchase by the Moravians of a 100,000-acre tract of land in Piedmont, North Carolina, from Lord Grandville in 1753 was the beginning of the establishment of the church there.[16] In that same year a contingent of brethren from Bethlehem, under the direction of Spangenberg, began the building of the first settlement, naming it Bethabara. It was intended to be a southern counterpart of Bethlehem. The area looked promising for evangelization among the settlers and nearby Cherokee, Catawba, Creek, and Chickasaw Indian tribes. However, the disturbances of the French and Indian wars, beginning shortly thereafter, thwarted the Indian mission and not until the early nineteenth century did the Moravian church in the South resume the project by a mission to the Cherokees in Georgia and Tennessee.

A second settlement, Bethania, was begun three miles distant in 1759. Neither of these developed into a settlement congregation, and it was Salem (now part of Winston-Salem), founded in 1766, which was destined to be the center of Moravian life in the South. Bethabara and Bethania continue to exist as village congregations, though in the latter twentieth century are more accurately described as a part of suburban Winston-Salem. Only three other congregations came into being during the colonial era, Friedberg, Friedland, and Hope. They are today thriving country congregations.

During the colonial era the Moravians had two classes of

16. The Moravians named their tract of land in North Carolina "die Wachau" after Zinzendorf's ancestral lands in Austria. It has been translated into English as "Wachovia."

adherents, communicant members and society members. Though similar to the European division between congregation and Diaspora members, it was different in America in that the society and the congregation were part of the same local group, forming an outer and inner membership. The arrangement was an adjustment to the absence of a state church at a time when Moravians were still not looking upon themselves as a denomination free to proselytize. Since many of those in the societies did not have access to the ministrations of the churches of their background, the Moravian church had to serve them in ways beyond those of the simple Diaspora fellowship. Hence American Moravian ministers baptized, buried, performed weddings, etc. outside of the circle of their own communicants, whereas in Europe the state church minister performed such services. These people so served, who did not submit to the discipline of the congregational life of the Moravians, formed the outer circles of membership.

THE TRAGIC STORY OF INDIAN MISSIONS

Moravian work among the Indians continued throughout the colonial period against increasingly overwhelming odds. Missionaries were visiting Indian villages while their colleagues were still breaking ground for the first buildings at Bethlehem. Despite these frequent personal contacts, there were no mission stations established in the area until 1746. The renowned David Zeisberger, then twenty-three years of age, was singled out for Indian mission service in 1744 and in the following year was sent up the Hudson Valley with Frederick Post to learn the language of the Indians there. Public opinion in that vicinity was most unfriendly and the two missionaries soon found themselves in a New York city jail where they stayed for seven weeks until Governor Thomas of Pennsylvania intervened to secure their release. Later that same year, 1745, Bishop Spangenberg, Zeisberger, and others made a notable journey to Onondaga, the Iroquois capital near present-day Syracuse, to renew the treaty between Zinzendorf and the six nations of the confederacy.

It soon became apparent that Shekomeko and its two filials in Connecticut were doomed because of hostile white neighbors. The church decided to remove the converts to Pennsylvania. Before they had picked a site some of the Christian Indians lived at Bethlehem. Others refused to leave their homes and the New York and Connecticut efforts languished for a few more years. In 1746 a station was established at the junction of the Mahony Creek and the Lehigh River, thirty miles above Bethlehem. To this they gave the name Gnadenhuetten (tents of grace). It was soon a flourishing agricultural settlement with its farm production supplemented by an abundant supply of fish and game. Already by 1748 there were some 500 Indians under the care of the mission, many of them gathered from itinerant work over a wide area.

Tragedy was soon to strike. Stirred up by the French, the Indians of New York and Pennsylvania grew restless and hostile toward the growing number of whites. Braddock's defeat at Fort Duquesne on July 9, 1755, filled the colonists with fear. Moravians, because of their friendship with the Indians, were under suspicion as allies of the French. Their converts at Bethlehem and Gnadenhuetten were in the hapless position of being regarded as a threat to their white neighbors.

On the evening of November 24, 1755, a band of raiding Shawnees struck Gnadenhuetten, killing eleven persons on the staff and setting fire to the buildings. The four who escaped, together with some seventy of their Indian converts, made their way to Bethlehem within the next few days. The Lehigh Valley was terrorized by continuing raids on outlying farms and villages. Bethlehem, Nazareth, and Easton became cities of refuge. Bethlehem was suddenly forced to feed and house three times the normal number of people during the next two months. By the end of January the crisis had eased and all but sixty of the refugees had returned home or gone elsewhere. Meanwhile Gnadenhuetten had been looted and completely destroyed.

During the height of the trouble the Moravians demonstrated that their pacifism did not stand in the way of their taking defense measures. Under Bishop Spangenberg's direction they erected a stockade to protect the more exposed portions of the settlement. For a while there were two watchtowers with guns mounted on swivel turrets. Armed guards stood sentry at night, calling to one another and occasionally firing their rifles to warn possible attackers that the place was on the alert. Farm workers in the fields also had armed protection.

The Indian outbreak brought extensive defenses under the direction of the commonwealth to the Lehigh Valley. A string of forts was erected along the Blue Mountain frontier. Governor Morris appointed Benjamin Franklin to be in charge of this operation, which brought him to Bethlehem on several occasions. In his autobiography he comments at length on the Moravians, expressing surprise to Spangenberg at their defense preparations when they professed to be pacifists. Franklin failed to make a distinction between reasonable measures of defense and offensive warfare, which distinction did not seem inconsistent to the Moravians.

During these critical years the Indian population at Bethlehem swelled to over one hundred. To better their situation a new village at the northwestern outskirts of the town was established in 1758. Here at Nain, as it was named, most of the Indians lived for the next six years. Conditions having quieted down considerably by 1760, some of the people at Nain were transferred to a station called Wechquetank, thirty miles to the northwest, just beyond the Blue Mountains.

The outbreak of Pontiac's War in 1763 again threatened the lives of Indians in the Lehigh Valley, and in the following year both Nain and Wechquetank were vacated and their inhabitants removed to an island in the Delaware River at Philadelphia, under the protective custody of the commonwealth. The toll from disease was heavy in this confinement, and in 1765 the survivors under the leadership of missionary Zeisberger moved to a new station, Friedenshuetten, (tents of peace) on the Susquehanna River, 120 miles north of Bethlehem. Thus ended Moravian missions in the greater Bethlehem area, and a new phase of this enterprise began.

Meanwhile during the 1750s Bethabara in North Carolina was also being subject to the troubles accompanying the war. Surrounded by a stockade, the settlement was known locally as the "Dutch Fort." Like Bethlehem in the North, it became a place of refuge for neighboring settlers, though on a lesser scale. Some of these people, impressed by the friendly reception they received, joined the Moravians and became the nucleus of a second nearby congregation called Bethania. The disturbances, as previously noted, delayed Indian mission work in the South to the next century.

The life of Friedenshuetten on the Susquehanna was brief, only seven years, but during that time it flourished and its location on a trade route extended its influence. Meanwhile Zeisberger, sensing the inevitable, traveled down the Allegheny River in western Pennsylvania to set up another station in 1767. Three years later he located still another on the Beaver River beyond Pittsburgh. Then in 1772 he secured land for Indian settlement in the Tuscarawas Valley of Ohio. Within a year the Pennsylvania stations were evacuated and in their places arose Schoenbrunn (beautiful spring) and a second Gradenhuetten. Lichtenau (meadow of light) followed in 1776 and Salem in 1779.

For a few short years these peaceful communities reflected their picturesque names. Farming was the chief source of livelihood, but there was continued reliance upon hunting and fishing. Many of the Indians learned to read and write and proved themselves capable of adopting the white man's culture and religion. The American Revolution brought uneasiness to the mission, but for five years nothing serious happened. The missionaries have been credited by some historians with keeping these displaced Delawares neutral when their inclination was to ally themselves with the English forces. This was an important factor in the eventual American victory.

In the fall of 1781 the stations in Ohio were evacuated upon the arrival of English troops. The missionaries had to go all the way to Detroit to clear themselves of charges that they were American spies, and although cleared, the enforced evacuation was disastrous. During the winter of 1781–1782 the refugee Christian Indians almost starved at a temporary encampment on the Sandusky River in the northern part of the state. Having left unharvested corn at Gnadenhuetten, some 150 of them returned to the vicinity in early March to gather what food they could. A company of American militia out to avenge the recent deaths of some white settlers, supposedly at the hands of Indians, brutally murdered ninety of these Christian Indians and six others who were with them. Locked up for the night in one of the log buildings of the mission, the defenseless refugees, including women and children, were struck down the next morning one at a time like so many cattle. Two boys escaped to report the tragedy. A hundred years later a memorial obelisk was erected on the spot. Visitors to the peaceful community park and God's acre in Gnadenhuetten read these lines inscribed upon it: "Here triumphed in death ninety Christian Indians, March 8, 1782."

For the next ten years the surviving Moravian Indian community eked out a miserable existence at several locations in northern Ohio and southern Michigan. Zeisberger and a few missionary colleagues heroically continued to minister to the disheartened exiles. Finally the opportunity came to move to territory friendlier to them, a reserve on the Thames River in Ontario. In April of 1792 the venerable Zeisberger, now past seventy, shepherded his charges to their new location. The move was the last chapter in the story of Moravian missions on American soil during the colonial era. Fairfield, as the new station was named, continued as a Moravian mission for 111 years, after which time the work was turned over to Methodists who later became part of the United Church of Canada. Fairfield, renamed Moraviantown in recent years, is today a small Indian community of farmers and commuters employed in nearby industries. It is a community aware of its tragic history, but proud of its survival and grateful for improving opportunities in a world at long last beginning to see all people as children of God.

MORAVIANS AND THE REVOLUTION

No account of Moravian beginnings in America is adequate without reference to the American Revolution. Before discussing this subject we must examine the background of Moravian pacifism. The original Unitas Fratrum, influenced by Peter Chelcicky, was strong in its pacifist stand, though by the end of the sixteenth century it had modified this considerably. At the time of its demise at the end of the Thirty Years' War many members of the church had participated in the religious wars of the preceding era. However, it appears that the refugees who came to Herrnhut, beginning in 1722, had reverted to a strong pacifist stance. Many others, not among the refugees, who became members of the Renewed Church, assumed this same position. Among such was John Ettwein, a native of Württemberg, later to emerge as the outstanding Moravian leader in America during the Revolution.

In early Herrnhut men subject to military service were permitted to hire substitutes, a practice which Zinzendorf sanctioned. But with reference to his estate as a whole he did comply with demands of the Saxon government for a certain quota of soldiers. How can we reconcile this with the church's application to the English Parliament in 1749 for exemption from bearing arms or taking an oath? The answer is that it was a matter of practicality, for in order to obtain recognition as a duly constituted religious body in England, certain specific things had to be requested. The above two exemptions reflected the opinion of the overwhelming majority of the Moravians at the time.

In America the constant threat of harm from the Indians made it difficult to maintain the position of absolute pacifism, as noted in describing the defense measures both at Bethlehem and in North Carolina during the Indian troubles of the 1750s. By the time of the Revolution the number of non-pacifist Moravians had grown, but the strong leadership of Ettwein overshadowed them. The pacifist stand was undoubtedly stronger than it would have been had Spangenberg remained in America.

The war found the Moravians in an awkward position, not only because of their pacifist heritage, but also because of their conviction that the powers that be are ordained of God. Furthermore they had special reasons for gratitude to England. The act of Parliament had removed obstacles to their mission work. They had strong ties with their brethren in Britain and in mission fields in English colonies. Believing their calling to be spreading the Gospel, eighteenth-century Moravians had little active interest in political affairs.

It is difficult to generalize on the Moravian position either with reference to warfare in general or with respect to this particular conflict. The Revolution revealed clearly that Moravians were by no means unanimous in their opinions and behavior. In the North, Bethlehem and Nazareth were strongest in initial opposition to breaking with England. In Lititz and the town and country congregations outside of the closed settlements many members sided with the colonists. Finally church leaders ruled that in the settlements, which would have included Lititz, members who took the oath required by the Test Act were to be excluded from communion. It is not clear whether this was strictly enforced. In some congregations communion was even omitted when feeling was running high on the subject.

Opposition to the Revolution was strong among the Moravians in North Carolina. Their Wachovia tract narrowly escaped confiscation because of their refusal to abjure allegiance to the crown and to swear allegiance to the colonial government. The lands were saved for the church by a special act of the state legislature early in 1779, which permitted the Moravians simply to affirm allegiance to the state. The church served the colonial cause by its care of the wounded, as it had done in the North. This won influential friends and helped prevent undue harassment in the anxious days before and after the battle of Guilford Court House.

Bethlehem's stand on the war was influenced by the presence of Ettwein, one of its resident pastors. His high regard for England together with his conviction about respect for government put him in the class of Tories at the outset of the struggle. He found it difficult to accept the Continental Congress as the supreme authority of the land. But he also felt that he would act contrary to the interest of the country and of peace if he actively opposed it. So he remained silent, making it clear, however, that Moravians owed loyalty to King George until events should prove that God had ordained that America be severed from England.

Other Moravian leaders from the start were convinced of the justice of the colonies' cause, but like Ettwein were reluctant to be active politically. As the war came to involve Moravian communities in a noncombatant role in providing care for the wounded, food and army supplies, sentiment became more and more pro-American. During the early stages of the Revolution Moravians in Pennsylvania were close to the battle lines. Bethlehem was on a direct route of travel between Philadelphia and New England. For a number of years leading military figures and members of Congress found themselves in the settlement, a stopover in their travels, or on official business. They usually stayed in the Sun Inn, well known for its comfortable lodging and good food. From December 1776 to March 1777 and again from September 1777 to March 1778 a general hospital of the American army was located in Bethlehem. From December 1777 to August 1778 such a hospital was also at Lititz. General Lafayette was nursed back to health in a Bethlehem home after being wounded in the Battle of Brandywine. For a brief period the town was also the location of an army depot. From August 1777 to March 1778 Hessian prisoners were confined in the Hebron church at Lebanon.

In the course of such service Ettwein and other Moravian leaders came to know top leaders of the country personally. Mutual feelings of respect were established. The presence of these leaders helped to prevent extremists from disrupting Moravians in their peaceful way of life. Before war's end and certainly soon thereafter, Ettwein had come to accept the new order gracefully and in retrospect is seen as a skilled diplomat who wisely guided his church through this difficult period. He retained his pacifist convictions, but behaved kindly and cooperatively for the common good with those who disagreed with him.

Yet the Moravian position on war and their distaste for the Revolution did pose a threat and at times subjected them to harassment. Some of the lower level military commanders were not as considerate of human rights as were their superiors. There were instances of rowdyism and destruction of property and crops on the part of soldiers encamped in the environs of Bethlehem. The presence of a military depot brought a rough element to the community. The burden of having a military hospital was heavy. During the second period of the hospital's stay all of the single brethren had to vacate their building and find makeshift quarters elsewhere. The continuing call for clothing, shoes, blankets, and bandages imposed a strain on community resources. Blacksmiths, carpenters, and tanners were kept busy meeting army requests for equipment and repairs. Depleted supplies were difficult to replace at a time when normal productivity was constantly interrupted.

Not least of the aggravations of the war was the behavior of some of Bethlehem's more immediate neighbors. On the county level governmental affairs had fallen under the control of the more radical supporters of the Revolution, particularly the Scotch Irish whose antipathy toward the Moravians was of long standing. They resented the brethren for their pacifism and their refusal to take oaths. The latter kept most of the Moravians from subscribing to the Test Act, which for a while threatened to jeopardize their title to property, which, as noted, was also the case in North Carolina. In 1779 Ettwein succeeded in having Moravians excused from the requirements of this act, after appeals to the Congress at York and Pennsylvania Assembly at Lancaster. In the meantime some of the brethren from Emmaus had been imprisoned in Easton for a period of several weeks because of refusal to take the oath. The church on several occasions paid heavy fines for some of its young men in Northampton County who refused to present themselves in Easton for military drill. There was frequent loudmouthed talk by irresponsible persons that the nest of Tories in Bethelehem should be cleaned out. However, the Moravians' conspicuous noncombatant service to the colonies kept the extremists from getting much of a following.

RESTRICTIVE CONSERVATISM

Immediately following the Revolution Americanization began in earnest on the part of the churches in general. Loosed from ties with the Old World, they rapidly set about becoming indigenous. American Moravians would have pursued the same course had they been free to do so. But disturbed by the spirit of freedom which began to express itself in America, the leaders of the church, with headquarters and ultimate authority in Germany, took measures to suppress it. The already highly centralized Moravian church became more so and was to retain this character for the next three quarters of a century.

Likewise more emphasis was laid on the exclusive settlements as the true center of Moravian life. The number of these settlements in Europe and America by this time had grown to over twenty. In America this meant that measures were taken to maintain the strictly regimented religious life in Bethlehem, Nazareth, Lititz, and Hope, New Jersey, in the North, and in Salem, North Carolina. Both foreign and Indian missions continued to radiate from these centers; the town and country congregations already established continued to exist, but little attention was given to starting new congregations. The Diaspora psychology of the European Moravians prevailed in a situation where denominational expansion was the only means of keeping pace with a growing nation. As Hamilton says on this subject:

> Had Ettwein and his associates enjoyed freedom of action even measurably comparable to that of Francis Asbury and Thomas Coke, or Samuel Seabury and William White, how different might have been the future of the Moravian Church in America. But just when the Methodist and Protestant Episcopal churches were making provision for logical expansion in America, the tendency to ultra-centralization in the Moravian Church caused it to ignore the opportunities presented in this land. The life and spirit of the settlement congregations in Europe, where full liberty of religion was unknown, became the unquestioned norm for Moravian work everywhere. The church authorities insisted on painstaking efforts to insure membership made up of indisputably regenerate individuals. The choir system, operating within strictly regulated settlement congregations was accepted as the desirable means of achieving this end.[17]

---

17. Hamilton, pp. 228–229.

MORAVIAN SCHOOLS

Yet certain developments within the church in the decades immediately following the Revolution revealed that forces in the other direction had been at work during the colonial era. Conspicuous was the opening of Moravian boarding schools to outsiders, beginning with their reorganization in 1785. Since then Moravian schools on the elementary and secondary level at Bethlehem, Nazareth, Lititz, and Salem have educated thousands of boys and girls whose families were not members of the Moravian church. The Moravians in America had from the beginning attracted attention for the way they educated their children. The growing number of people who through the Revolution had occasion to see Moravian life and schools were favorably impressed. They inquired about sending their own sons and daughters to these schools, giving to the Moravians an opportunity for service second only to their mission program.

It must be pointed out that the schools were not confined to the settlement congregations. There were schools in practically all of the town and country congregations as well. However, the above expanded program applied only to the settlements. Moravian churches elsewhere continued to educate their youth until the advent of public schools. Bethlehem, Lititz, and Winston-Salem continue to have church-related schools to the present day. The boys' school at Nazareth closed because of financial difficulties in 1929.

The need for more teachers and clergymen to take care of the growing number of students eventually called for Moravian ventures into higher education. The first of these, Moravian College and Theological Seminary, began as an extension of the curriculum at the Nazareth school. In 1858 the school was permanently located at Bethlehem. Higher education for women was offered by Moravians much later at both Bethlehem and Salem.

THE MORAVIAN HERITAGE

Handicapped as they were by continuance of the closed community much too long after the colonial era, the Moravians nevertheless escaped what might have happened, the fate of becoming a sect. Their missions, schools, and Diaspora concept kept them within the mainstream of historic Christianity. Actually the settlement plan, despite its drawbacks, helped them to maintain a higher level of culture in terms of music, literacy, art, and craftsmanship, brought from the Old World, than frontier settlers who came as isolated individuals or families.

Late twentieth-century America, in search of roots, finds early Moravian communities worthy of special study. Old Salem in North Carolina draws thousands of tourists to its restored eighteenth-century buildings and crafts. Bethlehem is in the early stages of such renewal under the organized direction of a project known as Historic Bethlehem. Lititz and Nazareth are beginning to feel the same incentive to recapture their past. What was once looked upon with suspicion, or at best with tolerant condescension, has come to be recognized as having something important to say to us in our modern predicament.

Colonial Moravians may be seen as a tiny minority which, as is so often the case with minorities, made a contribution to American life far beyond what might have been expected. In Georgia they started John Wesley on the way that led to Aldersgate, the importance of which to the English-speaking world need not be elaborated here. The Pennsylvania Synods were failures, but they did galvanize the participants into more rapidly organizing their churches. Even today their very failures are providing lessons to those achieving successes along ecumenical lines. Moravian missions to the Indians were a glorious dream and achievement with a tragic end. The massacre of ninety Christian Indians in Ohio has probably shamed many a white man into repentance for what his kind has done to those of other races. The influence of Moravians upon the Delawares was an important factor in saving the western frontier for the colonies. The humanitarian service of Moravian settlements certainly contributed more to the American cause than would have the service of their men in the military forces. These restored settlements, adjacent to twentieth-century industrial activity, witness eloquently to spiritual values which a secular society so desperately needs.

SELECTED BIBLIOGRAPHY–CHAPTER FOUR

Franklin, Benjamin, *Autobiography,* ed. Frank Woodworth Pine (1916)

Hamilton, J. Taylor and Kenneth G., *History of the Moravian Church—The Renewed Unitas Fratrum* (1967)

Hamilton, Kenneth G., *John Ettwein and the Moravian Church During the Revolutionary Period* (1940)

Levering, J. Mortimer, *History of Bethlehem, Pennsylvania* (1903)

Reichel, Levin T., *The Early History of the Church of the United Brethren (Unitas Fratrum)* (1888)

Sessler, Jacob John, *Communal Pietism Among Early Moravians* (1933)

Towlson, Clifford W., *Moravian and Methodist* (1957)

Weinlick, John R., *Count Zinzendorf* (1956)

———, *The Moravian Diaspora* (1959)

———, "Colonial Moravians, Their Status among the Churches," in *Pennsylvania History,* July (1959)

Yates, Ross, ed., *Bethlehem of Pennsylvania, The First One Hundred Years* (1968)

CHAPTER FIVE

RADICAL PIETISM IN AMERICAN HISTORY

by Franklin H. Littell

IN HIS BOOKS *The Rise of Evangelical Pietism* (1971) AND *German Pietism During the Eighteenth Century* (1973) Professor F. Ernest Stoeffler has given us the most authoritative and comprehensive treatment in English of a European movement which has had a massive influence on church life and thought in America. Certain of the basic teachings and practices of Pietism have spread far beyond the associations and churches which first gave channel to its renewal impulses. Indeed they are encountered frequently in church circles whose forefathers were basically hostile to Pietism. This is especially true of the characteristic Pietist emphasis upon a deeply personal, vitally significant experience of the living God.

Today we often encounter this teaching in an individualistic form, removed from the setting of the church and hostile to the organized life of the Christian community. In classical Pietism this was almost never the case, for profound religious experience was not then primarily a teaching: it was a reality of life. And even those preachers and teachers most critical of the religious establishments were devoted to a vision of the true church as the inspired community of God's people. The religious life expressed itself not in anarchy, and not in dogmatic assertions, but in a life of love for God and man. Predatory disregard for the rights of others had no place in the life style of those to whom the devout life was experienced, and not merely asserted as a religious dogma. The priesthood of all believers was not the freedom of each to be saved in his own way, let alone the right of each "to go to hell in his own way": it was rather the unlimited obligation which each had to seek the eternal well-being of all in God's inbreaking Kingdom.

The simple fact is that—until the rise of contemporary communes—Pietism was one of the three most influential sources of intentional community in American religious life. The other two impulses toward voluntary collectives were Utopian Socialism and Puritanism, and the interaction of Puritanism and Pietism was so substantial from the earliest years that Puritanism can hardly be considered a discrete force.

Studied separately, the various individuals and societies generally bracketed under "Pietism" display a bewildering variety of practices and teachings. Yet there were—even between such major parallel manifestations as the Herrnhuter, the Brethren, and the Communities of True Inspiration (Amana), and despite sometimes vigorous debate between their respective champions—fundamental areas of agreement. On nothing was there more general agreement than the conviction that the world of selfishness and acquisitiveness is condemned and dying, and that the New Testament order of brotherhood and mutual aid is God's way and will certainly triumph in the end. The Pietists said that since the "sects of Christendom" had accommodated to the spirit of the dying age they belonged to the structures which God's elect were leaving behind in their pilgrimage into the future.

Not all Pietists practiced Christian communism modelled on the church at Jerusalem. For that matter not all even separated from the state-churches: in the early decades, at least, gathering renewed Christians into house-churches on the primitive Christian model ("conventicles") did not prevent them from paying the church taxes and attending the public worship of God. With persecution by the state-church authorities, of course, the separatist impulse gained strength. But the Herrnhuters, at least, carried through to the present day a unique pattern of accommodation: in lands with established Protestant churches they remained renewal societies within the establishments, while on the mission fields (including North America) they founded a separate denomination. But in Herrnhut and Zeist, just as in Nazareth and Bethlehem, their intensity of conviction about the New Testament order of Christian community led them to practice for some time a full communal life.

The New Testament church was the normative, indeed the Golden Age of Christianity. They believed that Christendom then fell into sin and corruption when its leaders adopted the life style of worldly men and its peoples became committed to greed, war, and violence. They saw their own movement as a recovery of a spiritual power and life style that had been lost following the apostolic age. The vision of the distant past provided, in short, the program for the future: a Restitution of the true church.

This view of church history is technically called "primitivism."[1] "Primitivism" is the expression of civilized man's misgivings about his current condition and his future prospects, coupled with the myth of a glorious past from which descent into the present has been experienced. Sometimes, as in the myth of the Noble Savage, the "glorious past" is transferred to a distant scene among presumably unspoiled peoples. Or, as in the Robinson Crusoe myth, by means of removal to a desert isle the protagonist is able to grow into spiritual health uncorrupted by the institutions and compromises of decadent civilizations. The study and definition of primitivism was thoroughly developed by Professor A. O. Lovejoy of Johns Hopkins University and was elaborated by him and his associates in *The Journal of the History of Ideas.*[2] In my book *The Origins of Sectarian Protestantism* (1952, PB 1964), I made the first transfer of this typology from literary analysis to the study of radical Christian dissent.

The radical Reformers of the sixteenth century, without exception, spoke of a Golden Age, a Fall, and a Restitution in the history of the church. In doing this they overturned the periodization of church history which had governed Christian thought from the time of Augustine and Orosius. The "Golden Age" of the church was the New Testament period; the "Fall" of the church occurred at the time of the Constantinian establishment; the "Restitution" of the true church was identified with their own movements and/or events which were occurring

---

1. Franklin H. Littell, "Christian Primitivism: An Historical Survey," *Encounter,* vol. 20 (1959), 3:292–96.

2. A. O. Lovejoy *et al., A Documentary History of Primitivism and Related Ideas . . . in Antiquity* (1935), and George Boas, *Essays on Primitivism and Related Ideas in the Middle Ages* (1948).

in their own era. Using this typology, and keeping in mind contrast with the views of history dominant in Eastern O thodoxy, Roman Catholicism, and the "Magisterial Reforma-tion,"[3] we perceive that the primitivist periodization of church history was a governing intellectual force in radical Protes-tantism from Menno Simons through Gottfried Arnold and John Wesley to Charles Taze Russell.

The question before us is to what extent various leaders and groups in Pietism shared this view of church history and drew the consequences thereof in their theology and ecclesiol-ogy. Although Professor Stoeffler has warned that "it would be a great mistake if we took this approach to mean that these men must be interpreted primarily from the point of view of their ecclesiology,"[4] the working hypothesis is here ventured that the controlling factor in their thinking was eschatology, that integral to this eschatology was a certain periodization of church history, and that this periodization involved a norma-tive use of the early church. Most of all, the normative view of the early church gave them a clear guide into the future resto-ration of man's lost virtue. The Pietist communes, to which we shall turn in the latter part of this discussion, believed them-selves to be re-establishing in the final age of church history a style of life that had obtained when the church was at its best in the first age.

PRIMITIVIST PERIODIZATION

The limits of this paper prevent a presentation of the radically different view of Christian history which prevailed in the Latin church and which was carried over by the major Reformers, from that which dominated radical Protestantism. Suffice it to say that in pursuing the primitivist motif we would be rolling up a thread that would take us to Sebastian Franck as well as to Jakob Huter, to Paracelsus as well as to Dirck Phillipsz, to Johannes Campanus and Georg Witzel as well as to Pilgram Marpeck. And in this view, in spite of other fundamental differences between the radical Reformation and Pietism so well defined in Robert Friedmann's *Mennonite Piety Through the Centuries* (1949), the radical Reformation and Pietism were agreed.

---

3. George H. Williams, *The Radical Reformation* (1962), pp. xxiii–iv.
4. F. Ernest Stoeffler, *The Rise of Evangelical Pietism* (1971), p. 7.

Behind them, towering in the shadows, is the mysterious figure of Joachim of Fiore—the abbot and teacher whose students shattered the periodization of church history unchallenged since the time of the Church Fathers. The radical Franciscans used the intellectual weaponry of Joachim against the papacy, and from that time there has flowed an underground river of radical eschatology in the West.[5] In modern times it has surfaced repeatedly among persons and movements who have no knowledge of its origin, e.g., in Cotton Mather and his Age of the Triumph of the Eternal Gospel, in Karl Marx and his idea of the withering away of the state.

Among Pietist historians, Gottfried Arnold and Johann Lorenz von Mosheim were especially influential in popularizing the new eschatology. John Wesley esteemed von Mosheim on church history as he did Bengel on the Scriptures, and Wesley translated large sections of the *Institutiones historicae ecclesiasticae recentiores* (1741) and published them in his preachers' library. Arnold's *Kirchen- und Ketzer-Historie* (1700) profoundly impressed the formation of that sector of Pietism which came to be known as "Dunker" or "Brethren," and we shall quickly trace the outlines of his thought here. Churchly Pietism, which penetrated Reformed and Lutheran and Anglican establishments, is in many things of the same order as radical, sectarian Pietism. In the latter groups, however, the eschatological note—with its ecclesiological consequences—became controlling. Among the latter, Gottfried Arnold is a representative teacher.

Arnold was influenced by William Cave's *Primitive Christianity*, which he read in a German translation. But he reversed Cave's evaluation. Whereas for Cave (like Eusebius of Caesarea) the early church was a time of preparation for triumph with Constantine, for Arnold the unorganized and inspired earlier time was normative. Whereas Cave intended to restore the authority of the early councils and their creeds, Arnold located true religion among Jesus and the Apostles and Confessors before the theologians took over Christianity.[6]

> Worldly force, princes and powers have never benefited Christianity, which is indeed fundamentally different from the world, and they have always stained its purity.[7]

---

5. Ernst Benz, *Ecclesia Spiritualis* (1934); also his *Evolution and Christian Hope* (1966), Ch. III.
6. Wilhelm Freiherr von Schröder, *Gottfried Arnold* (1917), pp. 30f.
7. Eric Seeberg, *Gottfried Arnold* (1923), p. 68.

For Arnold, the true and early church consisted of house-churches or conventicles: the building of churches began with the Fall of the church. Until the "Fall" the only heresy was immorality; force was not used against heretics, but only reproach and disfellowshipping (the Ban). The early church knew no separation of clergy and laity, no hierarchy. The Fall brought the episcopal seizure of power and the rise of prideful ecclesiastical rulers. Arnold was the first church historian to treat sympathetically Julian "the Apostate," whom he interpreted as a victim of sectarian conflict and a champion of freedom of conscience.[8] Arnold also perceived a Fall in the Reformation itself, as the first great spiritual impact flagged and dogmatic Orthodoxy triumphed in the Formula of Concord of the Lutherans and the canons of the Synod of Dort of the Calvinists.

The antipathy to dogma and theology should be noted carefully, for here too the primitivist motif is controlling. In the early church the power of the Spirit was dominant and the fruits of the Spirit were many. Then the theologians took over. The theologians were the technical experts in the science of Christianity; as such, they were products of the Fall of the church. To this day, the same antipathy which leads the Amish Mennonites to avoid automobiles also controls their resistance to dogma and theology. In radical Protestantism there is often a curious sliding back and forth between the Fall of man—which introduced analysis, invention, calculation and compromise—and the Fall of the church—which brought into Christianity the same corrupting forces. And, as we shall see, for the radical Pietist communes the restitution of the true church is predictive of the coming restitution of all things to the original perfection of God's creation (Eden). Calculation and cunning are marks of the Fall of man and also of the Fall of the church, and Christ as the "Second Adam" reverses and overcomes them in both settings.

For Johannes Kelpius, at his retreat on the Wissahickon, the new age was at hand: sects, universities, and theologians would disappear; with the coming of the final age through great travail, the true church of the earliest times would return in glory with the universal restoration of all things.

> ... then all the Sons of God will shout for joy as they did in the Beginning, when God was all in all, as we will be all in all,

---

8. *Ibid.*, p. 83.

when again the End hath found its beginning. Amen! Hal-
leluiah![9]

It is utterly false to charge such "sectarians" with ignoring the
problems of the world and concentrating solely on individual
salvation. In the first place, they were not individualists. In the
second place, they resisted the claims and controls of this aeon
in order to live in readiness for the aeon close at hand, when
both church and world shall be redeemed. Even Etienne
Cabet, whose Utopian Socialist "Icaria" brought hundreds to
the New World to found a new society, and who had no use
whatever for the existing churches, called his program "true
Christianity."

In terms of Christian doctrine and life style, both
churchly and radical Pietists agreed that the Fall of the church
had flooded the Christian establishment with multitudes of
nominal Christians. For an individual to come alive he must be
turned around, he must break from culture-religion. This
"conversion" gave him "true knowledge" in place of ratiocina-
tion; through the experience he learned to profess "basic
truths" which could be experientially verified in place of giving
assent to dead propositions. But when turned around he became a member of a pilgrim community, a community which
lived and worked in anticipation of the early triumph of the
Kingdom of God.

The signs of the last times were many, and various
prophets laid differing weight upon the several signs of history's impending consummation: e.g., the renewal of the
church, the publication of the Bible for the people, the rise of
missions, the reunion of the churches, the defeat of Rome and
the triumph of Protestantism, the return of the Jews to the
Holy Land, the conversion of the Jews, the recovery of the
signs of the Spirit—even the discovery of America. Christian
self-knowledge, beginning with repentance, is the "door into
the sheep stall": by it the "new man" becomes a citizen of the
coming Kingdom, passing into the discipline of the true
church. Believers' baptism was usually the symbolic rite of this
passage, especially among the radical Pietists (as it had been
among the Anabaptists). But the end was not individual salvation: even in the churchly conventicles of Hamburg and

---

9. Ernest L. Lashlee, "Johannes Kelpius and His Woman in the Wilderness,"
in Gerhard Müller and Winfried Zeller, eds., *Glaube/ Geist/ Geschichte:
Festschrift für Ernst Benz* (1967), p. 335.

Frankfurt, as in the Christianized societies of Halle and Harvard, the eschatological vision of social redemption was kept alive. Whether in Gottfried Arnold or J. A. Bengel (who composed charts of salvation history), whether in August Hermann Francke or Friedrich Adolph Lange (who designed a scheme of dispensational ages), the passionate attention to history was pronounced.

As Koppel Pinson and others have shown us, when "the coming of better times" and the triumph of the "new man" was secularized, when a secularized eschatology moved from *Christengemeinschaft* to German *Volksgemeinschaft*, a potential for ethnic demonry was unleashed.[10] When Pietist movements retained their Christian discipline, however, using the Lesser and Greater Bans on the model of the New Testament church, *Geistigkeit* ("spirituality") kept its integrity and remained basically Christian.

THE PIETIST COMMUNES

Protestantism, particularly the radical Reformation, frequently has been accused of individualism and hence the proliferation of sects. This reproach is repeated toward Pietist schismatics by Professor Stoeffler:

> These enthusiasts made the proliferation of religious groups inevitable. Each had his own revelation from the Lord, each his set of subjectively validated norms of religious truth, each the conviction that he was God's favored instrument for saving his fellow men. Each, therefore, gathered about him a little band of followers. . . .[11]

Somewhat hesitantly, another explanation is here entered. Whatever the effect of Martin Luther's heavy emphasis on the individual conscience, whatever the results of human egocentricity among some of the prophets, it seems to me that the perennial source of division was the desperate necessity to be on the right track for the eschaton. This necessity brought an extraordinary psychological pressure upon groups, as well as leaders, to find the true life style for the time of preparation for the end. The right model for a restored church was imperative, for the restoration of the true church was preliminary to the

---

10. Koppel Pinson, *Pietism as a Factor in the Rise of German Nationalism* (1936), pp. 14f.
11. Stoeffler, p. 100.

impending restoration of all things. In the intense pressure-cooker life of the small groups, the mutual discipline of the general priesthood often led to explosion and fusion. As the social psychologists have amply documented for us, the personal interactions of members of a small society circular in form both greatly enhance the learning process and largely increase the chances of early division.

The "conventicles" in private houses obviously had the sociometric design of a circle. The meeting house at Amana, where the circle is squared, retains the same potential. However, the total communal life of the "Communities of True Inspiration" reduced fission to a minimum. Amana declined from Christian commune to modern corporation not through division but through the dying out of prophecy.

It is tempting, particularly in reference to such recurring concepts as androgynous primordial man in radical Protestantism, to discuss also the message of Ephrata, the Shakers, and Oneida. The radicals' view of the work of Christ, the "Second Adam," not only removed the curse of infant damnation; it also, exaggerated, led to the perfectionism of John Humphrey Noyes. The Second Adam had removed for all mankind the guilt of the First Adam, including the guilt of children until they reached "the age of understanding" (i.e., passed through puberty). Thereby freedom of choice was restored, along with the possibility of Christian progress within the fellowship. For those who lived close to the Bible, there were ample safeguards against any innovations which went beyond the Law. Among those Pietist communes here chosen for particular attention—Amana, Economy/Harmony, Zoar, Bethel, and Aurora—the Pietist emphasis on Bible reading and the use of devotional *Erbauungsliteratur* based on the Bible prevented the aberrations which made Noyes' sexual experiments a scandal.

Nevertheless all of the Pietist communes, with their intense group life, paid particular attention to the relations of the sexes. Amana separated men and women in the meetings and taught women to wear clothes that suppressed sex. The separatists at Zoar at first prohibited marriage altogether and later organized into a strict family pattern those who left the preferred celibate state. The women were, however, equal in standing to the men: they were also addressed in the familiar form ("thou," "du") and had the right to hold offices in the society. Bethel and Aurora had strong patriarchal leadership; indeed Dr. Keil taught that the patriarchal family was the model for all social governance. Celibacy was preferred, for love was due all members equally and sin arose with selfishness and separate possessions. In the teaching at Economy the basic doctrine was made explicit: Adam was bi-sexual before the Fall; sex and alienation entered with intermediate human history (post-Eden but pre-millennial); Christ was bi-sexual and brought an end to sexual tension and conquest among his true followers. After a revival in 1807 there was no more marrying at Economy, and no more children were born even though they continued to live in the same family houses. In Pietist communes generally, men and women treated each other with respect, often as equals, and tried by one means or another to eliminate the sexual tensions and separate family claims which seemed to threaten the good society.

*   *   *

All of these communes were primitivist, and all of them combined the matter of the Restitution of the true church with the impending restoration of all things to creation's original perfection. We will now summarize the key teachings and practices of those Pietist communes chosen as representative.

Amana, the "Communities of True Inspiration" that finally settled seven villages in Iowa (1855f.), arose from the preaching of Johann Friedrich Rock (ca. 1719). Their chief place of origin was the valley about the Ronneberg, north of Hanau in Hesse. They believed that the Spirit led his people through charismatics able to read and interpret the Scriptures. Christian Metz and Barbara Heynemann Landmann were such chosen *Werkzeuge,* and when no new prophet appeared upon the death of Barbara the society declined under a caretaker committee for fifteen years and finally became a joint stock corporation. The people of Amana were opposed to playing cards, musical instruments, "steeple-houses," and dancing. Tobacco, wine, and beer were enjoyed, along with plenty of good food prepared in communal kitchens. Especially, they believed that in the inbreaking new age the original genius of the primitive church would be recaptured.

> In the New Testament we read that the disciples were "filled with the Holy Ghost." But the same God lives now as then;

and . . . he will lead his people, in these days as in those, by the words of his inspiration.[12]

Economy (Pennsylvania), and for a time Harmony (Indiana, 1814–24), were settlements which grew out of the renewal work of a Swabian Pietist, Georg Rapp (1757–1847). Rapp sharply contrasted the corruptions of the economic and social order in Württemberg with what was taught in the New Testament. Persecuted, he and his followers migrated to the valley north of Pittsburgh and there prospered mightily. The "Harmonists" made and used moderately whiskey, beer, and wine, and they cultivated good music—both instrumental and vocal. After an 1807 revival they gave up tobacco. They also opposed dancing, jewelry, and fine clothes; some members abstained from eating pork. Rapp taught the eventual salvation of all mankind. He also constantly proclaimed the imminent return of the Lord. His last words, as he lay dying at ninety years of age, were these: "If I did not know that the dear Lord meant I should present you all to him, I should think my last moments come."[13]

Zoar (Ohio) was founded in 1819 as a Christian communist society, with Joseph Bäumeler as the leader. They were Pietists from Württemberg, whose separation from the Old World could only be accomplished by emigration. They especially opposed military conscription, which the duke of Württemberg had introduced in imitation of Napoleon, and they also opposed the requirement that children attend the public schools. (Prussia and Württemberg were then forerunners of universal public education.) They used musical instruments, but avoided dancing, pork, and tobacco. They allowed beer, coffee and tea.

Bethel (Missouri) and Aurora (Oregon) were founded in 1844 and 1855, respectively, by Wilhelm Keil. Dr. Keil was a Prussian who worked for a time with the German Methodists. Gathering a group of disaffected Rappites, he founded two highly successful communes. The primary goal was "the unselfish life": private property is sin. Obedient submission to

---

12. Charles Nordhoff, *The Communistic Societies of the United States* (Schocken edition, 1965), p. 43; the standard work on Amana remains Bertha Shambaugh's *Amana That Was and Amana That Is* (1932).
13. Nordhoff, p. 86; on the Rappites, cf. John A. Bole, *The Harmony Society* (1904); also John S. Duss, *The Harmonists: A Personal History* (1943), with critique by Karl J. R. Arndt in *The Western Pennsylvania Historical Magazine*, vol. 26 (1943), pp. 159ff.

God's will and to the communal order was the foremost virtue. Nordhoff reported Keil's words at the graves of his children, and these words plainly reveal the man's kind of faith:

> "Here," he said, "lie my children, all I had, five; they all died after they were men and women, between the ages of eighteen and twenty-one. One after the other I laid them here. It was hard to bear; but now I can thank God for that too. He gave them, and I thanked him; he took them, and now I can thank him too!" Then, after a minute's silence, he turned upon me the sombre eyes and said: "To bear all that comes upon us in silence, in quiet, without noise, or outcry, or excitement, or useless repining—that is to be a man, and that we can only do with God's help."[14]

Keil's followers were committed to nonresistance and simple living. At Bethel, liquor and tobacco were used; at Aurora, there was no liquor and few used tobacco. They were famous for their music, and their marching band from Aurora played at state fairs and even at a Presidential inaugural.

MAJOR COMMUNAL INSTITUTIONS

According to the radical Pietists, private property was a mark of the Fall of man—like war and violence and sexual tension. Before the Fall, the earth yielded her plenty for all living creatures; thorns and thistles were yet unknown, and hard labor was not necessary to survive and enjoy life. A singular case of corruption in the church at Jerusalem, of denial of the fellowship and offense to the Holy Spirit, was the selfishness of Ananias and Sapphira (Acts 5:1–11). In contrast to the company of the true church, where the Spirit visited with power (Acts 2:1–4; 4:31) those who completely shared this world's goods (Acts 2:44–45; 4:32), Ananias and Sapphira met death as self-seeking deceivers.

In contrast to some technological primitivists in radical Protestantism, the Pietist communes did not shun machines or industrial proficiency. Amana began with a system of workshops and ended with woolen mills, refrigerators, deep freezers, and micro-wave cookers. The Rappites began with workshops and developed an economy so sophisticated that at one time they sold a shortline railroad to Commodore Vanderbilt

---

14. Nordhoff, p. 319; the standard work is by Robert J. Hendricks: *Bethel and Aurora* (1953).

for five million dollars. The separatists of Zoar started with workshops, but seem to have done less well in expanding their businesses and holdings. Apparently their leadership was less imaginative, and the commune failed to develop an educational system and a culture comparable to the others. Nevertheless they were without debts, and members ate and dressed well if simply. Bethel and Aurora founded workshops of the usual kind—woolen mill, grist mill, sawmill, distillery, blacksmithy—and were famous for excellent fruit orchards and popular resort hotels. Both the Rappites at Harmony, Indiana, and the followers of Keil at Bethel were well known for the excellent wagons they made and sold to settlers moving westward. In fact, the reputation of the communalists for integrity of workmanship and honesty in business dealing seems to have been justly and widely known.

The attitude to sacramental and liturgical practices is also interesting, for infant baptism was early called into question in Pietism, while the Lord's supper was a major symbol of the common life. Even today the common meal is the major liturgical event in the new style communes.[15] The supper, which was usually followed by an agape meal (*Liebesmahl*), was a significant sign of the in-group ethos of mutual aid and of relationship outward to the hungry and wretched of the earth. Amana celebrated an occasional Lord's supper, followed by an agape meal; but they abandoned baptism. Economy was well known for its open hospitality to tramps on the road; an annual Lord's supper was celebrated each October. At Zoar neither baptism nor the Lord's supper was observed. At Bethel and Aurora there were irregular celebrations of the Lord's supper accompanied by the love feast. The general trend in the communes seems to have been away from formal observances. Pietism stressed true inward religion and depreciated the value of mere outward observances. In the communes, therefore, baptism tended to fade away, and liturgical communion—in effect superseded by the daily practices of the common life—became infrequent. When the eucharist was celebrated in its simplest form it was almost always accompanied by an agape or *Liebesmahl*.

On education of the young, the Pietist communes were in advance of the society at large, although public schools and

---

15. Cf. Franklin H. Littell, "Christian Faith and Counter-Culture: The Appeal of the Communes," *The Iliff Review*, vol. 30 (1973), 1:3–13

universal education were beginning to be established. In this the Pietists followed the same line as radical Protestantism from the sixteenth century on: the priesthood of all believers required a membership literate in the Bible, if nothing else— both male and female. Therefore they maintained their own quality schools, even though they resisted the claims of the public schools in the Old World and in the New. Opposition to the schools of the German and American states was due in part to their close connection with politically or socially established religion, and in part to their orientation to science and *Techne*.

At Amana the children were kept at school between the ages of six and thirteen. The emphasis was placed on reading, writing, and arithmetic—with the Bible and the Catechism the primary documents for mastering the first two skills. Among the Rappites, before the effects of celibacy were felt, a vigorous school system was maintained. For adults, attention was given to training in music; there were lectures, and also assemblies for discussion of matters leading to community decisions. At Zoar, from 1828 to 1845 all children over three years were placed in large houses under the care of persons with a special vocation for education; after the latter date, a year-round school was kept for all children to the age of fifteen. Bethel and Aurora were widely known for their musical programs, although the general cultural life was somewhat limited: the school taught the basics, but avoided the higher learning. Sometimes young people were sent out to master further technical skills in industry or agriculture, but no support was given to any who might crave humanistic learning.

The general attitude to learning is of a piece with that of larger churches influenced by Pietism, whose members for decades controlled state legislatures: they were quite willing to support major appropriations for state colleges of industry and agriculture, where students might master useful skills, but they were resistant to bills to strengthen the universities' attention to philosophy, social sciences, humanities, and religion. Technical proficiency was more than welcome; for wisdom, the oral tradition and the study of the Bible were deemed sufficient.[16]

---

16. Today the positions are somewhat reversed between the radical Protestant societies and the public schools; cf. Franklin H. Littell, "Sectarian Protestantism and the Pursuit of Wisdom: Must Technological Objectives Prevail?" Ch. III in Donald Erickson, ed., *Public Controls for Nonpublic Schools* (1969), pp. 61–82.

Even in the New World, where religious liberty was respected and the political covenant was in principle based on popular sovereignty, the Pietist communes were restrained toward politics. The people of Amana were nonresistants and did not vote. The Rappites did not vote, let alone hold public office. The people of Zoar were nonresistants and did not vote. Bethel and Aurora were also nonresistant and in Missouri the people tried to avoid politics; but being strongly opposed to slavery, in Oregon they voted solidly Republican and contributed several abolitionist political leaders to state politics. It might be mentioned too that in Oregon their second leader was "Professor" Christoph W. Wolff, a graduate of Göttingen and teacher of the first student from Oregon to enter Harvard (Henry T. Finck); Wolff was steeped in German Social Democracy as deeply as Dr. Keil was in Pietism, and his influence toward political activity was affirmative.[17]

The general priesthood, for which all were trained in the Bible and Catechism, was exercised in various ways and with varying degrees of intensity. At Amana there were three defined levels of Christian achievement, and an annual *Untersuchung* was made of all members to determine where they stood in spiritual progress. They read Matthew 16:19 to mean not Peter but the whole body of elders and teachers received the authority to loose and to bind. The covenant which all adults signed was worked out by the community itself. At Economy, Georg Rapp exercised great patriarchal authority among his people, and the covenant was written by an older member and signed by all. Yet the freedom of each remained such that in 1831 a false prophet, a fraudulent "Count Maximilian de Leon" (Bernhard Müller), succeeded in drawing off 250 of the 750 members and in wresting a substantial share of community property from the original commune. Rapp, with his ready wit and characteristic use of the Bible, commented, "and the tail of the serpent drew the third part of the stars of heaven, and did cast them to the earth" (cf. Revelation 12:9). The schismatic commune founded by the "Count" at Phillipsburg soon failed, whereas Economy went on to greater prosperity.

Zoar was the most overtly democratic of the communes considered. Even their own children were placed on probation for a time before they could sign the covenant. An article of

---

17. Hendricks, pp. 40f.

faith put it that since God was no respecter of persons they uncovered the head to none but God and bent the knee to no man. Opposed to all "ceremonies," including baptism and the Lord's supper, rejecting all preaching services, rigidly egalitarian, they apparently lacked effective instruments of group control—except of course for the common toil and the common life. Even though Wilhelm Keil was an autocrat, and Bethel and Aurora were committed to the patriarchal model as best for the society and also for the world, the records show that the major decisions were discussed and made by the whole community. When in 1872 Dr. Keil, growing old, divided the property which had for thirty years been held solely in his name among the heads of families it made no difference whatever in the conduct of the society. In contrast to the Socialist "Icarias" (Cabet) and phalanxes (Fourier), which were great in number but short-lived, the Pietist communes lasted for generations. In this too they parallel those characteristically Puritan societies of the common life—the Shakers and the Mormons.

THE VIEW OF HISTORY

Probably no one of the teachings and institutions of radical Pietism can be separated out as the single overriding principle—not conversion or rebirth, not restitutionist ecclesiology, nonresistance, plain dress, equality of sexes, mutual aid or communism, lay ministry, missions, believers' baptism, church discipline, covenant, democratic view of the dignity of every man, opposition to religious persecution and sectarianism, spiritual and experiential religion, or devotion to the word of God. Nor was the warp and woof of belief and practice which marked one group identical with that of another.

Yet there were themes that appeared again and again in radical Pietism, and most of them were present in the teachings of churchly Pietism as well—although sometimes in the latter situation they were inhibited by accommodation to institutional realities. It seems though that the most important common belief of the Pietist communes was an overpowering sense of the impending breakthrough of God and his final age in human history. They felt inwardly driven to prepare for this imminent event. Primitivists in their view of history and Biblicists in their pursuit of the Living Word, they drew from a picture of the ancient past the plan for the future. It was the view of the last things that dominated their mood and life styles. And even in this they were reliving the normative period of the past, for the early Christians too, before the church "fell," lived in joyful anticipation of the Second Coming (*parousia*) and the Restitution of All Things (*apokatastasis*).

With the establishment of Christianity as the official religion of the Roman Empire, the intense eschatology of the early age waned and a quite different view of history came to prevail. For Augustine, for example, who bracketed out an essentially timeless and soundproofed era between the ascension and the return of Christ, history in the intermediate period is either an anti-climax or a tiresome prelude. Real history in Augustine is intensely individual: at this level he was unsurpassed—in conceiving of personal history and defining it, and in personal awareness:

> ... in the Eternal nothing passeth away, but that the whole is present; but no time is wholly present: and let him see that all time past is forced on by the future, and that all future follows from the past, and that all, both past and future, is created and issued from that which is always present. ...

> There are three times; a present of things past, a present of things present, and a present of things future.[18]

There is here the half of a dialectic of history, one which leads readily to the intense *Nun* of the existentialists and the passion for freshness of the contextual ethicists. As for general history, conceived as the history of Christianity, Augustine and Orosius fastened upon churchly thought a periodization which leaves the middle period—between Christ's going and his coming again—essentially sterile.

In spite of his wrestling with the meaning of "the fall of Rome" (410), a meaning whose grandeur he spiritualized and whose concrete realities he relativized to the point of meaninglessness, for Augustine the age which began with the Christian church extends with no sudden changes or major events until the Second Coming and the end of human history as we know it. Thus life in this world is ultimately a tiresome postlude or a boring prelude, and the decisions we make here and now may be earnest in the personal sense; but in the end

18. Augustine's *Confessions*, Bk XI, ch. XIII, XX.

there are no cataclysmic, no earth-shaking events of general significance in the intermediate period.

The other half of a dialectic of history opens up as we meditate upon the eschatology of the radical Pietists. History was for them no cyclical or undulatory process, like the chronicles of the ancient Greeks or the civilizations of the Nile valley. Neither was it a flat plain traversed between two mountain ranges, between Alpine events as it were, with dramatic episodes occurring only within the soul of the sojourner. History was also an unfolding process—with a beginning, a direction, and a consummation. The relationship of each person to the process—his decisions, his style of life, his spiritual condition—was given meaning by the purposes of God in human history. The Christian man, with freedom of choice (by grace, not by nature) and a mandate to prepare himself with his brethren for imminent and decisive events, is right in the middle of the action. Moreover, Christian history is filled with dramatic events and critical periods, in which wrong turns have been taken as well as faithful witness sometimes made.

Without the balance of the emphasis upon this given moment of awareness and decision, a linear view of history can become dehydrated and formal—ending in charts and deterministic dispensations. But without a sure grip on the historical process, the individual's personal history and decision is not just relativized but made trivial.

For many of us in American Protestantism the churches have become a timeless void of abstract truths—whether propositional or "value-centered"—enlivened only by the celebration of natural liturgical events (birth, death, puberty rites, marriage) or occasional individual ecstasy. We have lost the sense of meaningful events that shape history, even such Alpine events as have recently occurred at our doorstep (e.g., the Holocaust, a restored Israel). The Pietist sense of history and its impending consummation saved them from such blindness and deafness.

In spite of human blunders, the radical Pietists were not so spiritually emasculated, so suspended from human history. They carried on the dialogue with the Book of History with passion, and they did not rest until they mastered and built into their hymns and prayers and life style what they understood the God of History to be saying to them and to be expecting of those who had ears to hear.

Our churches deplore selfishness and pass resolutions against the exploitation of the poor, but they do not practice mutual aid—let alone Christian communism. Our churches denounce war and violence, but they do not generally maintain the disciplines of nonresistance and peace. Our churches rail against worldliness and conspicuous consumption, but they excuse pomp and circumstance. Our churches talk about heaven, but they do not give priority to the Last Things.

The radical Pietists did not divide abstract "values" from the rule of life. No Docetists, they attempted to realize in their own bodies the import of what they professed with their tongues. They saw themselves as carriers of history. For this they are well worth study not only by those who enjoy reviewing the exoticisms of *Sektengeschichte* but also by those on a religious quest. The Pietist communards were among those, post-Augustinian and post-establishment, who look to a God who keeps his promises, who is not content to let his creation decline and collapse at the hands of wicked men in high places, who purposes a restoration of all things to their original perfection. The communes they founded were "Schools of Christ," within which men and women were readying themselves for the Kingdom of God which was at hand. In this setting, they were not only avid students of history: they were responsible protagonists.

SELECTED BIBLIOGRAPHY—CHAPTER FIVE

Arndt, Karl J. R., *George Rapp's Harmony Society, 1785–1847* (1965)

Bole, John A., *The Harmony Society* (1904)

Duss, John S., *The Harmonists: A Personal History* (1943)

Hendricks, Robert J., *Bethel and Aurora* (1953)

Hinds, William A., *American Communities* (1878)

Littell, Franklin H., "Primitivismus," in Littell, Franklin H. and Walz, Hans Hermann, eds., *Weltkirchenlexikon: Handbuch der Oekumene* (1960), cols. 1182–87

Nordhoff, Charles, *The Communistic Societies of the United States* (1965). First published 1875

Noyes John H., *History of American Socialisms* (1966). Reprint of 1870 edition

Randall, Emilius O., *History of the Zoar Society* (1971). Based on 3rd edition of 1904

Shambaugh, Bertha M. H., *Amana That Was and Amana That Is* (1932)

CHAPTER SIX

PIETISM, THE WESLEYS, AND METHODIST BEGINNINGS IN AMERICA

by F. Ernest Stoeffler

WHETHER THE METHODIST REVIVAL IS SEEN IN RELATION TO Whitefield or to the Wesleys it must be kept in mind that these men were not the originators but the product of the revival movement which swept across large segments of Protestantism during the late seventeenth and early eighteenth centuries. The fires of religious enthusiasm which had burned high in England during the Cromwellian period had long since begun to die down. At least part of the reason was that, beginning with the Restoration, there was a strong socio-political reaction against the rampant religious individualism of the earlier period. The uncompromising nature of that reaction was expressed by the Act of Uniformity of 1662, the Conventicle Act of 1664, the Five Mile Act of 1665, as well as the expulsion of non-jurors in 1690. The various acts against dissenters during the early decades of the eighteenth century testify to the same corporate mind-set. Since religious revival and individualism are inseparable it is clear that the external conditions were not conducive to the commencement of extensive revivalistic tendencies during this period of English history.

On the intellectual level the English reaction against any kind of religious fervor was equally pronounced. During the period in question Deism had come into its own. Already in 1624 Edward Herbert of Cherbury (1583–1648) had enunciated the basic beliefs of what came to be known as "natural religion." In the succeeding decades his rationalistic approach

184

to religious reality found fertile soil among English churchmen. The resulting movement eventuated in John Locke's famous *Reasonableness of Christianity* in 1695, to be followed by a veritable frenzy of attempts to make Christianity "reasonable." The result of it all was a religious climate, marked by rationalism and even agnosticism, which stands in marked contrast with the rising tide of Pietist fervor noticeable on the Continent during this same period of time.[1]

THE RELIGIOUS SOCIETIES

These markedly rationalistic tendencies in the religious life of pre-Wesleyan England were counteracted to some extent by the rise of the so-called "religious societies."[2] The forming influence during the inception of the religious society movement seems to have been the preaching and general religious concern of the renowned Dr. Anthony Horneck (1641–1697), a Continental who had come to England in 1661. This being the case, Horneck's own religious background becomes important.

Having been born at Bacharach in the Palatinate Horneck grew up in Reformed Pietist circles. In time he was sent to the University of Heidelberg to study under Friedrich Spanheim the Younger (1632–1701), who during his younger years had belonged to Jean de Labadie's band of youthful followers. Not only was Horneck in touch with Labadism through his teacher, however, but according to Martin Schmidt he also absorbed Labadist piety by being associated with that remarkable woman, Anna Maria van Schuurman.[3]

---

1. This must be admitted though one may not wish to follow the well-meant overstatements regarding the deplorable state of English church life prior to the Wesleyan revival by historians like J. W. Bready in his *England: Before and after Wesley* (1938), part 1, pp. 19–160.
2. For the religious society movement in England see J. W. Simon, *John Wesley and the Religious Societies* (1921); also J. W. Legg, *English Church Life from the Restoration to the Tractarian Movement* (1914). All accounts of this subject go back to Josiah Woodward's *Account of the Rise and Progress of the Religious Societies in the City of London,* which was available to me in the German translation published in 1700.
3. Martin Schmidt, *John Wesley: A Theological Study* (1962), vol. 1, p. 33. For the piety of Anna Maria van Schuurman and her mentor, Jean de Labadie, see the author's *Rise of Evangelical Pietism* (1965), pp. 162–169; H. L. J. Heppe, *Geschichte des Pietismus und der Mystik in der Reformirten Kirche, namentlich der Niederlande* (1879), pp. 240–275; Anna Birch, *Anna van Schurman, Artist, Scholar, Saint* (1909). During his younger years Horneck

When he came to England, therefore, he brought with him this
kind of piety, which is a mixture of early Reformed Pietism and
Romanic spirituality. That he never freed himself from this
approach to personal religion is immediately evident in all of
his works. This is true in spite of the fact that Horneck consciously attempted to subject his earlier understanding of the
religious life to the outward requirements of membership in,
and loyalty to, the Church of England.

   This early connection with Labadism may well explain,
in part at least, why the religious societies of England during
and after the days of William and Mary were so entirely hospit-
able to the kind of mystical spirituality which is associated with
Port Royal and the Quietism stemming from Molinos. It was
the members of these societies who were open to the religious
inspiration coming from Continentals like de Renty, Poiret,
Pascal, Antoinette Bourignon, Fénelon, Brother Lawrence,
Molinos, John d' Avila, Gregory Lopez, Saint Cyran, Madam
Guyon, Armelle Nicolas, as well as some of the older mystics
such as Thomas à Kempis *et al*.

   At this point it should also be pointed out, perhaps, that
even some of the native devotional writers who were read by
the members of the societies owed a great deal to Continental
models. In this connection one might mention, for instance,
William Law's indebtedness to Fénelon and Madam Guyon
(later also to Jacob Boehme), and Henry Scougal's dependence
on the theology of the Scottish Episcopalian Robert Leighton,
who in turn had found his religious awakening among the
Jansenists of France.

   G. C. Cell and others have made considerable effort to
demonstrate the indebtedness of the Wesleys to the Puritan
tradition. It would obviously be doing violence to the events of
history not to recognize such a debt. At the same time, however, it would be equally questionable not to recognize that the

----

was a friend of both Labadie and Spener. After he had emigrated to
England he identified himself closely with the Church of England. In 1670
he was preacher at the Savoy, in 1689 chaplain to William III, and in 1693
prebendary of Westminster. Among his important books are: *The Great
Law of Consideration*, etc. (1676); *The Happy Ascetic—or the Best Exercise*
(1681); *Delight and Judgment, or the Great Assize* (1683); *The Fire on the Altar*,
etc. (1683); and *The Crucified Jesus, or, a Full Account of the–Sacrament of the
Lord's Supper* (1686). He was buried at Westminster Abbey. All accounts of
his life seem to go back to Richard Kidder's biography of Horneck pre-
fixed to the latter's *Several Sermons Upon the Fifth of Matthew*, which was
available to the author in the 3rd ed. (1717).

kind of spirituality here discussed did not also enter the Wesley household through its long-standing connection with the society movement. It is well known that both Samuel and Susanna Wesley were enthusiastic supporters of the societies of their time.[4] Thus the kind of mystical-pietistic spirituality under discussion became a prominent ingredient of the life style of the Wesley home. Having been picked up by both John and Charles Wesley during their childhood, it became an important aspect of their religious self-understanding during their days at Oxford. This was quite natural since its theological emphases were completely congenial with the mystical traditions within both Puritanism and Anglicanism.

The implication of all this is, of course, that the religious indebtedness of both Wesleys, as well as that of the entire Methodist movement, reached back beyond Aldersgate to the Reformed Pietism of Labadie on the Continent.[5] Under the circumstances we are not surprised to find that John Wesley decided to include extracts of Horneck's works in his *Christian Library,* and that many of the Continental authors mentioned above, such as de Renty, were his lifelong favorites.

What has been said would seem to give us a clue to the life style of both John and Charles Wesley prior to 1738. On the one hand it was the highly internalized piety of the Labadist movement. Yet, it was not Labadism in its pure form. Among the members of the religious societies it had long since become mixed with the practical, outgoing, ethically sensitive, duty-oriented type of piety which had been the mark of the native Puritan tradition. For that reason the religiously motivated efforts of the Wesleys during their Holy Club days had two foci—spiritual exercises *and* concern for the neighbor. Before Aldersgate holiness to the Wesleys consisted of rigorous concentration upon the interior religious life, coupled with profound concern for the poor. By a relentless effort not to neglect either one of these two poles of their religious en-

---

4. See L. Tyerman, *The Life and Times of the Rev. Samuel Wesley* (1866), pp. 203–228; also G. V. Portius, *Caritas Anglicana, or, an Historical Inquiry into Those Religious and Philanthropical Societies That Flourished in England Between the Years 1678 and 1740* (1912), pp. 24, 128–131.
5. For a helpful discussion of Romanic influences upon John Wesley's religious self-understanding see Jean Orcibal, "The Theological Originality of John Wesley and Continental Spirituality," tr. R. J. A. Sharp, in R. Davies and G. Rupp, *A History of the Methodist Church in Great Britain* (1965), pp. 83–111.

deavor they hoped to work out their salvation with fear and trembling.[6] It was a combination of pious striving which yielded considerable fervor and dedication, but little religious certainty and less joy. Hence it made the preaching of the younger Wesleys as zealous and as pedestrian as that of their father. No movement such as historic Methodism could conceivably have sprung from it.

MORAVIAN INFLUENCES

While the influence of the older Continental spirituality upon the Wesleys has received relatively little attention, the Moravian sources of Methodist piety and practice have been widely investigated, both from the Methodist and from the Moravian side.[7] Still it is necessary at this point to give some attention to it. In an effort to do so it may be best to begin with the familiar Aldersgate experience of John Wesley.

It is not surprising, of course, that the question of what happened at Aldersgate, and of its significance, has been beclouded by the varying interpretations of the founder of Methodism. Like other great men in history John Wesley has become a symbol of the religious self-understanding of a multitude of people. Hence the scholars who represent this multitude during a given period of time tend to find in him whatever satisfies their religious needs and supports their interests. Thus Tyerman, writing at a time when Methodism was content to think of itself as a movement of reform by means of concentration upon the religious renewal of individuals, had no difficulty in according John Wesley's Aldersgate experience, as well as its Moravian sources, full value. As a result of the humanistic penetration of the religious consciousness of Methodism Aldersgate gradually came to be regarded as a liability rather than an asset. Hence there arose what we might call the revisionist interpretations beginning with Umphrey Lee in which the Aldersgate account gradually becomes a "pious legend,"[8] and the Moravian influence takes

---

6. Very interesting here is Richard Morgan's letter to his father describing the concerns of the Holy Club in 1734. See *The Letters of the Rev. John Wesley*, ed. John Telford (1931), vol. 1, pp. 147–150. (Hereafter cited as LJW.)

7. The most extensive discussions of the relationship between Methodists and Moravians are still A. W. Nagler's *Pietism and Methodism* (1918), and C. W. Towlson's *Moravian and Methodist* (1957).

8. A. C. Outler, ed., *John Wesley* (1964), p. 51.

on only secondary significance. With the rise of a more universal interest in Methodism and its founder, the catholicizing interpreters, of which Piette is typical, began to come into their own. As may be surmised, neither Aldersgate nor its Moravian antecedents have any special significance in this context.

The various revisionist interpretations, whether inspired by humanistic or catholic interests, are generally based on John Wesley's alleged silence about Aldersgate in later years. Aside from the fact that this oft-mentioned silence is only relative and is thus itself a serious problem, any interpretation based on what a man did not say is notoriously inconclusive.[9] From the point of view of historical scholarship it would seem to be far safer to put the emphasis on those parts of Wesley's *Journal* and *Letters* in which he recorded his day-to-day impressions as he actually lived through his religious experience in the spring of 1738. Later recollections and omissions, clouded as they were by controversy and rationalization, simply must be treated as far less reliable.

If these methodological assumptions are justifiable both John Wesley's 1738 experience, and its Moravian antecedents, must be regarded as of major importance to the religious self-understanding of Wesley, as well as of early Methodism.

The familiar story which lies behind the Moravian influence on the religious maturation, the theology, and the ecclesiastical practice of the Wesleys begins with their embarkation for Georgia on October 14, 1735, and ends with the "stillness controversy" in 1741. Since it has been meticulously recorded in John Wesley's *Journal,* and since it has been rather carefully researched, it needs no retelling. All we can hope to do in this connection is to point up a number of significant facts.

It would be difficult, indeed, to get around George Cell's assertion that the basic happening in John Wesley's life during the spring of 1738 was his acceptance of the Reformation doctrine of salvation by faith alone, thus becoming experientially certain of a right relationship with God.[10] This change was so utterly crucial to him that ever afterwards he was in the habit of dividing his religious pilgrimage into two parts—before and after 1738. What is important in this con-

9. For what is still a cogent argument against putting too much emphasis on John Wesley's silence is found in E. Rattenbury, *The Conversion of the Wesleys: A Critical Study,* pp. 118–151. The best summary of the argument for the significance of Wesley's silence is that of A. C. Outler, pp. 1–39.

10. G. C. Cell, *The Rediscovery of John Wesley* (1935), pp. 161f.

text, however, is that it was the Moravians, notably August Gottlieb Spangenberg and Peter Boehler, who laid the groundwork for this experience.

The day after the Wesleys had landed in Georgia John met Spangenberg, who asked him what proved to be a very disconcerting question, namely, "Do you know Jesus Christ?"[11] His contact with the Moravians on board the Simmonds had helped him to realize that his newly found friend used the word "know" in a sense previously quite unfamiliar to him and that, therefore, his own response consisted of "vain words." Hence the question continued to disturb him, its point being reinforced by the poignant sense of failure associated with his work in Georgia. After his return to England on Saturday, March 4, 1738, Peter Boehler convinced him that the missing ingredient in his personal religion was lack of faith, but that he should continue to preach it until he possessed it.[12] The following Monday he had thought the matter through and now decided to heed Boehler's advice. During the coming weeks Wesley and Boehler carried on various "affectionate conversations."[13] Out of these conversations came the famous heartwarming experience of May 24.

John Wesley, being the kind of man he was, decided to test the validity of this experience for some time to come. In the process of testing it he experienced periods of doubt the importance of which has been exaggerated by some of his recent interpreters. In actuality, however, such doubts are quite normal to a person's religious experience within the Pietist tradition, the literature on them being extensive. Furthermore, these religious scruples would have been less noticeable had it not been for the subsequent strains between John Wesley and the Moravians. The really significant fact here is that in spite of his disenchantment with the Moravians he continued to regard his 1738 experience as a water-shed, both in his religious pilgrimage and in his ministry, to the end of his life.[14]

---

11. *The Journal of the Rev. John Wesley,* ed. N. Churnock (1909–1916), vol. 1, p. 151. (Hereafter cited as JJW.)
12. JJW, vol. 1, p. 442.
13. In addition to the appropriate sections in vol. 1 of John Wesley's *Journal* see also "Peter Boehler, Bishop of the Brethren's Church," in *Transactions of the Moravian Historical Society,* vol. 2, pp. 193–218.
14. It is significant that at the age of eighty-six John Wesley still acknowledged the part which Peter Boehler had played in his religious maturation. See L. Tyerman, *The Life and Times of the Rev. John Wesley* (1871–1872), vol. 3, p.

It was his contact with the Moravians, then, which gradually turned Wesley the seeker into Wesley the possessor of that experiential "knowledge" of God which Pietists universally considered basic to the religious life.

Without this religious experience of John Wesley (as well as of his brother Charles) in the spring of 1738 Methodism as we know it from the study of its early history could not have arisen. Every record we possess indicates that in 1738 John was given a new message which then sent Methodism on its way. Both consciously and deliberately the early Wesleyan movement made the experience of "the Kingdom of God within" the touchstone of what is "real" and of what is not "real" in personal Christianity.[15] In doing so it was the direct heir of Continental Pietism as initially transmitted to the Wesleys by the Moravians.

So much for the Moravian influence on the actual religious experience of John Wesley in 1738. More problematical is the question of that influence on the Wesleyan theology as such. The roots of John Wesley's religious thought cannot be confined to one religious tradition without doing violence to what really happened. They run back into the Anglican as well as the Puritan traditions, the mysticism of Tauler, the *German Theology*, Thomas à Kempis and William Law, Richard Baxter and Henry Scougal, as well as the Romanic spirituality so widely appreciated on the Continent at the time. Since John Wesley was eclectic in his tastes, pragmatic in his theological inclinations, and decidedly individualistic in his evaluation of the work of others it is difficult to trace the historical lineage of specific theological beliefs.

By the same token, however, it would be difficult to gainsay the fact that those aspects of John Wesley's theology which are most closely related to his 1738 experience do not bear the hallmark of Moravian ancestry. We are thinking, of course, of his lifelong insistence on salvation by faith alone, on

---

595. This acknowledgment of his indebtedness to the Moravians for his 1738 experience had also been conveyed to his associates. Note Joseph Benson's reference to the influence of Peter Boehler in his memorial sermon for John Wesley, preached July 26, 1791 (printed by J. Thompson, 1791), p. 9.

15. See John Wesley's introduction to *Hymns and Spiritual Songs, Intended for the Use of Real Christians, of All Denominations,* of which the title itself is significant. The reference here is to the 8th edition (1761). This was the hymnal regularly used by Methodist people until 1780 and beyond.

assurance (or "the witness of the Spirit"), and, to a degree at least, on perfection (or "holiness").

John Wesley was acquainted, of course, with article 11 of the Articles of Religion of his own church, which speaks of justification by faith alone. It is significant, however, that he acknowledges in his *Journal* (as does his brother Charles) that it was the Moravians who first pointed out to him the actual meaning of this on the level of personal religious faith.[16] It was only *after* Peter Boehler and others had expounded to him the nature of such faith, as an instantaneous gift of God which carries its own certainty of divine acceptance, that he discovered that his own church had taught this all along. Before 1738 he had accepted it on the intellectual level. After that date it had become an indispensable aspect of his own religious life. Hence he continued to insist on it.

To what extent the Pietist understanding of salvation by faith alone became part of his message is evident in his *Sermons*. It is significant to find, for instance, that in the sermon which John Wesley deliberately put first in the 1771 edition of his *Works* he gives a definition of religious faith which had grown directly out of his 1738 experience. It is "a sure confidence," he says, "which a man hath in God, that through the merits of Christ *his* sins are forgiven, and *he* [is] reconciled to the favor of God." It hardly needs to be pointed out how close these words are to the famous statement in his *Journal* regarding his religious experience on May 24.

What we have here, then, is a deliberate attempt by John Wesley to make the *Moravian* understanding of the Anglican article on religious faith basic to Christian proclamation. This is so obvious that further documentation is superfluous. Many of the sermon titles in themselves tell the story: "The Almost Christian," "Awake Thou that Sleepest," "Justification by Faith," "The Marks of the New Birth," etc. Even more telling, however, is the fact that when in 1748 he published his sermon "On the Circumcision of the Heart" (first preached before the university on New Year's Day, 1733) he added to that sermon a section on personal religious faith which again harks back to his 1738 experience under the influence of Peter Boehler.[17] Not only that, but when Wesley

---

16. See JJW, vol. 1, pp. 454f.; also Peter Boehler's account of his dealings with John Wesley in "Peter Boehler, Bishop of the Brethren's Church," pp. 203f.

17. *Wesley's Standard Sermons*, ed. E. H. Sugden (1921), vol. 1, p. 445.

published the second volume of what became his *Standard Sermons* he decided to put this sermon, with the revised paragraph on personal faith, at the head of that edition.

What about John Wesley's concept of personal religious certainty known historically under the heading of "assurance," or "the witness of the Spirit"? That he felt constrained to emphasize this all through his ministry can hardly be doubted. This in spite of the fact that it was an aspect of theology which in his day was particularly apt to mark him as an "enthusiast." Thus in an early letter he spoke of it as the "main doctrine of the Methodists."[18] Later (by 1767) he had modified this judgment, though he continued to regard it as a "momentous truth."[19] In his sermon on the subject (sermon 10), which was probably written in 1746, he makes his well-known distinction between rational certainty concerning one's religious state and direct certainty. The latter he characterizes as follows: "The Spirit of God does give a believer such a testimony of his adoption, that while it is present in the soul, he can no more doubt the reality of his sonship, than he can doubt of the shining of the sun, while he stands in the full blaze of his beams." It must be assumed that the sermon in question, as well as other allusions to the same doctrine which we find in his *Standard Sermons*, was inserted into this collection of theologically authoritative discourses for didactic reasons.

While there can be no question about John Wesley's continued adherence to this doctrine, the problem of its origin is not entirely clear. Yates appears to be too quick in identifying it with the Moravians.[20] The fact is that when John Wesley speaks of "assurance" in his sermon "On the Circumcision of the Heart" (1733) he sounds very much as he does in his post-Aldersgate sermons. What we must surmise, therefore, is that he gained an insight into the possibility of direct religious certainty from the mystical literature which he had read.[21] During his pre-Aldersgate days he had accepted this possibility intellectually exactly as he had accepted article 10 of the Articles of Religion. What he received from the Moravians, therefore, was not really the doctrine of direct religious certainty,

18. LJW, vol. 2, p. 64.
19. *Wesley's Standard Sermons*, vol. 2, p. 343.
20. A. S. Yates, *The Doctrine of Assurance With Special Reference to John Wesley* (1952), pp. 20f.
21. See for instance Francisco de Losa's *Life of Gregory Lopez* (Paris ed. of 1638), pp. 102f. It is well known that this was a favorite devotional book of John Wesley during his earlier days and always remained so.

but rather the conviction that he himself could possess this certainty,[22] and that this should be the privilege of Methodist Christians in general. The people who had actually pointed him in this direction were Spangenberg in America, Boehler in England, and Michael Linner in Germany. His teaching on direct religious certainty, therefore, is the result of his reading of the New Testament in a religious perspective received from the Pietists.

More problematical is John Wesley's somewhat ambiguous emphasis on "perfection." This is a doctrine about which his brother Charles developed all sorts of misgivings, though John continued to regard it as "the grand depositum which God has lodged with the people called Methodists."[23]

One of the problems has to do with what John Wesley really believed about this subject—this in spite of the fact that he made numerous efforts to clarify his position. In reading his variously revised desideratum on the subject[24] the reader gains the impression that he meant to make at least the following assertions: (1) That the words "perfection," "sanctification," and "holiness" mean essentially the same thing. (2) That perfection has both a religious and an ethical aspect, consisting basically of love for God and man. (3) That perfection implies a wholly regenerated motivational center in man (the "heart"), which makes willful sinning impossible. (4) That the regeneration of man's "heart," however, does not preclude errors of

---

22. Note his famous Aldersgate statement, "And an assurance was given *me* that He had taken away *my* sins, even *mine,* and saved *me* from the law of sin and death" (JJW, vol. 1, p. 476). Note also his reference to this experience in his sermon on "The Witness of the Spirit," probably written around 1746 and its content reaffirmed in 1767 (*Wesley's Standard Sermons,* vol. 1, p. 208).

23. LJW, vol. 8, p. 238, written in September of 1790. Since his doctrine of perfection was undoubtedly of major importance to John Wesley and since large segments of the Methodist tradition have taken differing positions with respect to its meaning and significance it has been widely discussed both during the nineteenth and twentieth centuries. Besides the steady stream of doctoral dissertations which continue to appear on the subject the more important recent works dealing with it are: R. H. Flew, *The Idea of Perfection in Christian Theology* (1934); W. E. Sangster, *The Path of Perfection* (1943); H. Lindström, *Wesley and Sanctification. A Study in the Doctrine of Salvation* (1946); J. L. Peters, *Christian Perfection and American Methodism* (1956); and L. G. Cox, *John Wesley's Concept of Perfection* (1964).

24. *A Plain Account of Christian Perfection.* It has been published at various times and is found in *The Works of the Rev. John Wesley* (1829–1831), vol. 11, pp. 366–449.

judgment, so that we cannot properly speak of "sinless perfection." (5) That the new birth and perfection are both conceptually and temporally distinguishable one from the other. (6) That perfection as God's instantaneous gift and perfection as the Christian's progressive achievement are aspects of the same religious experience which must be held in tension with each other.

If this is essentially what John Wesley taught the question still remains, How did he come to hold this conviction? From our point of view it would seem that we must take him seriously when in his *Plain Account of Christian Perfection* he attributes this doctrine chiefly to his early mentors—Jeremy Taylor, Thomas à Kempis, and William Law, though his failure to give any credit at this point to the representatives of Romanic spirituality, many of whom he frequently mentions in his *Journal*, throws some doubt on the historical accuracy of his recollections.

In any case, the only link one can discover here between the Moravians and Wesley's understanding of the doctrine under discussion has to do with the idea of perfection as God's instantaneous work. Law and the other models whom he mentions made no such distinction. Their emphasis had been on the age-old, arduous road of self-conquest, which under the stern ideal of complete love for God and man, and on the basis of the most strenuous "spiritual exercises," leads to ever higher levels of religious and moral attainment. It had been Peter Boehler who had first made John Wesley aware of a "perfection," or state of renewal in man's Godward relationship, which is both instantaneous and divinely given.[25] In this connection it is interesting to find that in a conversation between Wesley and Zinzendorf, recorded in Wesley's *Journal*, the founder of Moravianism is on record as opposing Wesley's tendency toward what the former regarded as an ethical perfectionism. What the Moravians did for him, then, was to make him realize that the "habitual disposition of the soul" toward "holiness" (see his sermon on the "Circumcision of the Heart") is not simply a human achievement but also a divine gift. That Wesley accepted this religious insight is indicated in his sermon

---

25. John Wesley was aware of the scriptural promise, of course, that "whatsoever is born of God does not commit sin." It was Peter Boehler, however, who first drew his attention to the significance of this for himself (JJW, vol. 1, pp. 454f.).

on "Salvation by Faith," preached at Oxford in June of 1738. In it he speaks of the gift of faith through which "they are saved from the *power* of sin, as well as from the guilt of it." If later he taught that a second divine act is necessary for "entire sanctification" this only strengthens our argument. We recognize, then, in John Wesley's teaching on Christian perfection an element which came originally from Luther, was transmitted to him by the Moravians, and was then added on by him to the *amor Dei* tradition of catholic Christianity which he had received from his earlier religious mentors, notable among them being the representatives of Romanic spirituality.

METHODIST BEGINNINGS IN AMERICA

Thus far it has been our endeavor to point out those formative factors with regard to John Wesley's religious maturation, as well as his theology, which are indicative of a direct relationship with Continental Pietism. We have indicated that even his pre-Aldersgate religious development was indebted to Romanic spirituality which was channeled through Anthony Horneck's Labadist connection into the English societies, the piety of which helped to shape the religious devotion of the Wesley household. We have also attempted to show the connection between the early Moravian understanding of Christianity and certain basic aspects of Wesley's theology— specifically his understanding of salvation by faith alone, religious certainty, and Christian perfection. The question now before us is how this early Pietist *depositum* in the belief-system and the religious attitudes of John Wesley was enforced upon his early followers in America.

It is common knowledge that American Methodism severed itself formally from John Wesley's control and set up its own ecclesiastical organization during the Christmas conference of 1784. Henceforth it looked preeminently to its own indigenous leadership in all matters—except that of doctrine. In a very enlightening article Frank Baker, speaking of the doctrinal beginnings of American Methodism, says of John Wesley, "The one area where his influence persisted was that of doctrine."[26] This is borne out by the fact that practically all doctrinal material which was officially made available to early

---

26. "The Doctrines in the 'Discipline,'" *The Duke Divinity School Review*, vol. 31, p. 40.

American Methodists was either written or approved by John Wesley.

The question is, of course, What specifically constituted the "established standards of doctrine" which, according to the early *Disciplines,* must be accepted by American Methodists? To answer this question fully would lead us too far afield.[27] There can be no doubt about the fact, however, that early American Methodism always regarded Wesley's *Standard Sermons,* his *Notes Upon the New Testament,* and his revision of the Anglican *Articles of Religion* as basic theological guides.

In speaking first of the *Articles of Religion* it needs to be pointed out that, though they were kept in the *Discipline,* and were even moved to the front of the *Discipline,* their influence on early American Methodism was more negative than positive. The reason is that they contain nothing specifically related to the religious dynamic of historic Methodism. They simply indicated to the fathers of the movement that Methodism is not severed from the stream of the historically continuous religious self-understanding of Christians. The doctrines which have been mentioned above, and which gave distinctiveness to the theological ethos of early Methodism, are mentioned in the *Articles* only casually and in very general terms. This being the case, they are of little interest to this study. Thus we are left with John Wesley's *Standard Sermons* and his *Notes Upon the New Testament* as the most basic repositories of Christian theology for American Methodism during the days of its incipiency.

Indeed, the so-called *Standard Sermons* and the *Notes Upon the New Testament* were designated by John Wesley himself as the two fundamental criteria of Methodist doctrine and

---

27. The chief problem here is whether or not the polemical tracts included in the *Discipline* from 1788 on are part of American Methodism's "established standard of doctrine." We take for granted that this was not the case since the General Conference of 1812 mandated that they be published separately, since they were then published as *Interesting Tracts,* and since they finally disappeared from view altogether. For a brief and very helpful study on early American Methodism's doctrinal standards see Frank Baker's "Doctrines in the Discipline; A Study of the Forgotten Theological Presuppositions of American Methodism," *Duke Divinity School Review* (Winter 1966), pp. 39–55. Equally helpful is C. A. Rogers' article on "The Theological Heritage of the Early Methodist Preachers," *Duke Divinity School Review* (Autumn 1969), pp. 196–208. Unfortunately L. H. Scott's essay in vol. 25 of *Religion in Life* on "Methodist Theology in America in the Nineteenth Century," which is based on his unpublished dissertation at Yale, does not deal explicitly with our period (pp. 87–98).

practice. This was done in his *Model Deed* which was incorporated in the *Large Minutes* of 1763. They were accepted as such by American Methodists when at the first Methodist conference held in America (1783) they decided to use Wesley's *Minutes* as their guide. In this way the *Sermons* and the *Notes* became the unquestioned doctrinal standards of the frontier preachers. While American Methodism gradually began to depreciate those standards in favor of the *Articles of Religion* it should be noted that this was not the case during the period in which we are interested.

The Pietist *depositum* in the *Sermons* has already been pointed out in connection with our discussion of the Moravian influence on John Wesley. Hence we need not do so again. Through them the Pietist understanding of salvation by faith alone, of assurance, and to a degree of perfection, entered the religious self-understanding and practice of early American Methodists.

The second basic source of theology for Methodists in general, and for American Methodists in particular, requires some discussion. This, as has been indicated, consisted of John Wesley's *Notes Upon the New Testament,* which first came out in 1755. Since long before this date Wesley had decided to be a "man of one book" we are not surprised to find that he had planned this type of doctrinal standard for his followers many years before. According to his *Journal* he was finally able to begin this rather monumental task on Sunday, June 6, 1754. To his delight, however, he presently discovered Johann Albrecht Bengel's (1687–1752) *Gnomon,* which had first been published in 1742. Regarding this work Wesley made the following significant remark in the introduction to his *Notes:* "But no sooner was I acquainted with that great light of the Christian world (lately gone to his reward) Bengelius, than I entirely changed my design, being thoroughly convinced it might be more service to the cause of religion, were I barely to translate his *Gnomon Novi Testamenti,* than to write many volumes upon it. Many of his excellent notes I have therefore translated; many more I have abridged, omitting that part which was purely critical, and giving the substance of the rest." Thus we find that while Wesley also used the expository works of the Dissenter Philip Doddridge (*Family Expositor*), of the Calvinist John Guyse (*Practical Exposition of the New Testament*), and of the mystic and high-churchman John Heylin (*Theological Lectures at Westminster Abbey With an Interpretation of the Four Gospels*), a large segment of his borrowed expositions are from Bengel.

To the student of eighteenth-century Pietism it hardly needs to be pointed out that Bengel was the originator of South German (Swabian) Pietism and the one expositor of the Bible whose authority on biblical interpretation was well-nigh universally acknowledged by Continental Pietists.[28] Among the immense amount of literature produced by early Pietism one of the most influential books was undoubtedly the *Gnomon,* in the production of which the quiet preceptor of Denkendorf had spent more than two decades of painstaking labor. Through this work, ↑hen, the influence of Continental Pietism reached directly into the conceptual framework of the second doctrinal standard of early Methodism, both in Europe and in America.

Quite obviously a minute comparison between the *Gnomon* of Bengel and the *Notes* of John Wesley would far exceed the limits of this study. Only a few general observations are possible. For one thing, it must be remembered that Wesley was constitutionally incapable of following anyone else's opinions fully. Hence we must not expect a slavish translation of Bengel. Furthermore, Bengel wrote consciously for scholars, Wesley for his sincere but often unlettered lay preachers. Again, Bengel wanted to be as explicit and as intellectually convincing as possible in his explanations. Wesley, on the other hand, meant to produce a commentary which would be as brief as possible, which could be printed cheaply and distributed widely. Finally, Bengel wanted to save the credibility of the Bible for the world of critical scholarship while Wesley was interested mainly in broadcasting its message to a needy world. Under the circumstances we find that Wesley's *Notes* display a certain amount of independence of Bengel. His comments on the gospels especially seem to have been ready in substance before he discovered Bengel.

Still, there is overwhelming evidence that Bengel's *Gnomon* was Wesley's constant companion while he wrote the bulk of his *Notes.* Sometimes he uses almost the exact words of the Swabian author. Thus the comment on Romans 1:8 in the *Gnomon* is, "This phrase, *my God,* expresses faith, hope, love,

---

28. For a brief theological biography of Bengel see the author's *German Pietism During the Eighteenth Century* (1973), pp. 94–107. For the most painstaking analysis of the theological sources of John Wesley's *Notes* see D. Lerch, *Heil und Heiligung bei John Wesley, dargestellt unter besonderer Berücksichtigung seiner Anmerkungen zum Neuen Testament* (1941).

and, therefore the whole of true religion." Wesley's comment on the same passage is, "My God—This very word expresses faith, hope, love, and consequently all true religion."[29] More often he simply extracts Bengel's ideas and expresses them more succinctly than the Latin original.

The question is, What is there in Bengel's *Gnomon* which appealed so profoundly to the founder of Methodism? Several related answers are possible. On the one hand, Wesley must have felt a profound kinship of spirit with his German counterpart—this in spite of the obvious personality differences between the imperious, activity-oriented Englishman and the retiring, research-oriented Swabian scholar. In the writings of both men one finds an uncommon devotion to a way of life which is centered in love for God and man. Both of them are eminently sane and practical in their attempt to understand and apply the insights of the Gospel. To both of them only those aspects of theology are worth discussing which have experiential significance. Above all, both of them meant to be men of one Book with respect to thought as well as practice.

Perhaps even more important is the fact that Wesley found himself in substantial theological agreement with Bengel. There are differences of emphasis, of course. But the things that really seemed to matter—man's fallen state, the need for salvation with respect to both this life and the life to come, the understanding of the assurance of salvation, the religious life as a life of progressive striving for holiness, the understanding of holiness as centered in love for God and man, the need for community among earnest believers, and the rejection of every kind of accommodationism to the religious and ethical standards of the world at large—both men held passionately in common.

However, while there was a good deal of theological agreement between Bengel and Wesley the former had achieved what the latter had not had time to achieve, namely, a worldwide reputation for biblical scholarship. This is what commanded Wesley's lifelong respect for the great expositor. What we find in the *Notes,* therefore, is that whenever the author discusses difficult scriptural passages, or crucial points of theology, he has recourse to the *Gnomon.* Thus his explana-

---

29. J. A. Bengel, *Gnomon Novi Testamenti,* 3rd ed. (1773), p. 527; John Wesley, *Explanatory Notes Upon the New Testament* (1900), p. 517.

tions of passages taken from the Book of Revelation are almost entirely dependent on either Bengel's *Gnomon* or on his *Ordo Temporum.* [30] In his controversy with William Warburton, Bishop of Gloucester, he based his interpretation of the "children of light" passage on Bengel.

In general we may say, then, that Bengel had little to do with the maturation of Wesley's religious beliefs. By the time the latter came upon the writings of the German scholar his own theology was already fairly well established. What Bengel did primarily for Wesley, and through him for early Methodism, was twofold. As one of the central symbols of the classical Pietist movement on the Continent, and as one of the foremost religious scholars of the day, his essential agreement with Wesley gave theological support to the Wesleyan movement. Then too, as the most universally trusted biblical scholar of the day, the same agreement gave the Wesleyan revival intellectual support as well. [31] Bengel thus undergirded the religious and intellectual self-confidence of Wesley and his co-workers. In doing so he helped to fashion early Methodism into a very effective counterforce against the widespread Rationalism of the day.

What we have attempted to do, then, in our reference to Wesley's *Standard Sermons* and our discussion of his *Notes* is to show that both of these officially designated standards for the theological self-understanding of early Methodism owed a considerable debt to the older movement of Continental Pietism.

Through the *Sermons* and the *Notes* Pietism had its impact not only on early Methodism in general, but on early American Methodism in particular. It has already been pointed out that these two repositories of religious insight and practice were quickly accepted as the basic doctrinal standards of early American Methodism. The reason was that whatever other differences existed between American Methodists and their founder these did not extend to matters of theological import. The remaining question here is, then, What evidence

---

30. He gives his opinion of Bengel's chronology in his letter to Peard Dickinson on June 24, 1788 (LJW, vol. 8, p. 67). It should be said, however, that while Wesley more or less shared Bengel's understanding of events to come he had reservations about Bengel's famous date of 1836.

31. About Wesley's respect for Bengel's scholarship see his letter to Joseph Benson on December 8, 1777, in LJW, vol. 6, p. 291. There are few people whom Wesley accorded such unqualified approval.

is there that the *Sermons* and the *Notes* were not only accepted in America as doctrinal standards, but actually used as such? At least some indication of an answer to this question can be gained through trying to determine the availability of these materials during the early years of American Methodism. Unfortunately this task is somewhat difficult since there seem to be large gaps in our knowledge of the religious materials which were read by Wesley's early followers in America.[32]

We must assume, of course, that when Methodist preachers began to arrive on these shores from England in 1769 they brought both the *Sermons* and the *Notes* with them. From the early journals, particularly that of Thomas Rankin, we know that shipments of Wesley's books were soon received in America and systematically distributed. It would be amazing, indeed, if the two doctrinal standards under discussion had not been among these. According to the chronicler Jesse Lee one of the early preachers, namely Robert Williams, had at least some of Wesley's sermons printed in America prior to the 1773 conference.[33] It is certain that Wesley's four volumes of sermons were printed in America in 1783, and his *Notes* in 1791–1792. According to Frank Baker's *Union Catalogue* both the *Sermons* and the *Notes* continued to be published thereafter every few years during the early decades of the nineteenth century. Thus even a partial knowledge of early Methodist theological literature in America indicates that the official standards of doctrine were widely available to Methodist preachers.

These standards were not only available, but the general understanding among early Methodists in America was that they were meant to be read thoroughly and absorbed. The initial question, for instance, in the *Discipline* of 1781 asks: "What preachers are now determined, after mature consideration, close observation, and earnest prayer, to preach the old Methodist doctrine, and strictly enforce the discipline, as contained in the *Notes,* sermons and minutes published by Mr. Wesley?" In the *Discipline* of 1787 section 17 has to do with the profitable use of time. Here the admonition is given that the preachers are to rise early in the morning and to read "partly

---

32. Very helpful in this connection is Frank Baker's *Union Catalogue of the Publications of John and Charles Wesley* (1966). See also J. P. Pilkington, *The Methodist Publishing House,* vol. 1 (1968).
33. Jesse Lee, *A Short History of the Methodists in the United States of America* (1810), p. 48.

the Scriptures with Mr. Wesley's *Notes*, partly the closely practical parts of what he has published." Though the wording of this mandate was subsequently amended so as to require the reading of "the scriptures with notes," it remained in the *Discipline* during the entire period with which we are concerned. It may, in fact, be assumed that the *Notes* were not really replaced as the basic guide to scriptural interpretation in early American Methodism until the advent of Adam Clarke's *Commentary* became available in America in 1826.

If the "closely practical parts" mentioned above refer primarily to Wesley's *Sermons*, as was probably the case, we find that the doctrinal standards which relate Methodism to Continental Pietism were as important in America as elsewhere.[34] Through their required study the link between the two movements remained intact. Little wonder that they became essentially alike in both their basic theological emphases and their understanding of the religious life.

Once we are aware of the historic connection, and hence of the affinity in theology and piety between the two movements, we begin to appreciate why a considerable number of other sources of religious insight which Wesley made available for his followers are translations and/or abridgments of Pietist materials. This is the more remarkable since English and Scottish divines had produced an astounding wealth of devotional literature, a literature which was both known and easily available to Wesley. If he thus went beyond it in trying to provide his followers with material in "practical divinity" the reason was primarily ecumenical. He wanted to demonstrate that what he had come to regard as "genuine Christianity" was not limited either geographically, ethnically, or temporally, that, in fact, his own revival was in historic continuity with Continental Pietism.

From this point of view it is significant to find that in the very first volume of his *Christian Library*[35] he included an extract of John Arndt's *True Christianity*, introduced by a letter

---

34. Nor were they replaced until the influence of the British theologian Richard Watson began to make itself felt when his *Theological Institutes* were published in America in 1829. Up to that time the only systematician in American Methodism had been Roger Shinn, who in 1813 had published his *Essay on the Plan of Salvation*. The latter was little more, however, than a systematic re-statement of the theological insights of the *Sermons* and the *Notes*.

35. We used the London edition of 1819.

to the queen written by the Halle Pietist Anthony William Boehm (1673–1722). The latter had previously translated Arndt into English. To anyone acquainted with the literature of Pietism it hardly needs to be pointed out that Arndt's *True Christianity* was the most widely read devotional book among Continental Pietists.[36] In Pietist circles Arndt held the position among devotional writers which Bengel held among expositors. Wesley's choice in this instance is not surprising since Arndt, like Wesley, thought of authentic Christianity as revolving around the two foci of the new birth and the life of holiness.

August Hermann Francke (1663–1727)[37] was a name well known and highly esteemed in the household of Samuel and Susanna Wesley. As we note in his references to him the same esteem had rubbed off on John Wesley. Thus he tells us in his *Journal* that already on his way to Georgia he read Francke's *Pietas Hallensis,* in which the latter described the amazing charitable and missionary endeavors of Halle. Presently Wesley moved on to read Francke's devotional tract *Nicodemus; or a Treatise on the Fear of Man.* He appreciated its message so much that in Georgia he abridged it and then later included his abstract in the *Christian Library.*

Through these two tracts, then, the influence of the Pietist movement entered early Methodism's understanding of "practical divinity." In addition there are the literary monuments of Romanic spirituality which Wesley felt impelled to include in his *Christian Library.* These were as dear to the hearts of many Pietists on the Continent as they were to Wesley. Hence they, too, constitute a common bond between the two movements. Among the devotional tracts of this category included in the *Library* are letters by or about Don Juan d'Avila, Archbishop Fénelon, and Brother Lawrence, as well as *Pious Reflections* by Fénelon, the *Treatise of Solid Virtue* by Antoinette Bourignon, *The Happy Ascetic* by Anthony Horneck, *The Life of Gregory Lopez* by Francis Losa, the anonymous *Mother's Advice to Her Daughter,* and the *Spiritual Guide* by Miguel de Molinos.

In this connection it should be stated, however, that the

---

36. For a discussion of John Arndt see the author's *Rise of Evangelical Pietism* (1965), pp. 202–217. See also W. Koepp, *Johann Arndt. Eine Untersuchung über die Mystik im Luthertum* (1912).
37. For a brief theological biography of Francke see the author's *German Pietism During the Eighteenth Century* (1973), pp. 1–38.

Christian Library appears to have had only a limited influence on early Methodism's religious climate in America. While the *Minutes* of the Christmas Conference of 1785 admonish the preachers to read it there seems to be no evidence that it was ever published as such in America. The main reason for this omission is probably to be sought in the fact that the American frontier situation made such an ambitious publishing venture impractical. With respect to the contents of the *Christian Library,* therefore, American Methodists were dependent on imported copies and on the bits and pieces which were circulated as individual treatises. That such items did circulate among American Methodists we know. Exactly how much influence they had on the religious climate within the denomination remains a problem.

In general we may say, then, that Pietism did exert its characteristic theological influence on early American Methodism through John Wesley's *Sermons* and his *Notes,* while the question as to how much such influence it exerted on Wesley's American constituency through his other writings and abridgments remains problematical. Having discussed this it would now seem to be in order to give at least some attention to any organizational continuities which may exist between the older movement of Continental Pietism and American Methodism. In the realm of polity, too, Wesley had had an opportunity to make observations both at Halle and at Herrnhut during his visit on the Continent.

In speaking of polity it may be sufficient to summarize the rather careful studies and cautious conclusions of C. W. Towlson,[38] since it would seem to be quite unnecessary to go over the same ground again. Towlson concludes that there was a certain amount of borrowing by John Wesley from the Moravians with respect to the following practices: the organization of a small group of believers into "bands," which in the early days seems to have been an effective way of providing Christian fellowship, as well as incentive for religious and moral growth. There is little evidence, however, that this institution had much appeal in America, though Jesse Lee does mention the rules which are to apply to "band" meetings. Early practices which were observed among Methodists in America were the holding of love feasts and of watch-night services. There can be little doubt but that they constituted a continua-

---

38. Towlson, p. 185.

tion of an earlier Moravian institution which Wesley had observed at Herrnhut. The same is probably true of the *conference,* an ecclesiastical arrangement through which the organizational genius of the Moravians was perpetuated in Methodism throughout the world. While field preaching and lay preaching may not have been copied from the Moravians, Wesley's observation of the use made of it by the *Unitas Fratrum,* and possibly other Pietist groups in Germany, probably strengthened his resolve to employ them in his own work. That both field preaching and lay preaching were features of early American Methodism needs no documentation.

As we have seen, the religious societies were known in England since the time of Horneck. Thus they were nothing new to John Wesley. Here, too, however, his observations of the Pietist *ecclesiola in ecclesiae* on the Continent, and especially at Herrnhut, probably strengthened his resolve to organize his followers on this model. It should not be forgotten in this connection that the Moravian Diaspora societies were tied together in the person of Zinzendorf the way the English societies were not. It was this organizational principle of a multitude of religious societies under the control of one person which appealed to Wesley and which he certainly used in both England and America as long as he could.

Somewhat more problematical is Towlson's attempt to show a connection between Wesley and the acknowledged missionary zeal of the Moravians.[39] In the first place, it is a question whether Wesley was really that much interested in world missions, America excepted. Then, too, he had models of missionary activity in his own church, as well as in Francke's enterprise at Halle. As has been mentioned above, he had already acquainted himself with the latter's *Pietas Hallensis* on his way to Georgia. Thus the Moravian contribution to Methodist practice in this sector was probably minor.

CHARLES WESLEY AND METHODIST HYMNODY

At this point some attention needs to be given to Methodist hymnody, and in that connection to Charles Wesley, the chief source of Methodism's early hymns. The reason is, of course, that during the half-century under discussion here the theological self-understanding of American Methodists was prominently influenced by the hymns they sang. If, indeed, we

---

39. *Ibid.,* pp. 180f.

read John Wesley's prefaces to his hymn collections we find that this is precisely what he had planned. The hymns were meant to give a full "account of Scriptural Christianity." As was the case in Moravianism, and in the whole Pietist movement on the Continent, they were not only to stimulate religious devotion but to enforce right doctrine and to caution "against the most plausible errors." Their function was didactic, in other words, in the sense that they were meant to guide the Methodist enterprise theologically both in England and America.

Already on his trip to Georgia, and during his stay in Georgia, John Wesley had been profoundly impressed by the joyful spirituality of Moravian hymns. There was simply nothing comparable to them in England at the time. Hence we are not surprised to find that, having acquired a reading knowledge of German, he began to translate a whole series of them from the *Gesangbuch der Gemeinde in Herrnhut* (1735) and to set them to tunes taken from the famous Pietist *Geistreiches Gesangbuch*, compiled by Johann Anastasius Freylinghausen, who had published the first part of it in 1704. Whatever else his Georgia experience did for John Wesley, therefore, it made him aware for the first time of the power of the hymnody of Pietism, which had long since established itself on the Continent. It is obviously not insignificant to find that the very first hymns of Methodism were translations of Pietist originals which were sung to long-established Pietist tunes.

Far more important than John Wesley, however, is Charles Wesley if we look at early Methodism from the point of view of the formative influences of its hymnody.[40] The latter, like his brother, had come under the influence of the Moravians in England. The result was that a few days before his brother he had a religious experience very similar to John's. It was on May 21 that he wrote into his *Journal*, "I now found

---

40. For an excellent discussion of Charles Wesley's hymns see J.E. Rattenbury, *The Evangelical Doctrines of Charles Wesley's Hymns* (1941), and Frank Baker, *Representative Verse of Charles Wesley* (1962). See also J. L. Nülsen, *John Wesley und das deutsche Kirchenlied* (1938). For a representative collection of Charles Wesley's hymns one must turn to his *Hymns and Sacred Poems*, 2 vols. (1749). For the most important exemplar of early Methodist hymnody see John Wesley's *A Collection of Hymns for the Use of the People Called Methodists* (1780). John Wesley's *A Collection of Hymns for the Lord's Day* (1784) was sent in sheets to America to be used by the newly organized Methodist Episcopal Church. From 1821 on *A Collection of Hymns for the Use of the Methodist Episcopal Church*, edited by Nathan Bangs, was the official Methodist hymnal in America for several decades.

myself at peace with God and rejoiced in the hope of loving Christ." This was a milestone in his religious life which he celebrated over and over again in his hymns. Thus in a stanza which was later omitted from his famous hymn "O for a Thousand Tongues to Sing" he wrote on the first anniversary of his 1738 experience:

> Then with my heart I first believed,
> Believed with faith divine;
> Power with the Holy Ghost received
> To call this Savior mine.

Thus had passed away for him what afterwards he referred to as ten long years of "legal night." Referring to the same experience he says elsewhere:

> I woke; the dungeon flamed with light,
> My chains fell off, my heart was free,
> I rose, went forth, and followed Thee.

Out of this experience came the bulk of early Methodism's hymnody. Under the circumstances it would be strange indeed if that hymnody did not emphasize those facets of man's religious life and experience most closely related to it. That Charles Wesley's many hundreds of hymns and sacred poems meant to do precisely that is a matter of record.

What needs to be pointed out here, however, is that to anyone acquainted with Continental Pietism the Pietist, and specifically the Moravian, influence upon Charles Wesley's hymns is immediately and unmistakably apparent. We find it, first of all, in the wide variety of hymns which celebrate his change of status from that of a religious seeker to that of one who has found what his heart desired. Documentation is problematical here because of the almost endless number of allusions to this experience with which his hymns are replete. Joyfully he sings:

> Happy the soul to Jesus joined
> And saved by grace alone:
> Walking in all his ways they find
> Their heaven on earth begun.[41]

This was the promise which Peter Boehler had held out to him, the authenticity of which he came upon experientially in 1738,

---

41. *A Collection of Hymns for the Use of the People Called Methodists* (1780), hymn 15, stanza 1.

which he, too, had regarded as a "new doctrine" until he later discovered that it was actually imbedded in the formularies of his own church.

The note of religious certainty, furthermore, which permeates Charles Wesley's hymns, and which gave early Methodism perhaps its greatest appeal, is also based on this experience. The Gospel according to the Wesleys was biblical, to be sure, and by and large it was defensible according to traditional concepts of Protestant theology. Not only that, but it was sensitive to the needs of their generation. Quite as important, however, as all of these other characteristics was the fact that it was authenticated in personal experience and hence expressive of complete religious certainty. Wrote Charles Wesley:

> *What we have felt and seen*
> *With confidence we tell,*
> *And publish to the sons of men,*
> *The signs infallible.* [42]

This experience-centered proclamation of biblical insights is perhaps the very core of early Methodism's Pietist heritage. The verse in question could just as easily have been written by one of the Halle men, or by Zinzendorf, or by his disciple Peter Boehler, who had transmitted the religious perspective on which it is based to Charles Wesley in the first place.

What we have seen so far is that the hymns of Charles Wesley which early Methodists studied, memorized, and sang so enthusiastically on both sides of the Atlantic reinforced those religious insights which both Wesley brothers had received from the older Pietist movement on the Continent. There is an element in Charles Wesley's hymns, however, which is largely missing from the writings of John Wesley.

The reference here is to what has been called the "Lutheran" element in his Christology. That Luther had considerable influence on Charles Wesley's theology cannot be doubted, especially since the poet laureate of Methodism refers to it himself in his *Journal.* Yet the Luther who comes through the Christology of his hymns is essentially the Moravian Luther. His warm, childlike Jesus mysticism, which adores the "gentle Jesus, meek and mild," and is especially oriented toward the imitative contemplation of the suffering,

---

42. *A Collection of Hymns for the Use of the Methodist Episcopal Church* (1821), hymn 1777, stanza 2.

dying Lamb of God, is utterly typical of early Moravian theology. The following is only one sample of Charles Wesley's verses which expresses exactly the religious sentiments of eighteenth-century Moravians:

> Yes, Thou dear Lamb-like Son of God,
> Whom now with eyes of faith I view,
> Thou knowst, I in Thy steps have trod,
> And would to Calvary pursue,
> Through all Thy passion's stages run,
> 'Till Thou pronounce the Word, "'Tis done."[43]

John Wesley always seems to have felt somewhat uncomfortable in the presence of this contemplative, more or less romantic, approach to the Divine. Being the more practical and hard-headed of the two brothers, heir to the Puritans' grim striving toward a holy life, he deplored what he regarded as sentimental in the poetry of Charles and eliminated it whenever he could. Generally speaking Methodism has tended to follow John's lead in this respect. Under the impact of contemporary humanism Methodist scholars choose to regard this side of Charles Wesley's spirituality as a liability and hence to ignore it. It should be remembered, however, that during the years here under consideration, which was Methodism's period of greatest religious vitality, the heart-warming, Christ-oriented piety of Charles was highly treasured among the people called Methodists. That this was true in America is evident from the great number of such Christocentric hymns in the early American hymnals down through the *Methodist Pocket Hymnbook, Revised and Improved* (1802) to the *Collection* edited by Nathan Bangs, approved by the General Conference, and first published in 1821.

Whatever we may think of these hymns today it may well be that they are at least partly responsible for Methodism's appeal to the people at the frontier. Then as now there seems to have been a profoundly felt need to get away from the frightening, insensitive virility of an activist, success-oriented culture in order to make room for more emphasis on the tender side of man's being. Through much of the poetry of Charles Wesley *das ewig Weibliche* is joined to *das gänzlich Männliche* of his brother. One strongly suspects, therefore, that it was precisely this combination which accounts at least in part for early Methodism's broad appeal. There can be little doubt

---

43. Charles Wesley, *Hymns and Sacred Poems* (1749), vol. 2, hymn 4, stanza 1.

that even in later days Charles Wesley's "Jesus Lover of my Soul" has had as much (if not more) influence within American Protestantism as John Wesley's sober discourse *On Christian Perfection.*

Among those theological interpreters of the heritage of the Wesleys who choose to take history seriously there has been considerable dialogue about the question as to whether the greatest Wesleyan emphasis lay on "conversion" or on "sanctification." Whatever may be the answer to this question with regard to the Wesleys themselves it is clear that during the first fifty years of its existence, which are of concern to us here, American Methodism was concerned with both of these aspects of the religious life. The fact is that in the rough and tumble of frontier living the broader theological base which John Wesley had attempted to establish was lovingly and loyally, and quite unconsciously, narrowed down to proportions which were considered manageable under the circumstances. Presently the frontier preachers—Lee, Garrettson, Cartwright *et al.*—with Francis Asbury at the head, came up with three major religious concerns, namely, the finding of a new life in Christ, the believer's conscious certainty of its reality, and the need to express it ethically in one's private and public relations.[44] In other words, early American Methodism's central message had to do with the doctrines of the "new birth," "assurance," and "holiness" in the sense of the progressive ethical amendment of life.

The burden of our discussion thus far has been to indicate that the original impulses toward the Wesleyan emphasis on the first two of these doctrines—namely, on the "new birth" and on "assurance"—had their unmistakable origins in Moravianism. While the Wesleyan emphasis on "holiness" as a result of ethical striving had Puritan antecedents it was certainly supported by everything that Wesley had read in the sources of Romanic spirituality, Halle literature, and especially in the *Gnomon* of the Swabian Pietist Albrecht Bengel. Thus it

---

44. This is clearly indicated by the thoughtful reading of such accounts as Jesse Lee's description of the 1775 revival in Virginia (*A Short History of the Methodists,* 1810, pp. 54f.); of the many ejaculatory passages in Asbury's *Journal;* of Freeborn Garrettson's concerns in Maryland (*The Life of the Rev. Freeborn Garrettson,* compiled and edited by Nathan Bangs, 1828, pp. 62f.); and of the interesting section on "primitive" Methodism in the *Autobiography of Peter Cartwright,* with an introduction by C. L. Wallis (1956), pp. 61–66.

would seem that there is a definite historical connection, as well as a close theological affinity, between the most basic theological emphases of Continental Pietism and the theology which the American Methodist pioneers read out of John Wesley's *Standard Sermons* and his *Notes Upon the New Testament,* out of Charles Wesley's hymns and poems, and out of assorted edificatory tracts. This aside from the organizational borrowing which took place.

METHODISM AND GERMAN-SPEAKING SETTLERS

In order to gain a reasonably full understanding of the Pietist influence on American Methodism as it is now constituted it is not enough to look only at the religious heritage which stems directly from the Wesleys. There were other means of transmission which can no longer be ignored. In order to bring them into focus it is necessary to deal especially with the widely neglected subject of the German-speaking settlers whose beliefs and values began to blend in with the general religious atmosphere which prevailed at the American frontier. The reason for speaking specifically about immigrants of German-speaking stock is twofold. In the first place, the German-speaking sections of Europe were the seedbed of Pietism during the period under discussion. In the second place, for many and complex reasons, German-speaking immigration outnumbered that of the other ethnic groups, excepting the British, during the eighteenth century.

It was on August 20, 1683, that the first group of German-speaking immigrants arrived in the port of Philadelphia. Following the invitation of William Penn and of the *Golden Book* of Queen Anne they began to flock to the New World in ever-increasing numbers. While they settled in many different regions the preponderant number of them remained in Pennsylvania and in areas contiguous to it. Thus it is estimated that in 1751 about 90,000 of them had remained in Pennsylvania alone. We are not surprised to read, therefore, that on April 6, 1784, Pastor Helmuth of Philadelphia transmitted to Halle his belief that in a few years Philadelphia would be essentially a German city.[45] By 1790 there were upwards of 600,000 German-speaking people among a total American population of perhaps three and one-half million.

---

45. *Hallesche Nachrichten,* vol. 2 (1895), p. 748.

For socio-political and economic reasons the greater number of these early Germanic settlers came from the Palatinate, as well as from other areas of southwest Germany, and from German-speaking areas of Switzerland. These were precisely the regions in which Pietism had made considerable inroads among the people who began to look to America as the land of promise—namely, the peasants and the craftsmen. Hence many of the religiously inclined among them brought their Pietist convictions, together with their Pietist literature, with them.

The result was that in the German-speaking centers of Pennsylvania and vicinity, and extending south into Virginia, the general religious climate among Protestants of German-speaking ancestry was open to Pietist influences.[46] Here the Moravians had established the town of Bethlehem in 1742. While their early religious enthusiasm had cooled off considerably by the time the Methodists came on the scene, their basic religious self-understanding remained Pietist. The same is true of the German Baptist Brethren, or Dunkers, who under the leadership of Alexander Mack had come to Pennsylvania from the Pietist center of Schwarzenau. Among William Penn's settlers the Ephrata Society, too, had been established by Conrad Beissel, who had imbibed his mystical brand of Protestantism among the groups of radical Pietists in southwest Germany. The Pietist impulses emanating from the Dutch Reformed pastor Theodorus J. Frelinghuysen reached across the Delaware and struck a responsive chord among some of the members of the German Reformed population of Pennsylvania, who had already been introduced to Pietism in 1710 by Samuel Guldin. Among the Lutherans the Pietist tradition reached back to the Falckner brothers and to Anthony Jacob Henkel, and was later being vigorously promoted by Henry Melchior Muhlenberg, who had arrived in America in 1742. From our point of view it is obviously significant that already in 1741 Count Zinzendorf, the leader of the Moravians, thought he could actually unite a substantial number of German-speaking groups of Protestants in Pennsylvania on the basis of an essentially Pietist understanding of Christianity.

In speaking about the contact between Methodism and German-speaking settlers early in our history we actually need

---

46. Still helpful in this connection is J. F. Sachse, *The German Pietists of Provincial Pennsylvania* (1895). Also helpful is the author's *Mysticism in the German Devotional Literature of Colonial Pennsylvania* (1949).

to go back to the familiar story of Barbara Heck, Philip Embury *et al.*, who were Irish immigrants of German stock. It was Embury who in 1766 preached the first Methodist sermon in America. As far as we know, however, Methodist work among the German-speaking settlers lagged, though men like Henry Wiedner, John Hagerty, and later Simon Miller occasionally preached among them in their own language beginning about 1776. After almost a decade in the general superintendency Francis Asbury, too, began to show some concern for their religious welfare. The entry into his *Journal* for June 11, 1781, gives the first indication of what became a growing sense of responsibility on his part to take the Gospel to the German-speaking segment of the population. Referring to a group of people he came upon at a place called Patterson Creek he says, "Could we get a Dutch (his usual designation for German) preacher or two to travel with us, I am persuaded we should have a good work among the Dutch. I love these people; they are kind in their way."[47] In time he deliberately used itinerants who could speak German, notably Henry Boehm (1775–1875) and Jacob Gruber (1778–1850), to preach in the various German-speaking centers.

It was among the German-speaking friends and associates of Francis Asbury that the Pietist influences coming from the Continent merged with those within the Wesleyan heritage. Whether or not they found a religious home within the Methodist Episcopal Church at the time is of little importance. The reason is that the matter of church affiliation was so fluid that a man like Martin Boehm could be a bishop of the United Brethren in Christ while he was at the same time enrolled in a Methodist class.[48] Under the circumstances it becomes necessary to pay at least some attention to what we might think of as the German-speaking branches of the early American Methodist movement, though the rise of the United Brethren in Christ is covered elsewhere in this volume. This is especially important, of course, as a result of the recent merger of these groups with the Methodist Episcopal Church. In doing so we begin by looking briefly at the pioneers of the United Brethren.

The man whose name first comes to mind in this con-

---

47. *The Journal and Letters of Francis Asbury*, E. T. Clark, editor-in-chief (1958), vol. 1, p. 406.
48 See K. E. Rowe, "Martin Boehm and the Methodists," *Methodist History*, vol. 8 (July 1970), pp. 49–53.

nection is the above-mentioned Martin Boehm (1725–1812). As his son Henry, Asbury's German-speaking assistant, tells us in his *Reminiscences,* it was his ancestor's adherence to the Pietist way of life which forced the Boehm family to leave its native Switzerland. In the Palatinate the family joined the Mennonites, the religious tradition in which Martin was reared. Like many other Palatines at the time, the Boehms emigrated to Pennsylvania. Here in 1756 he was chosen by lot to become a Mennonite preacher. Soon after this event he went through a characteristically Pietist conversion experience, the immediate circumstances of which unfortunately escape us. It would be difficult not to surmise, however, that he had come in contact with some of the representatives of German Pietism in Pennsylvania of whom mention has been made above.

This supposition is strengthened by the fact that Boehm now sought the fellowship of other Protestants of Pietist inclination, such as the "New Lights" of Virginia. The Pietist fervor had evidently been transmitted to the latter from Theodorus Jacobus Frelinghuysen,[49] via the Log College and Samuel Davis, and was then fanned into flame by George Whitefield. After the famous meeting in Long's barn (probably 1767) near Lancaster Boehm also sought the friendship of Otterbein, whose contribution will be discussed presently. The Pietist influences, so broadly represented among the German-speaking population of the Middle Colonies, were thus channeled into the church of the United Brethren in Christ of which he became bishop in 1800. The same kind of piety was funneled into the Methodist Episcopal Church through his above-mentioned son Henry, who under the supervision of Asbury worked tirelessly among the German-speaking people of his day. The latter's Pietist inclinations are evident from that section of his hand-written *Journal* which is preserved in the Drew University Library, some of it in German script.

More directly demonstrable than that of Martin Boehm is the Pietist background of Philip William Otterbein (1726–1813). As a result of J. S. O'Malley's careful investigation of the religious background of Otterbein little needs to be done here but to summarize O'Malley's conclusions regarding that heritage.[50] Philip William Otterbein (like other members of the

---

49. For a careful study of his Pietism see J. Tanis, *Dutch Calvinistic Pietism in the Middle Colonies* (1967).
50. J. S. O'Malley, *Pilgrimage of Faith: The Legacy of the Otterbeins* (1973).

prominent Otterbein family) received his theological education at the Reformed academic center of Herborn. During his
student days, as well as those of his brothers, Herborn was still
under the influence of the great Pietist theologian of the Reformed communion, Friedrich Adolph Lampe.[51] Here he was
made aware of the cardinal emphases of Pietism—the need for
a personal acceptance of the salvation offered in Christ, the
religious certainty which may accompany such acceptance, and
the holy life which must follow—and of these emphases as
being the basic message of the Bible.

It appears, however, that Otterbein originally accepted
this Pietist understanding of Christianity as a piece of intellectual equipment only. After Michael Schlatter had brought him
to America in 1752, however, he entered upon a religious
quest not unlike that of the Wesleys before 1738. It finally
eventuated in his experiential acceptance of the Pietist understanding of Christianity which he had been originally taught at
Herborn. Here again the records are missing, but it must be
remembered that Otterbein, too, would naturally move among
German-speaking settlers who were pietistically inclined. It
was these contacts which presumably brought about the religious change in him which has been mentioned.

From our point of view it is significant to find that after
he had gone through this religious experience he found that
he did not really differ from the Methodists of his day. Between him and them there was the same concern for biblical
Christianity, and essentially the same Pietist understanding of
the nature of biblical Christianity. Hence it is interesting to find
Francis Asbury recording in his *Journal* on June 18, 1776, that
there are very few people with whom he can find so much unity
and freedom of conversation as with Otterbein. The feeling
between the two men was mutual. If they finally ended up in
separate religious organizations the reasons for such separation were ethnic, not theological. What Otterbein said to Martin Boehm, namely, *Wir sind Brüder,* he could have said with
equal justification (and probably did, though in English translation) to Asbury. The point here is, of course, that what united
these men was their Pietist heritage.

Together Boehm and Otterbein, assisted by men like
George Adam Geeting (1741–1812) and Christian Newcomer

---

51. For a summary of his theology see O'Malley, pp. 115f. See also the author's
German Pietism During the Eighteenth Century (1973), pp. 224–233.

(1749–1830), brought into being the church of the United Brethren in Christ. Their understanding of the Christian faith, and of the nature of Protestantism, though influenced more directly by Continental Pietism, was indistinguishable from that of Asbury and his co-workers. Like their "brethren" in the Methodist Episcopal Church they chose to order their fellowship largely on the Wesleyan model. The difference between them was basically one of mission, the United Brethren feeling called to proclaim the Gospel primarily among German-speaking settlers, who, they felt, were being neglected by the leadership of the Methodist Episcopal Church.

Not substantially different is the story of the rise of the Evangelical Association. Jacob Albright (1759–1808), its founder, had his Damascus experience under the tutelage of one of the lay preachers of the United Brethren in Christ, Adam Riegel. "Gradually," he recorded in his autobiography, "every anguish of heart was removed—. God's Spirit bore witness with my spirit, that I was a child of God."[52] Presently he became aware of the kinship of his newly found understanding of the Gospel with that of the Methodists. He was so favorably impressed also with their seemingly practical organization that he chose to adopt it in substance. Because of the essentially Anglo-Saxon orientation of the Methodist Episcopal Church, however, his followers, too, felt the need for a separate corporate existence. Thus the Evangelical Association took its rise at a meeting held in 1802. It was Pietist in theology, essentially Methodist in polity, and dedicated to work primarily among the German-speaking population of the Middle Colonies and Virginia.

Our attempt in this discussion has been to show how Pietism, which antedated Methodism, imparted to the Wesley brothers an experiential understanding of the Protestant doctrine of salvation by faith alone, and of a kind of personal religious certainty which both Wesleys freely acknowledged as distinctly "new." We have tried to point out, furthermore, how the Wesleyan emphasis on "Scriptural holiness," and on a biblically based religious restorationism in general, found support in the pietistically oriented religious climate which had come into being, as well as in the Pietist literature which had been created. We have tried to show, finally, how in America the Pietist elements implicit in early Methodism merged with

---

52. Quoted by R. W. Albright, *A History of the Evangelical Church* (1942), p. 35.

Pietist influences coming more directly from the Continent, thus creating jointly the general religious climate which prevailed within the total orb of Methodist origins in America during the first half-century of Methodist work on this continent.

Rather strong evidence for the cogency of this thesis is found in W. H. Naumann's careful study of the theological self-understanding of both the United Brethren in Christ and the Evangelical Association.[53] As the German-speaking members of these churches read their devotional books they found no difficulty whatsoever in reconciling the piety coming from Methodist sources with that which they read out of Arndt's *Wahres Christentum* or Johann Jacob Starck's *Täglisches Handbuch in guten und bösen Tagen*. When they compiled their early hymnals they were not aware of any theological discrepancies between the hymns of Charles Wesley and the hymns introduced from Pietist hymnals. If, on the other hand, one reads the journals of Francis Asbury and the early Methodist itinerants one looks in vain for any awareness of a difference between the ideals of Wesleyan piety and those of the "German brethren." What we are dealing with, then, when we are talking of Methodist origins in America is a confluence of Puritan and Pietist impulses, the resulting evangelicalism being as closely patterned on its Pietist as on its Puritan model.

The thesis of this entire volume is that in seeking to evaluate the influence of Christian belief and practice on American institutions it is out of keeping with the evidences of historical development to focus exclusively on Puritanism. It goes without saying, of course, that in studying the early phases of our social, political, and cultural history the latter cannot be ignored. Neither, however, can the religious movement with which this study is concerned. A look at Methodist origins in America confirms the fact that American evangelicalism as we find it in our history during the eighteenth and nineteenth centuries is a product of both of these older movements. It is Puritanism and Pietism together which, in concert with a plurality of other factors, share the credit, as well as the blame, for the aspirations, the dreams, the values, the goals, and the

---

53. W. H. Naumann, *Theology and German American Evangelicalism: The Role of Theology in the Church of the United Brethren in Christ and the Evangelical Association,* dissertation at Yale (1966).

moral blind spots of that strange ethnic amalgam we call America.

Quite unwittingly Methodist historians especially have been guilty of a certain ethnic narrowness in their historical interpretation. The time for such intellectual confinement would seem to be past, however. Americans in general are just beginning to be aware of the fact that whatever excitement, distinctiveness, and perhaps even promise there is in our American culture is in large part the result of its pluralistic ethnic origins. In that belief the present study was undertaken. In its widest implications it is meant to point out that a denomination which shares in the ethnic diversity of our nation must, among other things, increasingly recognize the pluralistic nature of its origins.

SELECTED BIBLIOGRAPHY–CHAPTER SIX

Albright, R. W., *A History of the Evangelical Church* (1942)

Asbury, Francis, *Journal and Letters,* E. T. Clark, editor-in-chief (1958)

Baker, E. W., *A Herald of the Evangelical Church* (1948)

Baker, Frank, "The Doctrines in the *Discipline;* a study of the forgotten theological presuppositions of American Methodism," *Duke Divinity School Review* (Winter 1966), pp. 39–55

Barclay W. C., *Early American Methodism, 1769–1844* (1949)

Bengel, J. A., *New Testament Word Studies* (1971)

Bett, Henry, *The Hymns of Methodism* (1945)

Boehm, Henry, *Reminiscences, Historical and Biographical,* ed. J. B. Wakely (1866)

Bucke, E. S., ed., *The History of American Methodism* (1964)

Cameron, R. M., "John Wesley's Aldersgate Experience," *Drew Gateway,* vol. 25 (1955), pp. 210–219

Carroll, H. K., *Francis Asbury in the Making of American Methodism* (1923)

Cartwright, Peter, *Autobiography of Peter Cartwright,* intro. by C. L. Wallis (1956)

Cell, G. C. *The Rediscovery of John Wesley* (1935)

Drury, A. W., *History of the Church of the United Brethren in Christ* (1924)

Garrettson, F., *The Experiences and Travels of Mr. Freeborn Garrettson* (1791)

Hatfield, J. T., *John Wesley's Translation of German Hymns* (1896)

Hough, S. S., *Christian Newcomer: His Life, Journal and Achievements* (1941)

Lee, Jesse, *A Short History of the Methodists in the United States of America, Beginning in 1766 and Continued Till 1809* (1810)

Lerch, Daniel, *Heil und Heiligung bei John Wesley, dargestellt unter besonderer Berücksichtigung seiner Anmerkungen zum Neuen Testament* (1941)

Lindström, Harald, *Wesley and Sanctification: A Study in the Doctrine of Salvation* (1946)

Nagler, A. W., *Pietism and Methodism; Or the Significance of German Pietism in the Origin and Early Development of Methodism* (1918)

Naumann, W. H., *Theology and German American Evangelicalism,* dissertation at Yale (1966)

Nülsen, J. L., *John Wesley und das deutsche Kirchenlied* (1938)

O'Malley, J. S., *The Otterbeins: The Postlude to Pietism,* dissertation at Drew University (1970). Published in 1973 under the title *Pilgrimage of Faith: The Legacy of the Otterbeins*

Outler, A. C., ed., *John Wesley: A Representative Collection of His Writings* (1964)

Peters, J. L., *Christian Perfection and American Methodism* (1956)

Rattenbury, J. E., *The Conversion of the Wesleys: A Critical Study* (1938)

———, *The Evangelical Doctrines of Charles Wesley's Hymns* (1941)

Rogers, C. A., "The Theological Heritage of the Early Methodist Preachers," *Duke Divinity School Review* (Autumn 1969), pp. 196–208

Schmidt, Martin, *John Wesley: A Theological Biography,* tr. N. P. Goldhawk, vol. 1 (1962)

———, *John Wesleys Bekehrung* (1937)

Strickland, W. P., *The Life of Jacob Gruber* (1860)

Sweet, W. W., *Religion in Colonial America* (1942)

Tanis, James, *Dutch Calvinistic Pietism in the Middle Colonies* (1967)

Towlson, C. W., *Moravian and Methodist* (1957)

Weissbach, Jürgen, *Der neue Mensch im theologischen Denken John Wesleys* (1970)

Wesley, Charles, *Hymns and Sacred Poems* (1749)

_____, *The Journal of Charles Wesley*, ed. T. Jackson (1849)

Wesley, John, *A Christian Library*, etc. (1819–1827)

_____, *Explanatory Notes Upon the New Testament* (1900)

_____, *The Journal of the Rev. John Wesley*, ed. N. Churnock (1909–1916)

_____, *The Letters of the Rev. John Wesley*, ed. J. Telford (1931)

_____, *Wesley's Standard Sermons*, ed. E. A. Sugden (1921)

_____, *The Works of the Rev. John Wesley* (1829–1831)

Yates, A. S., *The Doctrine of Assurance, With Special Reference to John Wesley* (1952)

CHAPTER SEVEN

THE BRETHREN IN EARLY AMERICAN CHURCH LIFE

by Donald F. Durnbaugh

INCLUSION OF A CHAPTER ON THE BRETHREN IN A BOOK ON Pietism is not self-evident. For many of the 250 years of their life in North America such an identification would have been rejected. The Brethren—known variously as New Baptists, Dompelaars, Tumplers, Dunkers, German Baptist Brethren, and since 1908 officially as the Church of the Brethren—have often thought of themselves as other than Pietist.

Nineteenth-century spokesmen contended that the Brethren were in apostolic succession from the early Christian church. A German journalist was given this interpretation when he visited the Dunkers in Southern Ohio in 1851. Upon asking a venerable elder for the origin of the Brethren, he was told "that it began with the apostles and was the history of the invisible church of God." (Another contributor to the discussion claimed that the history began with the Waldensians.)[1] A concise statement of this position is found in a book issued by Dunker printer and preacher J. E. Pfautz (1804–1884), as one of the brief sketches of "all religious denominations in the United States of North America" (1878):

---

1. Donald F. Durnbaugh, "The German Journalist and the Dunker Love-Feast," *Pennsylvania Folklife*, vol. 18 (Winter 1968–1969), p. 46. The excerpt is from the third chapter of Moritz Busch, *Wanderungen zwischen Hudson und Mississippi, 1851 und 1852* (1954). This has been recently published in English translation: Norman H. Binger, ed., *Travels between the Hudson and the Mississippi, 1851–1852* (1971).

German Baptists

This denomination arose as follows: John the forerunner of Jesus, was the first Baptist, then Jesus Christ and his apostles; in this way the Church of Christ upon earth was founded and organized in Palestine, then planted elsewhere under heavy persecutions and martyrdom. [Here follows a long list of martyrs from the first to the 16th centuries.] In the 17th century, the persecuted Christians found a refuge in the valley in the alps in the western part of Piedmont, where they lived unharmed for a short time; however, they were soon again atrociously persecuted. Then in the 18th century, in the year 1708, a place of freedom was found near Schwarzenau, where some of the apostolic Christians assembled and again organized a church; but soon afterwards they were again persecuted and dispersed, a part to Holland and Crefeld, the rest to Friesland. Then in the year 1719, they came from Friesland to America and landed at Philadelphia. Then in the year 1729, their brethren from Holland and Crefeld followed. In this way, the Church of Jesus Christ arose and came to America which at this time has been extended over almost all of the United States.[2]

In his direct linking of the Brethren to the early church by way of the persecuted Waldensians (although not naming them directly) Pfautz was echoing a claim popular among denominational controversialists of his day. Other religious bodies, both of sectarian and churchly character, were using the argument to demonstrate their superior ecclesiastical credentials. A Baptist polemicist used the same lineage in 1869 to show that it was the Baptists, not the Brethren, who were the true church. Since the Brethren admitted an organization in 1708, they were "about 1675 years too late to be the church founded upon a rock, against which the gates of hell never were to prevail."[3]

Henry Kurtz (1796–1874), one-time Lutheran pastor and foremost Brethren publisher in the nineteenth century, accepted the same interpretation. He began to publish installments of a history of the Brethren in his periodical, *The Gospel Visitor*. However, he never came to the actual history of the

---

2. John Eby Pfautz, "The Pennsylvania Churches and Sects (1878)," tr. Don Yoder, *Pennsylvania Folklife*, vol. 17 (Winter 1967–1968), p. 45. Pfautz' original publication was *Eine Deutsche Concordanz über das Neue Testament von Jesu Christo ... Auch eine kurze Anmerkung von allen Religions-Verfassungen in den Vereinigten Staaten von Nord-Amerika* (1878). Pfautz was confused on the sequence of Brethren migrations.

3. M. Ellison, *Dunkerism Examined* (1869), p. 14.

Brethren. In his Germanic thoroughness, he devoted so much attention to tracing the annals of the church in the wilderness, especially that of the Waldensians, that the history was never completed. As late as 1954, a leading Brethren historian, Floyd E. Mallott, defined the Brethren as a "company of Christians who seek to live according to the pattern of the primitive Christians." He began his story with sketches of Bernard of Clairvaux, Francis of Assisi, and Peter Waldo.[4]

Brethren self-understanding took a new course at the turn of the nineteenth to the twentieth centuries with the publication of Martin G. Brumbaugh (1862–1930). One of the first Brethren to earn a doctoral degree (at the University of Pennsylvania), he became there a professor of pedagogy to begin a career in education and public service which was to bring him to the governorship of the Commonwealth of Pennsylvania in 1915. Brumbaugh wrote in 1899 what has often been called the first history of the Brethren. It was primarily a collection of sources originally gathered by the industrious farmer-librarian-antiquarian, Abraham Harley Cassel (1820–1908). Brumbaugh's eloquently written book linked the Brethren not so much to the Pietists as to the Dissenters of the sixteenth century—to the "most ardent product of the reformation" upon whom fell the "full power of church and state" so that the "flaming torch of persecution nightly lighted the valley of the Rhine for a hundred miles." For Brumbaugh, it was these "sturdy, devout, God-strengthened men and women" who had "heroically suffered and died for the religion they loved" who should be seen as Brethren ancestors. In a word, it was not a Pietist but an Anabaptist lineage.

One reason Brumbaugh denied categorically that any of the Brethren were Pietists was that he mistakenly equated Pietism with some of the excesses of the radical Reformation, with the Münsterite rebels and discredited enthusiasts of the

---

4. [Henry Kurtz], "The Church in the Wilderness," *The Monthly Gospel-Visitor*, vol. 1 (May, 1851), pp. 17–20 and succeeding issues; Floyd E. Mallott, *Studies in Brethren History* (1954), pp. 15, 17–20. Albert T. Ronk, *History of the Brethren Church* (1968), provides some evidence on Waldensian activity in Germany, concluding that "Waldensian influence may well have been found in Schwarzenau" (pp. 33–34). He also refers to the speculation by Stephen A. Bashor, writing in 1893, that missionaries from the Greek Orthodox church active in Western Europe may have provided the Brethren with a link to the early church.

Reformation era. He did concede that the Brethren shared some doctrines with the "better elements" of Pietism, that they found some items of value in the writings of Spener and Francke, and that Ernst Christoph Hochmann von Hochenau was an intimate of the early Brethren; this justified a second chapter of his book on the "Pietistic Pathfinders." He correctly pointed out that when the Brethren "separated from prevailing creeds they were no doubt tempted to go the extreme of denying all organized functions" and thereby to join the ranks of the radical Pietists, but in fact they rejected this option.

Basically, Brumbaugh was concerned to emphasize the independent, creative genius of the Brethren. Although he placed them in the Anabaptist tradition and admitted Pietist influence, he wished primarily to show their uniqueness: "They knew all of the sects already organized, but found in none the sum of doctrines their study of the Bible compelled them to believe. They created a new denomination because they found nowhere a body of believers fully living the Christ life." Again, "It will be seen that the new congregation at Schwarzenau studied all shades of faith, and then turned from Ecclesiasticism and Pietism alike to carve out a new and distinct order of faith and practice. They were debtors to all, and followers of none."[5]

This position of Brumbaugh was gladly echoed by Brethren church leaders of the early twentieth century during a process of change which saw the Brethren leave their withdrawn and sectarian posture and increasingly take up a stance in American church life as a denomination like others. John Flory, author of a valuable study on Brethren literary activities, followed Brumbaugh's interpretation. Flory held that "none of the leaders of the German Baptists [i.e., Brethren] had ever been Pietists, although they held more in common with them than with any of the other dissenting sects of the time. . . ." He defined the German Baptists as "those who protested against the oppression, errors, and lack of spirituality in the established Protestant churches of the early eighteenth century" and yet "could not go full lengths with the Pietists . . . and make Christianity wholly a matter of spirit." This being the case, "the

---

5. Martin G. Brumbaugh, *A History of the German Baptist Brethren in Europe and America* (1899), pp. 3, 5–11, 12–28. The most recent study of Pietism is F. Ernest Stoeffler, *German Pietism During the Eighteenth Century* (1973).

only course left for them was to organize a church in which piety and spirituality might have free course, and yet in which they could practice all the rites and ordinances taught in the New Testament."[6]

Flory's explanation presaged the theory of Brethren origins most often put forth today. That is to see the Brethren as a movement shaped by radical Pietism which adopted an Anabaptist view of the church. A creative tension between these two influences, balanced on a fulcrum of Protestant faith, is thought to provide the best explanation of the Brethren character. Pietism is recognized as the matrix of Brethren origins, Anabaptism as a tradition consciously adopted by early Brethren. This would explain, for example, why the more fervent Brethren were able to attract Mennonites into their fold (Pietism) and also why the Brethren resemble the Mennonites so much in their beliefs and practices (Anabaptism).[7] This was illustrated early in Brethren history by a contemporary from the camp of the radical Pietists (critical of all church organization) who compared the Old Anabaptists (Mennonites) with the New Baptists (Brethren) in Germany:

> The congregations of the Old Anabaptists had undergone an improvement and enlargement from the New Baptists. . . . One must profess concerning the Old and New Baptists, that they have a great superiority over the common mass of the large sects in outward, orderly, honorable lives of virtue. They enjoy physical blessing, peace, and preservation from all that is idle, in their simple agricultural pursuits. The Old Baptists do not seek to enlarge themselves outside of their family, but rather remain in their old simplicity, the simple lay ministry, the house-meetings, the unlearned salvation system, the simple administration of the Sacraments, and the lowly farming and artisan life, etc. The New Baptists, however, want to make themselves large and broad among the

6. John S. Flory, *Literary Activity of the German Baptist Brethren in the Eighteenth Century* (1908), pp. 3, 29–30.
7. The discussion has been carried on primarily in the journal *Brethren Life and Thought (BLT)*. See especially, Donald F. Durnbaugh, "The Genius of the Brethren," *BLT*, vol. 4 (Winter 1959), pp. 4–34 and (Spring 1959), pp. 4–18; Vernard Eller, "On Epitomizing the Brethren," *BLT*, vol. 6 (Autumn 1961), pp. 47–52; Allen C. Deeter, "Membership in the Body of Christ as Interpreted by Classical Pietism," *BLT*, vol. 9 (Autumn 1964), pp. 30–49; and Dale W. Brown, "Membership in the Body of Christ as Interpreted by the Heritage of the Brethren," *BLT*, vol. 9 (Autumn 1964), pp. 63–77.

awakened souls with powerful teaching and converting to the
new baptismal peculiarity and necessity.[8]

The first Brethren spoke highly of the Mennonites and considered joining them, but decided against it on the grounds
that the Mennonites did not teach immersion baptism and had
moreover lost the zeal ("first love") of their forefathers.
Brethren history, nevertheless, parallels that of the Mennonites both in geographical areas of settlement and life styles.[9]

If this basic adherence to an Anabaptist view of the
church (discussed elsewhere at length) is accepted, it is possible
here to look more closely at the Brethren relation to Pietism.
The thesis will be that the Brethren can be understood as
emerging in and being shaped by a series of awakenings or
revival movements, not unlike but earlier than those described
in the religious history of America among the English-
speaking communions.

THE BRETHREN AND PIETIST AWAKENINGS

Brethren rootage in Pietism is irrefutable. Their early self-
descriptions portray this clearly. More recent scholarship has
filled in the background. Not surprisingly, the most detailed
studies have come from German scholars. The classic treatment in many ways is still that of Max Goebel in his history of
the Reformed churches in Westphalia and the Rhineland
(1849–1860). The fullest modern discussions are found in the
books by Heinz Renkewitz and Friedrich Nieper, the former in
his definitive monograph on E. C. Hochmann von Hochenau,
the latter in his study of the religious backgrounds of early
Germantown settlers. Nieper was guided in his research by the
dean of Pietism scholars, Wilhelm Goeters, who unfortunately
committed to print very little of his massive knowledge of
Pietism in both its churchly and radical forms.[10]

Still unsurpassed for immediacy and perceptiveness is

8. J. S. Carl and others, eds., *Geistliche Fama* (1730–1744), I, 10, pp. 86–89.
9. This is discussed in Donald F. Durnbaugh, "Relationships of the Brethren
   with the Mennonites and Quakers, 1708–1865," *Church History*, vol. 35
   (1966), pp. 35–59.
10. Max Goebel, *Geschichte des christlichen Lebens in der rheinisch-westphälischen
   evangelischen Kirche* (1849–1860), especially vol. 3, pp. 235–267; Heinz
   Renkewitz, *Hochmann von Hochenau (1670–1721): Quellenstudien zur Geschichte des Pietismus* (1935); Friedrich Nieper, *Die ersten deutschen Auswanderer von Krefeld nach Pennsylvanien* (1940).

the sketch on Brethren origins penned by Alexander ("Sander") Mack, Jr. (1712–1803) for the second edition of his father's writings (1774). Mack relied on papers left by his father, Alexander Mack, Sr. (1679–1735), the first Brethren teacher of the word or minister, and by Peter Becker (1687–1758), first minister in North America, as well as on descriptions of early times given him orally by these and other brethren. Several quotations from Mack's story show that the Brethren began as the result of a revival or awakening, and also reveal the spirit of the founders:

> It pleased the good God in his mercy, early in the beginning of this (18th) century, to support his "grace that bringeth salvation, and which hath appeared to all men," by many voices calling them to Awake and repent, so that thereby many were aroused from the sleep and death of sin. These then began to look around them for the truth and righteousness, as they are in Jesus, but had soon to see with sorrowful eyes that great decay (of true Christianity) almost in every place. From this lamentable state of things they were pressed to deliver many a faithful testimony of truth, and here and there private meetings were established beside the public church organization, in which newly awakened souls sought their edification.

These gatherings, deemed illegal under the state church system, were disrupted by governmental measures incited by an "envious priesthood." Participants were compelled to seek refuge in those areas in the Germanies where limited freedom of religious conscience was found. The major asylum was the county of Wittgenstein where the pietistically inclined ruling family set aside land around the village of Schwarzenau on the Eder River for religious refugees. Although the county was economically backward and its land stony, hundreds of dissenters gathered there until "this place, which had been but little esteemed, became so much changed, that in a few years it became a place extensively known."

Those who gathered formed a heterogeneous mix of territorial backgrounds and religious ties, united only by common distaste for the established churches. Some withdrew to isolated hermitages in the Wittgenstein mountains; others became disillusioned with the lack of unity and returned to their former church affiliations. Others, who became the first Brethren, decided to go forward in establishing a religious community. One reason was that they were concerned to follow Christ's injunctions; when they read the passage on discipline in Matthew 18 they saw that this "could not be reduced to a proper Christian practice, because there was no regular order yet established in the church." They had been expelled from and had broken with their former churches, but had nothing in their places.

> Under these circumstances some felt themselves drawn powerfully to seek the footsteps of the primitive christians, and desired earnestly to receive in faith the ordained testimonies of Jesus Christ according to their true value. At the same time, they were internally and strongly impressed, with the necessity of the obedience of faith to a soul that desires to be saved. And this impression also led them at the time to the mystery of water-baptism, which appeared unto them as a door into the church, which was what they so earnestly sought. . . . Finally, in the year 1708, eight persons consented together, to enter into a covenant of good conscience with God, to take up all the commandments of Jesus Christ as an easy yoke, and thus to follow the Lord Jesus, their good and faithful shepherd, in joy and sorrow, as his true sheep, even unto a blessed end.[11]

Almost all of those who became Brethren had been baptized into the Reformed church (principally in the Palatinate), with a few coming from the Lutheran church. The language of Mack's account makes it clear that it was a Pietist type of awakening which brought them to a feeling of dissatisfaction with the institutional church. As they met in homes for simple Bible study, singing, and testimonies, they found themselves accused of criminal activity. When they persisted, the government drove them from their homes. Yet they were not content to stay apart as did the radical Pietists. Those who became Brethren stressed the necessity of following the commandments of Jesus Christ, which to them meant baptism, church discipline, and mutual aid.

Prior to the late summer baptism of 1708 which marked the beginning of the Brethren, they sent out a letter to Pietists

---

11. The quotations on pages 21, 22–23, are taken from the edition by Henry Kurtz and James Quinter (1860), which combines the original German with a parallel English translation. Kurtz' justification for a new edition was: "When we came to examine into the former english translation published Philadelphia 1810, consequently fifty years ago, we found in order to do justice to the work that we would have to make an entirely new translation, which was first made as literal as possible by the writer of this [a native German], and then revised by his english co-laborer [James Quinter], so that we spared no pains, to make our brother, being dead long ago, speak yet as intelligibly to all as possible" (p. 6).

in the Palatinate. The letter revealed that the visit of two "strange brethren" had brought to a head the desire for baptism which several had been feeling for some time. "Dear brethren," they wrote in announcing their intention of baptizing, "what is then better than being obedient and not despising this commandment of the Lord Jesus Christ, the King of all glory? This, especially as we have left all sects because of the misuse concerning infant baptism, communions, and church system, . . . We profess that they are rather man's statutes and commandments. . . . But as Christ, our head and keeper, lowered himself into the water, we must of necessity as his members, be immersed with him."[12]

A corroboration of Mack's account is found in a later eighteenth-century description written by the Quaker historian, Samuel Smith. On the eve of the Revolution, Smith was eager to narrate the histories of other religious bodies who shared a peace witness with the Society of Friends. His account of the Brethren is based on interviews with members in Pennsylvania. The revival note is clearly discernible in his description:

> They declare that the most ancient among them have been awaken(e)d here and there in Europe from their profound sleep of sin by the voice of God in and about the year 1705. . . . (B)eing then quicken(e)d by the light of Christ to a sense of their degenerate evil condition, they began to see a reformation necessary; many of them being taught by the Calvinists from their youth out of the Heidelberg Confession had given them high notions of the purity that ought to be in those who were converted to God, with the sense of their own evil condition. . . . (I)n consequence of it they began to see that the ministers were not yet converted, and tho' they were freely admitted to the communion table, they say they observed them to be a covetous people, and often worse. For these reasons, they determined to depart from under their tuition, and daily searching the holy scriptures, after the practices of the first and best Christians, they became in time to have a particular gift of prayer. (A)fter they could no longer say the prayers which before they had learn(e)d by heart, they went into the fields and prayed by themselves. (W)hen they met together,

---

12. Donald F. Durnbaugh, ed., *European Origins of the Brethren: A Source Book on the Beginnings of the Church of the Brethren in the Early Eighteenth Century* (1958), pp. 115–120.

> (they) bowed their knees in fellowship, praying and proph-
> esying as they thought the spirit gave them utterance.[13]

The striking thing about this portrayal is the parallel with the beginnings of the Great Awakening in colonial America. The realization of personal sinfulness, the criticism of unregener-ate ministers, the unwillingness to commune with a mixed multitude, the rejection of formalized prayers and liturgies, the meetings outside the church structures for small prayer fellowships—these are hallmarks of the revival spirit.

Although the sources are limited for tracing the per-sonal pilgrimages of those who became Brethren, one story has been preserved which may well have been typical. A simple fisherman and later soldier named P. J. Peterson from Altona in northern Germany had been raised without schooling or religious instruction. During his military career, the "prompt-ings of the Father drew him inwardly to repentance" so that he applied for a release. This he finally received after great diffi-culty. After returning home he resolved to live a better life but was unclear how to do this. He attended church diligently and once heard a preacher speak on the future punishment of the godless. Peterson sought out the pastor and implored him to show him the way to salvation. The pastor put him off, citing the pressure of his duties. When Peterson persisted, the pastor told him, "There is a book called the New Testament. You buy that and read it. The way to heaven is described correctly and infallibly therein." Peterson asked if the book could be found in Altona, and was told that several stores had it. He im-mediately secured a copy and prevailed on some school chil-dren to show him how to read. After two weeks' work with a primer, Peterson was able to read on his own and began to study the New Testament. When he read there about the baptism of the early Christians, he asked his acquaintances if there were any people who still baptized in that fashion. He was informed that there were such at Krefeld. Going there at once, he convinced the Brethren of his sincerity and insisted on immediate baptism even though it was winter. A hole was

---

13. Samuel Smith, *History of the Province of Pennsylvania*, ed. William M. Mer-
    vine (1913), pp. 180–181. Most of Smith's account of the Brethren was
    reprinted in Donald F. Durnbaugh, ed., *The Brethren in Colonial America*
    (1967), pp. 14–21.

chopped in the ice and he was baptized. He lived until ninety years of age in the Brethren faith.[14]

THE AMERICAN BEGINNINGS OF THE BRETHREN

Following the first baptisms at Schwarzenau/Eder in 1708, the Brethren expanded rather rapidly in that area, in the Marienborn district, in the Palatinate, and into Switzerland and the Low Countries. The congregation in Marienborn was forced to leave in 1715 because of their public baptisms. This group found refuge in Krefeld for a time before moving to Pennsylvania in 1719. The larger congregation near Schwarzenau removed to Surhuisterveen in Friesland in 1720, whence they came to the American shores in 1729. By 1735, the bulk of the young Brethren movement had been transplanted to North America, although there are references to co-religionists on the Continent until the mid-eighteenth century.

The first Brethren, then, arrived in Pennsylvania in 1719. It was four years before they came together for baptisms and a love feast on Christmas Day, 1723. Some Brethren historians have found this interval a matter of embarrassment. The unfriendly chroniclers of Ephrata wrote that it was religious controversy among the former Krefeld members which kept them apart. Others put forth reasons of geographical distance and the problems of establishment in a strange environment. Morgan Edwards (1722–1795), the well-informed Baptist pastor and historian who included the Brethren in his researches, accepted this view: "The first appearing of these people in America was in the fall of the year 1719, when about twenty families landed at Philadelphia, and dispersed themselves, some to Germantown, some to Skippeck [Skippack], some to Oley, some to Connestogo [Conestoga], and elsewhere. This dispersion incapacitated them to meet for public worship; and therefore they began to grow lukewarm in religion."[15] One clue that the dispersion was not complete is the land record which shows that John Gumre (Gomorry) bought a tract of land, along the Wissahickon River, in 1720 for

---

14. *Brethren in Colonial America*, pp. 533–537.
15. Morgan Edwards, *Materials Towards a History of the Baptists in Pennsylvania both British and German, Volume 1* (1770), p. 64. The Edwards material on the Brethren is reprinted in *Brethren in Colonial America*, pp. 173–191,

himself and for the "congregation of the brethren." It was on this site, now in Fairmount Park, that the first baptisms were performed in 1723.[16]

Whatever the cause of the delay, it is known that in the fall of 1722 Peter Becker with several companions from Germantown visited the scattered brethren; this "was attended with a great revival, in so much that societies were formed wherever a number of families were in reach of one another" (Edwards). The account by the Ephrata chroniclers is comparable: "They travelled through the regions of Shippack [sic], Falckner's Swamp, Oley, etc., and wherever they came they communicated to their brethren how they were minded, with their approval, to begin to organize a meeting. . . . When they came home, they began to hold meetings alternately at Peter Becker's and Gomorry's, until the advance of winter prevented them."[17]

The occasion of the eventual organization, love feast, and baptism was the report in the summer of 1723 that Christian Liebe had arrived in Philadelphia to preach. Liebe (1679–1751), a leader in the Krefeld congregation, was well known because of his sentence as a galley slave on the Mediterranean, from which he was freed after a time through the intervention of the Dutch Estates General. A number of "newly awakened persons" from the Schuylkill region (primarily of Mennonite background) came to the Philadelphia area only to be disappointed by learning that the report of Liebe's arrival was erroneous. However, the Germantown Brethren invited the visitors to meet with them. Being much edified, the Schuylkill group continued the contacts begun in this manner, and in the fall of 1723 asked to be baptized.[18]

This request posed a difficult problem for the Germantown Brethren, as they did not consider themselves a fully organized congregation. After due deliberation, they asked Peter Becker, known for his fervency of prayer, to be their minister, and it was Becker who performed the first Brethren

---

including information from subsequent printed and manuscript volumes. Comments from the Ephrata viewpoint are found in Lamech and Agrippa, [pseud.], eds., *Chronicon Ephratense: A History of Seventh Day Baptists at Ephrata, Lancaster County, Penn'a*, tr. J. Max Hark (1889), pp. 15, 249–250.

16. William Hull, *William Penn and the Dutch Quaker Migration to Pennsylvania* (1935), pp. 219–220.

17. Edwards, *Materials*, p. 65; *Chronicon*, p. 22.

18. *Chronicon*, pp. 22–23.

baptism in America and officiated at the love feast which followed. In Brethren practice, this consisted of a period of examination, a literal washing of feet (after John 13), a meal, and the celebration of the eucharist.

A description of this and succeeding events is found in the Ephrata Chronicle:

> Through such divine happenings the Baptists [Brethren] in Pennsylvania became a congregation, and continued their meetings through that summer with great blessing and edification until the following winter prevented them. The next spring, of 1724, however, when they resumed their meetings there was given to them such a blessing that the whole region roundabout was moved thereby. Particularly among their youth was this movement felt, who now, to the great edification of their elders, began to walk in the fear of the Lord and to love the Brethren. And as the fame of this awakening spread abroad, there was such an increase of attendance at their meetings, that there was no room to contain the majority. The following summer again many among them were moved, and love feasts were held, through which many of them were impelled to join them, and so their communion experienced a speedy increase. [19]

A sign of the revival spirit was the decision of the Germantown congregation to undertake a general visitation of the hinterland. In the fall of 1724, the entire male membership of Germantown went on foot or on horseback into the "bush," held meetings, and organized two new congregations. This is told in detail in the Ephrata account.

Again, students of American history will be struck by the similarities of these developments to the later awakenings in New Jersey under Freylinghuysen and in New England under Edwards. Likely the only reason this has not been previously identified with the story of the Great Awakening is that it has been unknown. The Brethren were a small, German-speaking group of sectarian character, and had little impact on the broader English-speaking population. Those historians who have noticed the Brethren have done so in the context of describing other minority religious groups or by way of depicting the unusual Ephrata movement. There are indications that a change in historical interpretation in this regard is in the making. A significant article by Martin E. Lodge on the mainline churches of this period states in passing that "the German

---

19. *Chronicon*, p. 23.

Awakening was staged by the Dunkers and Moravians, two pietistic sects recently organized out of separatists from the established churches"; he also refers to the Dunkers and Moravians in mentioning German evangelism and the intellectual origins of the Great Awakening.[20]

A little-noticed analysis of the total involvement of the German groups in revivalism was written by an anonymous Lutheran for the *Evangelisches Magazin* in 1813–1814. He had his own explanation why the awakenings among the German population were not well known: "Many believe that the Almighty had effected his work among the English in a much more powerful and numerous way than among us [Germans]. If I investigate this all carefully, I cannot agree. There is not always the most fire where the most smoke is found. The customs, culture and personality of a nation cause great differences in the outward appearances of the works of grace. . . . It is not appropriate to the German character to have the newspapers trumpet abroad how many one has converted here and there." This critical Lutheran observation on Brethren beginnings in America is worth quotation:

> The first tempestuous movement to cause excitement came about among the old Brethren *[die alten Täufer]*, who resided from the Germantown area on into the country. The Brethren have always been diligent proselyters, and had recruited many who had belonged in Germany to all kinds of brotherhoods, especially to the Inspirationists and the famed Friedrich Rock. These people read all writings of the mystics— Bernier, Madame Guyon, Tauler, John of the Cross, Bertot, Molino, Arnold, etc. and even the writings of Jacob Boehme—mornings and evenings for their home worship, and this as regularly as their bibles. Otherwise, they were kind, loving people, full of good works which they performed, and the spirit of grace had his fire and hearth among them. They travelled, they preached as far as Virginia, they visited the brethren, spoke of repentance and conversion, and of the inward life, and considered themselves to be the centerpiece of the kingdom of God. Indeed, much good was instituted by them and living Christianity was planted by them, although the Enemy also sowed weeds.[21]

---

20. Martin E. Lodge, "The Crisis of the Churches in the Middle Colonies, 1720–1750," *Pennsylvania Magazine of History and Biography*, vol. 94 (April 1971), pp. 195–220, esp. pp. 196–197.
21. "Gestalt des Reiches Gottes unter den Deutschen in Amerika," *Evangelisches Magazin*, vol. 2 (1813), pp. 22–24; vol. 3 (1814), pp. 65–69, 129–138. The quotations are found on pp. 130–132.

RELATIONSHIP OF THE BRETHREN WITH
OTHER RELIGIOUS GROUPS

If the awakening which marked the beginning of the Brethren movement in North America was as striking as these commentators have stated, then it would follow that other contemporaries would have made comparable observations. A survey of the reports which have been received from those groups from which Brethren converts might come indicated that the Brethren expansion was indeed noticed. The phenomenon would naturally be assessed critically, for Brethren growth could come only at the expense of their own increase. The periodic reports sent by Lutheran clergy to their center at Halle and the letters and reports sent by German Reformed clergy to the Dutch authorities bear this out. Of course, Brethren inroads were but part of the picture. It is commonly accepted that representatives of the churches which enjoyed state protection in Europe found it difficult to accept the separation of church and state found in the Middle Colonies. Clergy were not able to adjust at first, and neither were lay members. The early lack of capable and conscientious clergy, the unwillingness of many Lutheran and Reformed migrants to take up the burdens of the voluntary support of ministers, the problems of distance, dependence on ecclesiastical authority abroad—all of these provided a situation which helped the sectarian groups to attract members. Their pattern of covenanted congregations using ministerial talent from among their own number on the so-called "free ministry" basis proved appealing to others, combined as it usually was with a style of life which was sober, neighborly, and honest.

Hence, we find Henry Melchior Muhlenberg (1711–1787), the Lutheran patriarch, writing at mid-century with a bitter pen about the attractiveness to his flock of the Brethren: "If one wants to be master of his own property and land, and still become something special, which has a better appearance than the usual church system, then one can be converted to the belief of the so-called Sunday Baptists [in contrast to the sabbatarian Ephrata community]. All one needs to do is memorize several verses from the Revelation of John about Babel, the Beast, and the Harlot, present along with this a good outward appearance, and be publicly baptized by them by immersion. . . . All that is necessary is to mock infant baptism, and condemn all others who do not agree with them, especially the clergy and church people. . . ."[22]

The ministers and elders of the German Reformed congregation in Philadelphia wrote in sorrow (1734) about the decline of true religion owing to the lack of orthodox pastors and the division of those on the scene: "The numbers of those who . . . have gone over to the Tumplers [Brethren], Sabbatarians and Mennonites and others is so large that it cannot be stated without tears in one's eyes." Johann Philip Boehm (1683–1749) reported ten years later that many formerly Reformed had concluded that the Reformed church could not be "maintained in this country principally because of our inability to support ministers" and thereby were scattered among "the Mennonites, the Tumplers (Seventh Day as well as Eighth Day Tumplers) and the like." A comparable report from the Monocacy church in Maryland mentioned in 1748 that several "have left the church and joined the Dunker sect." Earlier (1730) Boehm complained that the "Tumplers, although they are divided and had conflicting opinions, mainly about the Sabbath or Seventh Day, have a large following everywhere." The problem, said Boehm, is "nothing else but this great liberty" of religious activity, so unlike the accustomed situation in Europe.[23]

Brethren proved to be very appealing to the Mennonites with whom they came in contact. Their great resemblance in faith and ordinances made a transfer relatively easy. By most accounts, the Brethren were much more zealous and lively than the quiet Mennonites. The standard history of the Mennonites observes that the Dunkers "followed the Mennonites to their Skippack and Pequea settlements where their proselyting zeal gained a number of adherents to their faith." In fact, many names which have often been thought to have been typically Brethren, if traced back, reveal themselves to be of Mennonite origin. The colonial records of the Brethren contain many references to the Mennonites, often in terms of tension, despite, or perhaps precisely because of, their great similarities. During the Moravian synods, a final passage recommended that the Brethren unite with the Mennonites and come "to an

---

22. *Kurze Nachricht von einigen Evangelischen Gemeinen in Amerika,* second ed. (1750), p. 217.
23. The comments are taken from *Brethren in Colonial America,* pp. 131–136, originally published in William J. Hinke, ed., *Life and Labors of the Rev. John Phillip Boehm* (1916) and archival reports in the Dutch archives.

agreement on the mode of baptism. That would make one less sect in the country." Evidently the difference in manner of baptism seemed to be the only significant barrier.[24]

The zeal and activity of the Germantown brethren and their co-religionists in other areas seems to have ebbed in the mid-1730s, according to contemporary accounts. The arrival of Alexander Mack, Sr., in 1729 with some thirty families, had brought renewal. Morgan Edwards noted that the 1729 arrivals "both quickened them again and increased their number everywhere." However, Mack, Sr., died in 1735 and the impulse slackened.[25]

A Germantown member, Stephan Koch (1695–1763), has left a highly charged personal testimony of the period. Deeply upset by the death of a brother in the faith (Henry Traut) in 1733, he was reminded that he himself had not yet attained a true relationship with God; he reflected that others in the congregation had personally "witnessed the awakening at Schwarzenau" which explained why the "fire was still smoldering under its ashes." On May 3, 1735, Koch was walking in the orchard behind his house and experienced a vision.

> While I lamented thus to God it seemed to me as though suddenly a flame of God's voice struck into me, which entirely illumined me inside, and I heard a voice say to me, "Yet one thing thou lackest." I asked, "What is it then?" The answer was, "You do not know God and never have really known Him." I said, "Yes, that is so, but how shall I attain it?" Then it seemed as though I were beside myself. But when I came to again, I felt an inexpressibly pleasing love to God in my heart, and on the other hand, all anxiety, with all the temptation of the unclean spirits had vanished. Yes, it seemed as if all my transgressions were pardoned and sealed, and day and night there was nothing else in my heart but joy, love, and praise to God.

Alexander Mack, Jr., had known like feelings of unfruitfulness and was led by Koch also to this awakened state. As Mack was a

---

24. C. Henry Smith, *The Story of the Mennonites*, third ed. by Cornelius Krahn (1950), p. 547. The Moravian conclusion was published in *Brethren in Colonial America*, p. 286. Morgan Edwards, *Materials*, p. 94, reported that many Mennonites "desired a restoration of *immersion* and have gone off to the Tunkers for want of it" among their own community; of course, as a Baptist, Edwards believed that immersion was the correct form of Christian baptism. Other contacts between the Brethren and Mennonites are noted in Durnbaugh, "Relationships."

25. Edwards, *Materials*, p. 65.

ready speaker, according to Koch, "he began to speak in the meeting so powerfully that it was a marvel to hear him, and this aroused much notice in the congregation." Some were very edified, but others looked askance at the movement. One result was that the unmarried population associated with the congregation at Germantown began to meet on Sunday afternoons. "At last the spirit of revival came upon all who were assembled, so that one heard with astonishment how they praised God," although with some the experience did not last long.[26]

Some of the young men decided to live with each other in a kind of spiritual hermitage. These developments caused controversy as some of the leaders encouraged the movement and others thought it smacked of the spirit of enthusiasm. The revival at Germantown was noticed by others. August Gottlieb Spangenberg (1704–1782), then a missionary of the Moravian Brethren and later the leader of the movement, reported to his home base about the "new economy among the Brethren at Germantown" and that several of the unmarried brethren were "earnestly and intimately united in the Spirit." Though "tempted to leave the congregation" they "found it to be better to confess the truth and either suffer for it or conquer through it, and hoped for both at the same time." This had caused several of the older members to be "mightily awakened" and to humble themselves before the Lord. An interesting sidelight of Spangenberg's account is that several of the area separatists (including Johann Adam Gruber, Johannes Eckstein, and Christoph Sauer) were meeting with the Brethren in the wake of the revival. They spoke and prayed there in the public meetings, although did not affiliate as members.[27]

THE EPHRATA MOVEMENT

The chief criticism of the revival led by Koch and Mack, Jr., was that it tended toward a spirit of separatism like that of the Sabbatarian community at Ephrata, a painful schism among the Brethren of recent memory. The congregational leader Peter Becker, though sympathetic to their concern, specifically warned the young men about this. His warning was well advised, for almost all of those caught up in the revival

26. *Chronicon*, pp. 95–101; republished and discussed in *Brethren in Colonial America*, pp. 90–96.
27. *Brethren in Colonial America*, pp. 270–278.

at Germantown did in fact leave to join the Ephrata community, although not all stayed there permanently.

To understand this development, it is necessary to relate the way in which the famed Ephrata community was formed. During the expansionary movement of the Germantown Brethren in the fall of 1724, one of those baptized was Johann Conrad Beissel (1690–1768), then living as a hermit in the Conestoga area. Beissel's life and labors have been related in the *Chronicon Ephratense* (1786). Much of the volume revolves around the problem posed to the movement by Beissel's involvement with the Brethren. On the one hand, the chroniclers had to recognize the prior activity of the Brethren; on the other, they were concerned to justify the break between Beissel and the Brethren by painting the latter as arid legalists and spiritual adolescents. For this reason, the interpretations contained in the *Chronicon* are often painfully twisted, although factual matters are invariably trustworthy.[28]

Following an unusual religious pilgrimage in Germany, including association with a circle of Pietists in the Palatinate and with the Inspirationists and Brethren in the Wetterau and Wittgenstein, Beissel came to the New World in 1720. He had hoped to join the Kelpian-led community known as the Woman in the Wilderness, but found it had been dispersed by the time of his arrival. After a brief residence in Germantown as apprentice to the weaver Becker, he lived with a few associates in the thinly settled area of present-day Lancaster County. Not satisfied with his self-administered baptism, he allowed himself to be baptized by Becker, although not without intense spiritual struggle. His problem was accepting the rite from someone he deemed much inferior spiritually.

Beissel's gifts, in fact, were such that he was asked by the Germantown Brethren to be the leader of the new Conestoga congregation. Among other occasions, he was asked to officiate at a love feast at Whitsuntide called by Martin Urner in the Schuylkill area. Under Beissel's leadership "quite extraor-

---

28. An unsympathetic biographical treatment is Walter C. Klein, *Johann Conrad Beissel: Mystic and Martinet* (1942); the most comprehensive narrative about the Ephrata community is James E. Ernst, *Ephrata: A History,* ed. John Joseph Stoudt (1963), largely a collation of the *Chronicon* and Henry Sangmeister's diary. The most balanced appraisal is still Oswald Seidensticker, *Ephrata, eine amerikanische Klostergeschichte* (1883). The volumes by Julius Sachse, *The German Sectarians of Pennsylvania* (1899–1900), contain valuable material but are marred by the author's manipulation of the sources.

dinary powers of eternity manifested themselves," in the language of the *Chronicon*, "such as were never known before or after."

Very soon, tension built up between the Conestoga group led by Beissel and the other Brethren. Beissel so emphasized the Spirit that he refused to use the Scriptures as a basis for his teaching. He taught that marriage represented a fall from grace, and was responsible for several women leaving their husbands. He introduced the Sabbath and tolerated some of his followers who practiced circumcision, kosher meals, and other Jewish practices. These differences, compounded by the arrogance of Beissel, finally led to a rupture, with most of the Conestoga congregation following Beissel, and others adhering to the Germantown group. Mack, Sr., attempted to reconcile the split soon after his arrival from Friesland in 1729, but Beissel would not even speak with him. The judgment of the Ephrata chroniclers is apt: "Those who knew how affairs stood between the two congregations, know also that a close union between them was impossible; for they were born of different causes, since the one had the letter [Bible] for its foundation, and the other the spirit; and while both had the same Father [radical Pietism] they had different mothers."[29] Beissel dramatized the break by having himself baptized backwards (to give back the Brethren-acquired baptism) and then forwards again, following which he baptized the rest of his group.

Soon after this, Beissel left the Conestoga area to live by himself along the Cocalico brook, today's Ephrata. By 1732, a number of his followers had gathered about him, and the Ephrata community took form. Eventually, three orders were organized, the Solitary Brethren, the Solitary Sisters, and the "householders," married folk who wanted to participate in the community but who were not ready to accept the celibate life.

Despite this painful break, there is evidence that the Brethren and the Ephrata community were not without contacts throughout the colonial period. Particularly in the South there was much intermingling, so that it is often difficult to tell whether a certain congregation was Seventh-day or First-day Baptist (Ephrata or Brethren). While Ensign goes too far in claiming that the Brethren considered Ephrata a kind of religious order to which they could repair for spiritual renewal,

---

29. *Chronicon*, pp. 35, 50. On the schism, see the contemporary materials and discussion in *Brethren in Colonial America*, pp. 61–111.

it is equally off the mark to deny any relationship at all, as was asserted by many Brethren historians of a later date. It was irritating to many Brethren to be confused in the popular mind with the Ephrata movement, and in the attempt to set the record straight there were sharper categories established than the history of the eighteenth century justifies. Differences there certainly were in the style of spirituality, but there were many points of contact.[30]

The Ephrata movement is one of the most often written about in all of American colonial history, but at the same time one of the least understood. To this day there is no fully adequate interpretation either of the founder, Beissel, or of the movement itself. Its monastic-like practices, its superb cultural achievements, and its striking personalities have won it much attention, from journalist to folklorist to church historian, but much of the description has stayed on a shallow level. Admittedly, the Ephrata movement helped to ensure this by the peculiar language of Canaan they affected, steeped as it is in the vocabulary of Gottfried Arnold and Johann Georg Gichtel, and the master of both, Jacob Boehme. For present purposes, it is perhaps most important to note the impact which Ephrata made in terms of religious resurgence and spiritual vitality taking communal form. Perhaps it is appropriate to see Ephrata as a kind of eighteenth-century Taizé, as an expression of Protestant monastic spirituality with similar religious and artistic flowering such as draws thousands of seekers to the small Burgundian village today.[31]

The testimony of American and European travelers (recorded most conveniently in the anthology *Ephrata as Seen by Contemporaries*) is abundant that many shared Voltaire's observation that at Ephrata were found the most inimitable of men. Although judgment then as now was divided on the community and its founder, that Ephrata needed to be taken into consideration was clear. As Johann Peter Miller (1709–1796), a successor to Beissel, commented to the Swedish Lutheran pastor, Israel Acrelius:

30. C. David Ensign, "Radical German Pietism (c. 1675–c. 1760")" (Ph.D. diss., Boston University, 1955), p. 282. An instructive description of the intermingling of the two groups is Klaus G. Wust, "German Mystics and Sabbatarians in Virginia," *Virginia Magazine of History and Biography*, vol. 72 (July 1964), pp. 330–347. See also Elmer Lewis Smith and others, *The Pennsylvania Germans of the Shenandoah Valley* (1964).

31. Useful descriptions of the Taizé community are John Heijke, *An Ecumenical Light on the Renewal of Religious Community Life* (1967), and François Biot, *The Rise of Protestant Monasticism* (1963).

So, will you also see this poor place? But however poorly we live here, and although we live almost entirely to ourselves, yet we have the advantage of seeing the most distinguished people in the country; for no one comes to the land, who wishes to be honored for his knowledge and understanding, without visiting us in our isolated retreat, even though our visitors be the proudest people in the country.

As to the impression Ephrata made, there is no reason to doubt Morgan Edwards' report:

From the uncouth dress, the recluse and ascetic life of these people sour aspects and rough manners might be expected; but on the contrary, a smiling innocence and meekness grace their countenances, and a softness of tone and accent adorn their conversation, and make their deportment gentle and obliging.[32]

Edwards went on to admire their singing, which was praised literally to the heavens by those who heard it. The sophisticated Anglican rector, Jacob Duché, was but one of those who found themselves lacking for words to describe the effects of their singing. "It is impossible," wrote Duché, "to describe ... my feelings upon this occasion. The performers sat with their heads reclined, their countenances solemn and dejected, their faces pale and emaciated from their manner of living, their clothing exceedingly white and quite picturesque, and their music such as thrilled the very soul. I almost began to think myself in the world of spirits, and that the objects before me were ethereal. In short, the impression this scene made upon my mind continued strong for many days, and I believe, will never be wholly obliterated."[33] Recent attempts have been made to recapture the spirit of the Ephrata hymnody, but are doomed to relative failure because of the harsh regime imposed by Beissel upon the singers in order to gain the effects he wanted. In curious fashion, the untaught genius of Beissel in the musical area has been immortalized by Thomas Mann in his novel *Dr. Faustus*. His character Adrian Leverkukhn was introduced to Beissel's theory of music by an early teacher; some of his profoundest work (in the novel) was said to be inspired by the concept of "master" and "servant" notes, coined by Beissel. The exact literary sources for Mann's treat-

---

32. Felix Reichmann and Eugene E. Doll, eds., *Ephrata As Seen by Contemporaries* (1953), p. 54; Edwards, *Materials*, p. 75.

33. Reichmann and Doll, *Ephrata*, pp. 101–102.

ment have been determined.[34] Morgan Edwards quotes an unnamed close acquaintance of Beissel, whose appraisal is probably as balanced as can be obtained: "He was very strict in his morals and practiced self-denial and mortification to an uncommon degree. Enthusiastic and whimsical he certainly was, but an apparent devoutness and sincerity ran through all his oddities. He was not an adept in any of the liberal arts and sciences except music, in which he excelled."[35]

In some ways even more attention has been given to the unsurpassed abilities of the Ephrata community in artistic accomplishment, specifically in the skillful execution of *Fraktur* or illuminated manuscripts. Shelley, Stoudt, and other experts agree that no other group rivals the attainments of the sisters in this art form, although it was seen by Beissel as something of a poor substitute for those not apt at singing. "Fraktur illumination not only appeared in America first at the Ephrata Cloister in Ephrata, Pa., but also reached its greatest perfection there." The intense competition of collectors to secure examples of Ephrata art, or even that of the somewhat less ingenious daughter colony at Snow Hill, near Quincy, Pennsylvania, is testimony enough to this contribution. There is some evidence that contemporaries were less impressed with this exercise, seeing mostly a discipline of patience and painstaking, rather than great art.[36]

Other scholars give the community high marks for its schools, which were said to have been outstanding with respect to their classical curriculum. Watson wrote that many families from Philadelphia and Baltimore sent their children to Ephrata for training because of its reputation as a seat of learning

34. Thomas Mann, *Doctor Faustus,* tr. H. T. Lowe-Porter (1948), pp. 63–67. The sources were identified by Andreas Briner, "Conrad Beissel and Thomas Mann," *American-German Review,* vol. 26 (December 1959–January 1960), pp. 24–25, 32 and the note in vol. 30 (February-March 1964), p. 33; it was primarily based on Hans Theodore David, "Hymns and Music of the Pennsylvania Seventh-Day Baptists," *American-German Review,* vol. 9 (June 1943), pp. 4–6, 36.
35. Edwards, *Materials,* p. 78.
36. Donald A. Shelley, *The Fraktur-Writings or Illuminated Manuscripts of the Pennsylvania Germans* (1961), p. 101; John Joseph Stoudt, *Pennsylvania German Folk Art* (1966); Henry S. Bornemann, *Pennsylvania German Illuminated Manuscripts* (1937). Israel Acrelius noted in 1753 that the "younger sisters are mostly employed in drawing. A part of them are just now engaged in copying musical notebooks for themselves and for the brethren. I saw some of these upon which a wonderful amount of labor had been expended" (Reichmann and Doll, *Ephrata,* p. 53).

and fine arts. Ludwig Höcker, the schoolmaster, is also thought to have started the first Sabbath Schools in North America, sometime after 1739, with his afternoon classes in which he offered religious instruction and the three R's to neglected boy-scholars of the Ephrata neighborhood.[37]

One aspect of the life of the community has not often been appreciated, given the fascination of writers with the essential monastic intent of the members. This was the effort made by members of the community to help their settler-neighbors. Miller described this in a letter written late in his life (1790) speaking of the earlier years of the movement: "At that time, works of charity hath been our chief occupation; Canestogues [Conestoga] was then a great wilderness, and began to be settled by poor Germans, which desired our assistance in building houses for them; which not only kept us employed several sommers [sic] in hard carpenters-work, but also increased our poverty so much that we wanted even things necessary for life."[38] Dr. William Fahnestock, who wrote (1836) one of the better descriptions of Ephrata from the perspective of a descendant of a member family, had this comment: "Their doors were ever open to the weary traveller, and all visitors were cordially received and entertained, while they tarried, as is done in the *Hospices* of Europe. They gave all the necessary supplies to the needy, even their own beds, and to stripping their own backs to afford some shelter from the 'peltings of the pitiless storm,' to those who were exposed to the weather in inclement seasons."[39] Some of the harsher judgments rendered about the peculiarities of Ephrata might be tempered by the realization that the Solitary were mindful of the needs of those not of the community.

THE BRETHREN, EPHRATA AND THE MORAVIANS

The Brethren and the Ephrata movement had agreed to disagree, but they found common cause in the 1740s in their criticism of the Moravian Brethren. Although alike in many ways, the Brethren bodies and the Moravian Brethren found it

37. William M. Fahnestock, "An Historical Sketch of Ephrata; together with a concise account of the Seventh Day Baptist Society of Pennsylvania," *Hazard's Register of Pennsylvania*, vol. 15 (January–June 1835), pp. 161–167, reprinted in Reichmann and Doll, *Ephrata*, pp. 164ff.; John F. Watson, *Annals of Philadelphia in the Olden Time* (1857), vol. 2, pp. 110–112.
38. Published in Reichmann and Doll, *Ephrata*, p. 198.
39. Reichmann and Doll, *Ephrata*, p. 179.

difficult to work together. Both Brethren groups, however, were represented at the early ecumenical synods called in Pennsylvania at the behest of Count Ludwig von Zinzendorf, (1700–1760) in 1742. In the case of Beissel and Zinzendorf, part of the eventful split seems to have been a clash of strong personalities, even though they never met face to face. It is instructive to watch the change in tone in the references to Ephrata in the Moravian records. They start with use of glowing tones about the spiritual endeavors of Beissel and his flock. The final synod refers to Ephrata in scathing terms as a pack which stole the best members from the Brethren: "The Congregation of the Lord declares herewith that this sect organized in Conestoga with its two cloisters is merely a schismatic pack from the Dunkers, from whom they attempted to steal their baptism and calling. After they had accomplished this and by and by had alienated the loyalty of most of the sincere Dunkers with all kinds of pretense, they finally succeeded in seemingly creating an establishment. This, however, was in fact invented by the devil for the sole purpose of preventing in time the coming of the kingdom of Jesus Christ. . . . May the Lamb crush this satan to death soon!"[40] One of the reasons for this harsh condemnation is that the Ephrata community busied itself in print and orally in testifying against what they considered to be the machinations of Count Zinzendorf. They were especially opposed to the emphasis the Moravians placed on marriage as an ordinance of Christ, and the jubilant style of the Moravians. What was Christian joy to the Moravian Brethren was foolish frivolity and worldliness to the strict Ephrata members.

The Brethren were active in the synods until the third session which saw some Indian converts baptized, but not by immersion as the Brethren practiced it. They became suspicious that the ecumenical gatherings were in fact a device to increase the membership of the Moravian church, and are said to have begun holding their own yearly meetings as a result. At least two Brethren actually left to join the Moravians, Andreas Frey and Joseph Müller.

The final judgment of the synods about the Brethren

---

40. Quoted in *Brethren in Colonial America,* pp. 286–287. For background on the synods, see J. Taylor Hamilton and Kenneth G. Hamilton, *History of the Moravian Church* (1967), pp. 82–90; and John R. Weinlick, *Count Zinzendorf* (1956), pp. 151–169.

was not as harsh as about Ephrata but not very encouraging either. "The Dunker Church failed to prove its origin. . . . It is a congregation of God-fearing folk, who act after their conscience but without illumination, who are earnest and therefore appealing people."[41] They recommend, as previously stated, that the Brethren unite with the Mennonites to make one less sect in Pennsylvania.

Frey went to Europe with Count Zinzendorf, according to one source because the count wanted to use him to help bring some of the remaining Brethren in the Netherlands into closer association with the Moravians. The Pennsylvanian returned home full of disappointment following his sojourn among the Moravians, for he happened to have visited them during the time of emotional excess known in Moravian history as the "Sifting Period." Frey published at Germantown his critical reactions to what he experienced, much to the embarrassment of his former hosts. The exposé was republished both in Germany and also in English translation in London; it became a staple of anti-Moravian polemics. It has been used for that purpose as recently as 1950 in Monsignor Knox's *Enthusiasm.*[42]

The other adherent, Joseph Müller (1707–1761), was not only caught up by the Moravian movement but also stayed faithful to it, ending his days as a physician in Nazareth, Pennsylvania. He tried often to win his former brethren to the fold of the Lamb, only to meet with firm rejection. A Brethren reply of 1750 not only categorically rejected his appeals and beliefs, but pronounced excommunication, unless Müller were to repent his "idolatry, great and small errors, and clever and foolish fables." In that event, of course, he would "be dear to us as a brand plucked from the burning."[43]

Moravian records in the Carolinas mention the Dunkers from time to time, but largely in the context of Indian troubles or land transactions. Some later references indicate that there was little common ground religiously and some friction because of proselyting on both sides.

41. *Brethren in Colonial America*, p. 286; the entire section (pp. 267–320) deals with the relationship between the Moravians and the Brethren.
42. R. A. Knox, *Enthusiasm: A Chapter in the History of Religion* (1950), pp. 414–416. See in relation to this the explanations of S. H. Gapp, ed., *A History of the Beginnings of Moravian Work in America* (1955), pp. 130–135.
43. *Brethren in Colonial America*, pp. 302–315.

THE SAUER FAMILY

An active part in the Moravian controversy was played by the German printer, Johann Christoph Sauer (1695–1758). In some ways, he was Zinzendorf's chief opponent in America. This was for two reasons. The first was that Sauer was in close touch with personalities in Europe who were critical of Moravian activities there. This being the case, he quickly circulated the news of these controversies throughout the colonies, much to the disgust of Zinzendorf who had hoped to find a clean slate in the New World. The second reason for Sauer's policy was that he was a determined separatist in religious views, and therefore highly critical of any religious organization. Although intensely religious personally, Sauer was convinced that formalization of religious attachments would lead to tyranny over conscience. For radical Pietists such as Sauer, the very formation of a religious community was the Fall; sectarian and party spirit, excommunications and disciplining were bound to follow. This point of view made Sauer the terror of such figures as Muhlenberg and Boehm, and he was especially suspicious of a nobleman playing a religious role.[44]

Even well-informed sources have persisted in calling Sauer I (also spelled Saur and Sower) a member of the Brethren. The confusion arises from several sources. One is that there were three men, in three successive generations, named Christopher Sauer, all printers in Germantown. The latter two men were bona fide members of the Brethren. Careless writers have often combined the three, or at least the first two, into one personage. Many Brethren historians have claimed Sauer as one of their own, misled by an ambiguous reference in the *Chronicon Ephratense* and perhaps by a desire to enlist an outstanding personality in their ranks. A final reason for the confusion is that Sauer in fact was closely associated with the Brethren in Wittgenstein and in Germantown, and in basic religious beliefs. He attended their meetings at times, was a close friend of their interests, and generally held congruent religious principles, except for his insistence on separatism and

---

44. *Brethren in Colonial America*, pp. 315–319; Donald F. Durnbaugh, "Christopher Sauer, Pennsylvania German Printer: His Youth in Germany and Later Relationships with Europe," *Pennsylvania Magazine of History and Biography*, vol. 82 (July 1958), pp. 330–334.

individualism. This relationship suffices for including him in the present discussion.[45]

It is difficult to exaggerate Sauer's importance in the history of the American colonial period, because he influenced his peers in so many different ways. One way to put it is that he was for the German element in the colonies what Benjamin Franklin was for the English element. Brumbaugh has a classic passage to illustrate Sauer's ubiquity, with excusable hyperbole:

> Could you have entered any German home from New York to Georgia in 1754 and asked "Who is Christoph Saur?"—you would have learned that in every German home the Bible, opened morning and evening, was printed in 1743 by Christoph Saur; that the sanctuary and hearth were wreathed in music form by the *Davidsche Psalterspiel,* printed by Christoph Saur; that the family almanac, rich in medicinal and historical data, and containing the daily weather guide of the family, was printed by Christoph Saur in 1739, and every year thereafter until his death in 1758, and then by his son until 1778; that the religious magazine, prized with pious ardor and read with profound appreciation, was printed by Christoph Saur [II]; that the secular newspaper, containing all the current domestic and foreign news, linking the farm of that German with the whole wide world, was printed from 1739 by Christoph Saur; that the ink and paper used in sending letters to loved ones across the sea came from the shop of Christoph Saur, and was of his own manufacture; that the new six-plate stove, glowing in the long winter evenings with warmth and welcome, was invented and sold by Christoph Saur. That the medicine that brought health to the sick was compounded by Dr. Christoph Saur; that the old clock, telling the hours, the months and phases of the moon, in yon corner of the room, was made by Christoph Saur; that almost every book upon the table was printed by Christoph Saur, upon his own press, with type and ink of his own manufacture, and bound in his own bindery; that the dreadful abuses and oppression they suffered in crossing the Atlantic had been lessened by the heroic protests . . . of one man, and that man was Christoph Saur; that the sick emigrants upon landing at Philadelphia were met by a warm friend who conveyed them in carriages to his own

---

45. The evidence against the thesis of Sauer's Brethren membership is presented in Donald F. Durnbaugh, "Was Christopher Sauer a Dunker?" *Pennsylvania Magazine of History and Biography,* vol. 93 (July 1969), pp. 383–391.

house, and without money and without price nursed them to health, had the Gospel of the Savior preached to them, and sent them rejoicing and healed to their wilderness homes, and that friend was Christoph Saur; that, in short, the one grandest German of them all, loved and followed most devotedly, was Christoph Saur, the Good Samaritan of Germantown.[46]

Because of Sauer's personal integrity in refusing to print anything he did not know to be true, he won a great following among his readers. This meant that he had great political influence as well, which he was not adverse in employing. His basic strategy was to uphold the Quaker Party in the Pennsylvania Assembly, because as a strong pacifist he supported their resistance to war-making legislation.[47] The opponents of the Quakers recognized his pivotal role, and did what they could to diminish his influence. Franklin tried repeatedly to establish rival German-language presses, but without success until, later in the century, Johann Heinrich Miller was able to displace Sauer's son and successor. Muhlenberg described the situation in a report to Halle in 1748: "The Quakers, who are the foremost party in this province, have on their side the German book publisher, Christoph Sauer, who controls the Mennonites, Separatists, Anabaptists, and the like with his printed works and lines them up with the Quakers. All of these speak and write against the war and reject even the slightest defense as ungodly and contrary to the commands of Jesus Christ."[48] In 1765 the Lutheran leader wrote in the same vein, commenting that "the Germans had been so inculcated with the idea that if they failed to keep the Quakers in the government and elected in their place Englishmen from the Episcopal or Presbyterian churches, they would be deprived of their ancient rights and liberties and then they would be saddled with laws forcing them to engage in military drill to assist in defense against enemies, and also to pay a tithe to the ministers of the Episcopal church."[49]

---

46. Brumbaugh, *German Baptist Brethren*, pp. 374–376, originally presented in an address at Bellefonte, Pennsylvania, July 5, 1898.
47. See the discussion in Durnbaugh, "Relationships," pp. 43–48. The most thorough study of Sauer's political role is William R. Steckel, "Pietist in Colonial Pennsylvania: Christopher Sauer, Printer (1738–1758)" (Ph.D. diss., Stanford University, 1949).
48. Theodore G. Tappert and John W. Doberstein, eds., *The Notebook of a Colonial Clergyman* (1959), p. 30.
49. Tappert and Doberstein, *Notebook*, pp. 114–115.

A *cause célèbre* in this altercation was the noted Charity School movement, which attracted donors in England and the Continent. Ostensibly set up to provide instruction in English for the benighted children of the Pennsylvania peasants, the plan won support from Lutheran and Reformed clergymen (the potential schoolmasters) since it seemed to offer an outside means of support not dependent on the whims of reluctant parishioners. Sauer immediately attacked the scheme on two grounds: in the first place, he denied the picture painted by its proponents that the Germans were wretchedly ignorant and a menace to society; in the second place, he noted that the supporters of the project were the political opponents of the Quakers and suspected that the plan was a device to gain support for the war party. The scheme failed because one of its leading promoters, William Smith, was thought to be using it to further the cause of the Anglican church and because Sauer's criticism turned public opinion against it. Sauer had commented in a private letter that the real purpose of the plan was to get the "Germans to stick their necks out in the Militia in order to protect the property of Hamilton, Peters, Allen, Turner, Shippen and Franklin" who "care very little either for religion or for the cultivation of the Germans."[50] The press set up by the fund (again with the purpose of rivaling Sauer) published as one of its first issues a translation of the royal articles of war, which seemed to critics a very odd choice if the intent was the religious instruction of German children. The general conclusion of scholars studying the Charity Schools today is that Sauer was not far off in his assessment of its purpose, and that he did in fact play a chief role in squelching the plan.[51]

THE LITERARY CONTRIBUTION OF THE BRETHREN AND THE EPHRATA COMMUNITY

Increasing attention is being paid to the cultural achievements of the German-speaking population in the Ameri-

---

50. Dietmar Rothermund, *The Layman's Progress* (1961), pp. 171–172.

51. The most recent studies are Whitfield J. Bell, Jr., "Benjamin Franklin and the German Charity Schools," *Proceedings of the American Philosophical Society*, vol. 99 (December 1955), pp. 381–387 and Bruce R. Lively, "William Smith, the College and Academy of Philadelphia and Pennsylvania Politics, 1753–1758," *Historical Magazine of the Protestant Episcopal Church*, vol. 38 (1969), pp. 237–258. The older survey is Samuel E. Weber, *The Charity School Movement in Colonial Pennsylvania, 1754–1763* (1905).

can colonies. The dominant influence of the English culture long kept this development obscure and known only to
a few scholars. The "dumb Dutch" were thought to be rather
bovine, rural folk, able to produce at best a dialect-literature
suited to tall stories and jokes. The reaction to this on the part
of the filio-pietistic societies was little better, as they, like other
ethnic-based groups, sought to prove that their people had
contributed the finest leaders in cultural, political, and economic pursuits. Today when plurality is being celebrated and
the myth of the melting pot proclaimed, it is possible to appreciate better the achievements of the mixture making up
American society, including the German element.

The most complete study made thus far of the contribution of the Pennsylvania Germans in the poetic idiom is by John
Joseph Stoudt. Far from being country cousins in producing
poetry, according to Stoudt, the Germans in America were
writing "literate poetry executed in literary patterns of an
ancient cut, of a quality which their Anglo-Saxon neighbors
could not match, and in a quantity so astonishing that English
poetry pales by comparison." In sum, for Stoudt, "the Pennsylvania Germans, far from being compelled to assume a minor
role, took the lead in American colonial verse." This author
gives Conrad Beissel the palm as the most productive of poets
in the American colonies. Although other authorities have
called Beissel's admittedly prolific production mechanical and
banal, for Stoudt, in contrast, Beissel's work was without doubt
the most profound creation of colonial literature, English or
German. He rates him as "a mystic of rank equal to Boehme,
Tauler and Eckhart"—high praise indeed. Beissel's most significant trait was his ability to communicate both his goal and
the passion to seek it to other people. "The history of western
mysticism has given us many examples of individual mystics
whose spirit was infectious . . . but nowhere in modern times
was the spirit communicated with such fulness as at Ephrata."[52]
Those who cannot share Stoudt's high view of Beissel's genius
are left with the question: Why were so many colonial Americans of real ability—Johann Peter Miller, Conrad Weiser (for
a time), Ludwig Höcker, Johannes Hildebrand—attracted to

---

52. John Joseph Stoudt, *Pennsylvania German Poetry, 1685–1830* (1956), pp.
xxii–xxiii, lxviii–lxix. A more negative appraisal is found in F. Ernest
Stoeffler, *Mysticism in the German Devotional Literature of Colonial Pennsylvania* (1950), pp. 43–65. A general treatment is afforded by Earl F.
Robacker, *Pennsylvania German Literature* (1948), pp. 29ff.

Ephrata and kept there despite Beissel's difficult demands and imperious leadership?

Of the thirty poets singled out by Stoudt for special quality or quantity of production, a large number were members of the Ephrata or Brethren groups: Beissel, Michael Frantz, Ludwig Höcker, Mack, Jr., Miller, Johannes Preiss, Sauer, Jacob Stoll, and Michael Wohlfarth. Quite a few more are represented in his anthology with one or more pieces. The high point of Ephrata poetic production is seen in the series of hymnals, including the *Weyrauchshügel, Das Gesäng der einsammen und verlassenen Turtel-Taube* (1747) and the *Paradisisches Wunder-Spiel* (1754). Again, the enjoyment of these poems is hampered for many by the special language in which they are written. Particularly offensive to some modern eyes is the use of sensual imagery to attempt to portray the depths and heights of spiritual mysticism, not unlike the verses of the medieval mystics, and directly influenced by baroque literary tastes.

Although there were those in the two movements who studied formally, most of the writing was done by relatively unlettered folk. This makes the literary productivity a rather astonishing performance. Like the early years of the Quaker movement which saw a tremendous outpouring of publication, these movements motivated members to an unusually vigorous effort of writing. A bibliography of publications of the Brethren alone lists 54 different items before 1800. Ephrata literary production was even more fertile. Of the Brethren publications one of the more typical is the booklet called *Ein Geringer Schein des verachteten Lichtleins* (1747), written in answer to a German-language Quaker tract by Benjamin Holmes. The three points covered were: "On the Holy Scriptures," "On the True Conversion," and "On the Baptism of Christ." The first section begins: "The Holy Scriptures is a letter of God which he has written to the human race through the operation of his Holy Spirit."[53]

Alexander Mack, Jr. was the most prolific of the colonial Brethren authors. He left at his death (1803) many unpublished poems and other manuscripts. His two most ambitious

---

53. Bibliographical information is found in Donald F. Durnbaugh and Lawrence W. Shultz, eds., "A Brethren Bibliography, 1713–1963," *BLT*, vol. 9 (Winter and Spring 1964), pp. 3–177. The booklet *Ein Geringer Schein* was published in English translation in *Brethren in Colonial America*, pp. 428–447.

printed efforts were polemical in nature, attempted defenses
of the Brethren position on believer's baptism, church discipline, and basic doctrines. His opponent was the Reverend Dr.
Johann Christoff Kunze (1774–1807), Lutheran clergyman
and professor in Philadelphia and New York. Mack's first
writing, the *Apologia* (1788), incorporated Kunze's criticism of
Brethren baptismal practice with running rebuttal. Kunze
published a spirited rejoinder of 92 pages, which brought
forth a second work from Mack, *Anhang zum Widerlegten
Wiedertäufer* (1788), valuable as much for historical material as
for its line of reasoning. Actually, many of Mack's personal
letters written to give spiritual counsel to friends and inquirers
are other sources of evaluation for his character, marked as
they are by deep piety and concern for others.[54]

The most substantial Brethren treatises were printed in
1774; they were the second editions of the early writings by
Alexander Mack, Sr.: *Grundforschende Fragen, welche denen
Neuen Täuffern, im Wittgensteinschen, insonderheit zu beantwor-
ten, vorgelegt waren* and *Kurtze und einfältige Vorstellung der . . .
heiligen Rechten und Ordnungen desz Hauses Gottes.*[55] Because the
Brethren were reacting against what they thought of as
creedalism gone to seed and speculative theologizing, they
avoided anything like a systematic doctrinal statement. For this
reason, the two writings by Mack, Sr.—which are devoted to
answering controversial matters between themselves and the
radical Pietists—are as close to early basic statements on theology as can be found. Although often reprinted, they can
scarcely be called widely popular, and have not been determinative of the development of the Brethren in the way that
Calvin's *Institutes* have been for Presbyterians or even Wesley's writings for the Methodists.

Flory's characterization of the literary work of the
Brethren bears quoting: "They were earnest, thoughtful, practical men, who had to face stern facts and harsh realities, and to
them life was a very intense and serious matter. When they

---

54. There is a study of the poetic writing of Mack, Jr., by Samuel B. Heckman,
The Religious Poetry of Alexander Mack, Jr. (1912). The two apologetic
treatises are published in English translation in *Brethren in Colonial America*, pp. 469–547, with additional material on the controversy with Kunze.

55. The writings of Mack, Sr., were originally published in Germany in 1713
and 1715; the second editions were the work of Christoph Sauer II
(1774)—"A Brethren Bibliography," nos. 22–23. They are available in
English translation in several versions, most recently in *European Origins of
the Brethren*, pp. 321–405.

wrote they wrote because they had something to say; and the bulk of their writing is characterized by an earnest, sincere, rugged directness that gives it positive aim, and directs it to some definite mark."[56] There is little to be found of literary grace and style. They were plain men and wrote a plain style, often with pleasing results, but there was not a John Woolman among them.

With one notable exception, the literary output of these Brethren-related bodies had little impact outside their own fellowship. The exception is that of Christoph Sauer II (1721–1784), who had for his writings the platform of almanacs, newspapers, and a publishing house established by his father. The second Sauer announced upon the death of his father (1758) that although he would have preferred to have continued to earn his livelihood as a bookbinder, he was willing to take up the task begun by his father. He intended to conduct the enterprise in the same spirit—"for the honor of God, and for the well-being of this country." He noted that his father had earned the enmity of a number of highly placed individuals because of his independence and courage and that he could expect good and bad judgments himself.[57]

Politically, he charted the same course as the elder Sauer. His publishing policy remained much the same. His father had won a place in history by the publication of the first Bible in a European language in North America with his 1743 edition of the German Bible in Luther's translation. Sauer II added second (1763) and third (1776) editions before an English-language edition was published by a competitor in the colonies.

One innovation by the son was the publication at irregular intervals of the first religious magazine in American history, *Ein Geistlisches Magazien* (1764ff.). This is often noted in printing history because the twelfth issue of the second volume (1772) was printed with the first type cast in North America. The periodical was distributed free to subscribers of the news-

---

56. Flory, *Literary Activity,* p. 161; this appraisal is quoted with approval by Robacker, *Literature,* p. 25.
57. The statement on the implications of the death of the first Sauer is found in *Brethren in Colonial America,* pp. 378–380. Flory, *Literary Activity,* pp. 37–160, has an extensive discussion of the importance of the Sauer press, but mistakenly considers it to be a denominational publishing house. One of the more complete studies is Edward W. Hocker, *The Sower Printing House of Colonial Times* (1948).

paper, as Sauer II pointed out that the foundation of the print shop was laid "to the glory of God and my neighbor's good." He was troubled by the lack of religious instruction and the scarcity of good books in homes. He thought that some people might be willing to read a short piece in a magazine who would not take the trouble to read a devotional book. The *Magazien* published many hymns by Brethren and other authors and general edifying material, such as the rules for children's conduct by the colonial schoolmaster Christopher Dock (d. 1771).[58]

Sauer also made a contribution to the German population by all manner of educational materials through his several publications. This ranged from medical advice and the equivalent of first-aid manuals to instructions on writing, agricultural improvements, and financial transactions. Both father and son saw their printing business as a vehicle for improving the lot of their fellows and were quite inventive in finding ways to carry this out. Many specialized studies have detailed their creativity in a number of different fields. Although they tended to be critical of university products, they themselves furthered education by their long-standing support of the Germantown Academy. In any evaluation, the Sauer press would need to be considered an important part of the total colonial educational achievement.[59]

THE AMERICAN REVOLUTION

According to the calculations of Morgan Edwards, the Brethren numbered by 1770 some 1500 adult members, who lived in New Jersey, Pennsylvania, Maryland, Virginia, and the Carolinas. There is some evidence that Brethren had been active in Georgia at an early date, but no continuing congregation is known. Very full information, with exact names of members, is available for Pennsylvania and Maryland, thanks to Edwards. Only sketchy materials are provided for the

58. Flory, *Literary Activity,* pp. 145–157; see Hocker, *Printing House,* pp. 84–90, for information on the type foundry. Gerald C. Studer, *Christopher Dock, Colonial Schoolmaster* (1967), pp. 157–170, discusses Dock's authorship in the *Magazien.*

59. See, among others, Jean Moore Cavell, "Religious Education Among People of Germanic Origin in Colonial Pennsylvania," *Pennsylvania German Society Proceedings,* vol. 36 (1929), pp. 33–45; and Albert B. Faust, *The German Element in the United States* (1909), vol. 1, pp. 20ff.; vol. 2, pp. 96ff.

Southern Colonies, although detailed research now going on is filling in the details.[60]

The coming of the American Revolution was a major challenge to the Brethren. Although they gave support to the Quaker party in the Pennsylvania assembly earlier in the century, Brethren basically followed a pattern of non-involvement. They were reluctant to be engaged in affairs of the world and thought it safer to remain isolated from the currents of politics. Their attitude was that of Christian non-resistance. They believed in rendering unto Caesar that which was Caesar's and therefore paid legitimate taxes. They drew the line on personal involvement in actions contrary to the teachings of the New Testament as they understood it, and consequently would not defend themselves militarily or participate in warfare. (This attitude had cost several lives in the Indian attacks on the frontier, although they were ordinarily on good terms with the aborigines.) They kept aloof from the intense political activity of the Puritan clergy of New England, the anti-British preaching of the Scotch-Irish Presbyterians, or the crusades against a resident Anglican bishop, all of which contributed to the revolutionary spirit.

Moreover, the Brethren felt deeply obligated to the crown for the religious freedom which they had enjoyed, so unlike their early experience in Europe. When they arrived as immigrants, they had affirmed allegiance to the British king and his government and did not lightly swerve from this attitude. They were farmers and craftsmen and little bothered by the economic strains of the British mercantilist policy so upsetting to the merchants of the Atlantic seaboard. When war came, therefore, they were placed in a difficult position in knowing what posture to take. Was the new revolutionary government in fact the authority which Romans 13 taught them to obey? The problem came to the general church council held at Conestoga, Pennsylvania, in 1779, in the form of a decision whether members should take the "attest" or oath of

---

60. Published in *Brethren in Colonial America*, pp. 171–191. Statistical information on Brethren growth is found in Donald F. Durnbaugh, ed., *The Church of the Brethren: Past and Present* (1971), pp. 143–144. The basic study for Maryland is still J. Maurice Henry, *History of the Brethren in Maryland* (1936). Roger E. Sappington has authored two studies on Brethren in the Southern Colonies: *The Brethren in the Carolinas* (1971) and *The Brethren in Virginia* (1973). Several denominational histories dealing with geographical areas (districts) contain important material.

allegiance to the new government. The answer was that: "Inasmuch as it is the Lord our God who establishes kings and removes kings, and ordains rulers according to his own good pleasure, and we cannot know whether God has rejected the king and chosen the state, while the king had the government; therefore, we could not, with a good conscience, repudiate the king and give allegiance to the state."[61] Those who had affirmed allegiance to the new revolutionary government were to renounce this or face church discipline. There is evidence that in their perplexity some Pennsylvania Brethren sought guidance from British authority "praying that a general line of conduct might be pointed out to them, to conduct themselves" so that they would not be thought by the crown to be guilty of revolutionary activity. Muhlenberg commented on this in his *Journal* in May 1778: "Now many of the inhabitants are again in a predicament, especially the Quakers, Baptists [either Brethren or Mennonites], etc., who have been hoping all along that the might of England would conquer the land and protect these sects in their former liberties and accumulated possessions, leaving them settled and undisturbed on their lees, while only the Protestant church people would be turned into slaves."[62] At bottom, Brethren wished to remain neutral in the conflict between the revolutionary forces and the British government. Given the temper of the times, this was impossible. It is not surprising the insurgents considered them to be Tories and treated them as such. Incidents of economic hardship and brutal treatment have been recorded.

The fate of the Sauer family is instructive. Although Sauer II himself protested the Stamp Act (which affected him directly as a printer and publisher), he spoke out in no uncertain terms for the old government. He contrasted the benefits which had accrued to the Brethren and other dissenters under the king with an uncertain future under a new regime. As a pacifist, he was completely opposed to the use of force to bring about new political conditions. A pamphlet of 1765 which he wrote is typical of his attitude toward government: "It was undeniably a great blessing of God that for some eighty years

---

61. *Brethren in Colonial America*, p. 353; chapters 10 and 11 (pp. 341–423) are devoted to the Brethren in the Revolutionary period. There is valuable material in Rufus D. Bowman, *The Church of the Brethren and War, 1708–1941* (1944) and Peter Brock, *Pacifism in the United States* (1968), pp. 267–270.

62. Tappert and Doberstein, *Notebook*, p. 198.

this land has had such a good, peace-loving government, and that everyone has been able to worship God as he sees fit without any coercion of conscience or prohibition. No other land in the entire inhabited world is known that is as perfect as Pennsylvania has been up to now, under our proprietary government."[63]

Sauer's son, Christoph Sauer III, threw in his lot with the Loyalists. After the war he addressed a memorial to the king to secure some compensation for losses suffered. In this memorial he reported that his father and he "from a sense of duty to their sovereign and attachment to the British government" had "opposed to the utmost of their power the rising sedition as well by frequent publications in his paper as otherwise, until at length the Council of Safety of Pennsylvania summoned your memorialist and his father before them, and forbade them to print a newspaper or any political piece whatever [on December 16, 1776]." Sauer III stated that he and his father "became so obnoxious to the rebel rulers that they were obliged to secret themselves from the fury of their mobs which were exerted to seize on their persons and threatened to tar and feather them."[64] Before February, 1777, Sauer II turned over his publishing business to Christoph and to another son Peter. They chose to move the business to Philadelphia in the autumn of 1777 when it came under British occupation and printed for the crown.

Sauer III was captured in Germantown in December, 1777, while accompanying a detachment of British soldiers. He was exchanged for a powdermaker held prisoner by the British, which is some indication of the esteem in which he was held by the British authorities. When the British left Philadelphia, the young Sauer went to New York where he continued his labor in their behalf. One of his more important publications was an appeal to the Germans in the colonies, stressing the prosperity they enjoyed under British rule, the confusion attending the revolution, the ambition of revolutionary leaders, and the benefits they would enjoy if the British government could be re-established.

He was also engaged in attempts to rally Loyalists in rural areas, to provide intelligence for the British army, and to stimulate the British government to take steps to encourage

---

63. *Brethren in Colonial America*, p. 381.
64. *Brethren in Colonial America*, pp. 387–388.

Loyalism among those wavering in their political allegiance. His actions were lauded both during the war and after. The memorial he presented to the crown was supported by testimonials from high officials who stressed his value to the Tory effort.[65]

Sauer II followed a policy of neutrality, but in the heat of the period he was considered a traitor, especially when he moved to his sons in Philadelphia for a time during the British occupation. He returned to his home in Germantown before the British withdrawal, only to be seized and mistreated by the revolutionary party. On May 21, 1778, the revolutionary council meeting in Lancaster proclaimed a number of citizens to be traitors, including Sauer II and Sauer III. They were ordered to appear in court before July 7 to answer charges, failing in which they would be guilty as charged. Sauer was captured in his home and held in military captivity during much of this time, but was nevertheless held to have forfeited any defense against the charge of treason. Later in July officials dispossessed him and sold off at auction (in depressed continental currency) his large estate, despite their own ruling that such could not be carried out while children of the accused were still in their minority. Sauer did not take legal steps to stop the action, because of the Brethren policy of nonlitigation. The details of the confiscation are found in the printed records of the *Pennsylvania Archives.* The estate was valued at more than £10,000, indicating that Sauer was among the wealthiest Germans in the colonies. Following the loss of his worldly goods, Sauer earned his living as a bookbinder, taking pains to repay those friends who had loaned him money in his time of need. He died in 1784.[66]

The attitude of the Brethren during this period is best seen in the memorial which they presented along with the Mennonites to the Pennsylvania assembly in November 1775. After expressing gratitude for rights enjoyed in the past, they stated that they had "dedicated (themselves) to serve Men in every Thing that can be helpful to the preservation of Man's lives, but we find no Freedom in giving, or doing, or assisting in any Thing by which Man's lives are destroyed or hurt. . . . We

---

65. James O. Knauss, "Christopher Sauer the Third," *Proceedings of the American Antiquarian Society* (April 1931); *Brethren in Colonial America*, pp. 395–399, 405–423.

66. *Brethren in Colonial America*, pp. 400–405; Hocker, *Printing House*, pp. 90–110, believes that Sauer had only himself to blame for the confiscation.

are always ready, according to Christ's command to Peter, to Pay the Tribute, that we may offend no Man, and so we are willing to pay Taxes. . . . We are also willing to be subject to the Higher Powers, and to give in the manner Paul directs us, for He beareth the sword not in vain. . . . This Testimony we lay down before our worthy Assembly . . . letting them know that . . . we are not at liberty in Conscience to take up Arms to conquer our Enemies, but rather to pray to God Who has Power in Heaven and on Earth, for Us and Them."[67] With this attitude, the Brethren were not susceptible to appeals for recruitment to the rebel army. A local functionary wrote to the president of the executive Council at Lancaster in November 1777 that "the Grate Number of Quakers, Mananest and Dunkers in this County ocations the companey to be so hard filled up. The others in the upper end of the County which is mostly Irish people and Low Dutch goes Preetey Generall; . . . so many scrupolis peoples as we have ocations much hiring and deters the business much."[68]

These events in Pennsylvania were paralleled by Brethren experiences in other colonies. The Maryland Convention resolved upon receiving petitions from Mennonites and Brethren that the "several committees of observation may, in their discretion, prolong the time or take security for the payment of any fine by them imposed for not enrolling in the militia . . . and it is recommended to the committee to pay particular attention, and to make a difference between such persons as may refuse from religious principles, or other motives." In North Carolina, the Brethren, along with other peace church members, were forced to pay a threefold tax (November 1777) and to affirm loyalty and subjection to the state (1778), as well as to respond to special levies of blankets and clothes. Likely the Brethren in Virginia were treated in the same manner as the Quakers and Mennonites, who were first exempted from militia duty and later required to pay fines and furnish substitutes.[69]

Ephrata felt the impact of the war, both directly and indirectly. Long suspected of Romish leanings because of the monastic practices, the community felt public disfavor and

---

67. *A Short and Sincere Declaration, to Our Honorable Assembly* (1775); also published in German. This has often been reprinted.
68. Durnbaugh, "Relationship," pp. 49–50. See also Wilbur J. Bender, *Nonresistance in Colonial Pennsylvania* (1949).
69. *Brethren in Colonial America*, pp. 375–376.

suspicion. At one point, great quantities of the copies of the Mennonite book of martyrs, printed at the Ephrata press in 1748, were seized by the American authorities for use as gun wadding. This was thought to be a great evil by the peace-loving Ephrata members, who bought back as much as they could.[70]

True to its tradition of Christian charity and hospitality, the community threw open its doors in September 1777 to the wounded American survivors of the Battle of Brandywine. They tended the victims with moving devotion. A graphic description was left in the journal of a wounded officer:

> I came among this people by accident, but I left them with regret.... They all acted the part of the Good Samaritan to me, for which I hope to be ever grateful; and while experiencing the benefits of their kindnesses and attentions, witnessing the sympathies and emotions expressed in their countenance, and listening to the words of hope and pity with which they consoled the poor sufferers, is it strange that, under such circumstances, their uncouth garments appeared more beautiful to my eyes than ever did the richest robes of fashion, and their cowls more becoming than headdresses adorned with diamonds, and flowers, and feathers? Until I entered the walls of Ephrata, I had no idea of pure and practical Christianity. Not that I was ignorant of the forms or even of the doctrines of religion. I knew it in theory before, I saw it in practice then.[71]

The care given to the soldiers had serious repercussions on the community. Camp fever and other epidemic diseases spread among the military and 150 died. Ten of the solitary who tended them died, too, and three of the large buildings had to be destroyed because of infection. Some historians judge that the community, already in decline, never recovered from this loss.

Miller, the leader of the community following Beissel's death, interceded on behalf of numerous sectarians who ran afoul of the government because of their conscientious objection to war. He upheld the right of conscience in letters to American leaders, many of whom he had known through his membership in the American Philosophical Society. On another occasion, according to tradition, he won a reprieve from the American authorities for a tavern keeper sentenced

---

70. *Chronicon*, pp. 213–214; Reichmann and Doll, *Ephrata*, pp. 131, 181.
71. Reichmann and Doll, *Ephrata*, p. 115.

to death as a Tory, although the man was Miller's arch-opponent and enemy.

The effect of the Revolution upon Brethren was to heighten their tendency of isolation and separation from the world. These troubles encouraged the already present process of migration westward, where it was hoped they could live their faith undisturbed by outward events. Some historians of the Brethren have treated the post-revolutionary era as one of darkness and degeneration. Actually, it was a time of great activity, of expansion across the continent, of literary efforts and able leadership. Yet, it seems likely that the experiences of the revolutionary period delayed the time when the Brethren would feel themselves one with American society. They were reinforced in understanding themselves as a "peculiar people," pilgrims in a foreign land. Little noticed by the world, except for their unusual manner of dress and their prosperous farms, the Brethren entered the early national period as a small but growing body of believers, attempting to be faithful to the teachings of Christ as they learned them from the Scriptures.

They no doubt continued to appear to others in much the same way as the historian Morgan Edwards had described them in 1770:

> It is very hard to give a true account of the principles of these Tunkers as they have not published any system or creed, . . . They are *general baptists* in the sense which that phrase bears in Greatbritain; . . . General redemption they certainly hold, and, withall, general salvation; which tenets, though wrong, are consistent. They use great plainness of language and dress, like the Quakers; and like them will neither swear nor fight. They will not go to law; nor take interest for the money which they lend. They commonly wear their beards, and keep their first-day sabbath. . . . They have the Lord's supper with its ancient attendants of *love-feasts, washing feet, kiss of charity,* and *right hand of fellowship.* They anoint the sick with oil for recovery; and use the *trine immersion* with *laying on of hands* and prayer, even while the person baptized is in the water; which may easily be done as the party kneels down to be baptized. . . . Their church government and discipline are the same with those of the english baptists; except that every brother is allowed to stand up in the congregation to speak in a way of exhortation and expounding; and when by these means they find a man eminent for *knowledge* and *aptness* to teach, they choose him to be a minister, and ordain him with imposition

of hands, attended with fasting and prayer and giving the right hand of fellowship. They also have *deacons;* and ancient widows for *deaconesses;* and *exhorters;* who are licensed to use their gifts statedly. They pay not their ministers unless it be in a way of presents . . . ; neither do the ministers assert the right, esteeming it more *blessed to give than to receive.* Their acquaintance with the Bible is admirable. In a word, they are meek and pious christians; and have justly acquired the character of the *Harmless Tunkers.*[72]

SELECTED BIBLIOGRAPHY–CHAPTER SEVEN

Bowman, Rufus D., *The Church of the Brethren and War, 1708–1941* (1944); reissued with an introduction by Donald F. Durnbaugh (1971)

Brumbaugh, Martin G., *A History of the German Baptist Brethren in Europe and America* (1899); reprinted with index (1961)

Durnbaugh, Donald F., ed., *European Origins of the Brethren: A Sourcebook on the Beginnings of the Church of the Brethren in the Early Eighteenth Century* (1958); reprinted (1967)

Durnbaugh, Donald F., ed., *The Brethren in Colonial America: A Sourcebook on the Transplantation and Development of the Church of the Brethren in the Eighteenth Century* (1967)

Flory, John S., *Literary Activity of the German Baptist Brethren in the Eighteenth Century* (1908)

Henry, J. Maurice, *History of the Brethren in Maryland* (1936)

Hocker, Edward W., *The Sower Printing House of Colonial Times* (1948); Pennsylvania German Society Proceedings, vol. 53

Lamech and Agrippa [pseud.], eds., *Chronicon Ephratense: A History of the Community of Seventh Day Baptists at Ephrata, Lancaster County, Penn'a,* tr. J. Max Hark (1889); reprinted (1972)

Mack, Alexander, Sr., *A Short and Plain View of the Outward, Yet Sacred Rights and Ordinances of the House of God . . . Also*

---

72. Edwards, *Materials,* pp. 66–67.

Ground Searching Questions Answered by the Author, tr. Henry Kurtz and James Quinter (1860)

Nieper, Friedrich, *Die ersten deutschen Auswanderer von Krefeld nach Pennsylvanien: Ein Bild aus der religiösen Ideengeschichte des 17. und 18. Jahrhunderts* (1940)

Reichmann, Felix and Doll, Eugene E., eds., *Ephrata As Seen By Contemporaries* (1953); Pennsylvania German Folklore Society, vol. 17

Renkewitz, Heinz, *Hochmann von Hochenau (1670–1721): Quellenstudien zur Geschichte des Pietismus* (1935); republished with additions in the series Arbeiten zur Geschichte des Pietismus, vol. 5

Sappington, Roger E., *The Brethren in the Carolinas* (1971)

Smith, Samuel, *History of the Province of Pennsylvania,* ed. William M. Mervine (1913)

Stoeffler, F. Ernest, *German Pietism During the Eighteenth Century* (1973)

Stoudt, John Joseph, *Pennsylvania German Poetry, 1685–1830* (1956); Pennsylvania German Folklore Society, vol. 20

Wust, Klaus, *The Virginia Germans* (1970)

EPILOGUE–SOME TENTATIVE CONCLUSIONS

by F. Ernest Stoeffler

AFTER WORKING WITH THE MATERIAL IN THIS VOLUME ONE FINDS that a series of conclusions would seem to suggest themselves. They are tentative in the sense in which all historical generalizations are tentative; i.e., they are based on the current state of research and hence open to future revision in the light of further evidence.

Having made such a concession, however, it must also be affirmed that the conclusions based on the essays in this book necessarily challenge some of the older assumptions relative to the origins of our American religious heritage. Especially problematical becomes the thesis of our almost exclusive national indebtedness to the Puritan tradition, which was probably stated most baldly by T. S. Flynn (*The Influence of Puritanism on the Political and Religious Thought of the English*, 1920) when he wrote: "Puritanism made America (p. 99)"; or again, "England and America, the two most genuinely democratic nations in the world, could never have become what they are, had not Puritanism given them along with its political ideals that Godliness which was the very life of its life" (p. 110). Whether stated in terms of such exuberant triumphalism, or in the more guarded language of more cautious scholarship, this thesis appears to have become untenable. With reference to its influence on early American history Puritanism must share the field with Anglicanism, with the movement which presently concerns us, namely Pietism, as well as with the Enlightenment, Romanticism, etc., and subsequently with impulses coming out of Roman Catholicism and Judaism.

The Puritan influence implicit in the early American clerocracies seems to have weakened considerably during the course of the seventeenth century. This was true even in New England. To what extent Puritanism ever penetrated the religious self-understanding of the people of the Middle Colonies, of the Southern Colonies, and of the multitudes involved in the great westward migration, is a problem indeed. There can no longer be any doubt that the evangelicalism which became the dominant pattern for the individual and corporate religious self-understanding of American Protestants is heavily indebted to the Pietist tradition. Hence Pietism touched all segments of American society, as well as all geographical areas. And, furthermore, its influence continues to be felt, not only among sectarian groups, but among the broad majority of Protestant denominations in America.

Somewhat parenthetically it should also be pointed out that it was not one particular brand of Continental Pietism which held the field in our early history. As there had long been a tendency among church historians to stress only the influence of the major reformers and to discount the impulses which originated in the radical Reformation, so there has been a tendency to ignore the influence of the radical Pietists and to concentrate on what were deemed to be more acceptable manifestations of the same phenomenon. The fact seems to be that both church-related Pietism and radical Pietism influenced American life and institutions. Nor is it possible to differentiate sharply between the two with reference to their impact upon early American religion. While during the early days of our history radical Pietism informed especially the religious perspectives of the smaller Protestant groups its influence began to penetrate American Protestantism in general. A case in point is the rise of the denominational pattern of American churches. In this as in other instances whatever impulses in this direction came from New England Puritanism received powerful support not only from Enlightenment sources, but from the Pietist groups who looked askance at notions of religious establishment and the accommodationist understanding of the religious life which goes with such an establishment. Perhaps equally interesting in this context is the Brethren support of the Quaker position on war, which generated impulses that were never entirely lost by American churches.

More specifically, how does the Pietist heritage manifest itself in the general evangelical climate of American Protestantism? Perhaps most obvious here is the fact that by and large the American churches have been more interested in the "saving of souls" than in problems of theology, or ecclesiology. The traditional emphasis has been to help the would-be believer into a new state of being, and then to provide for him the kind of religious nurture which is designed to keep him in that state. While in some of the major denominations these emphases are somewhat muted at the moment this is obviously not a universal condition of American Protestantism, nor can it even be assumed to be a permanent one. This is especially true in light of the fact that the growing edge of Protestant Christianity in America is currently outside of these denominations and is thus very much given to the business of "saving souls," and of keeping them in the new state of being to which such efforts are expected to lead. It is true, of course, that these emphases were part of the Puritan tradition. The fact is equally clear, however, that it was Pietism which during the eighteenth century transformed the Puritan tradition in America into the kind of new-life centered evangelicalism which meets us in American religious history.

Equally typical of most American Protestantism is the rather pronounced experiential note which it has traditionally sounded. To the average American Protestant the essence of being religious is not a matter of theologizing, or merely of ethical conduct, or of cultural affiliation, or of being a part of a given religious group, or even of participating in certain modes of sacramental action. To him the use of the so-called "means of grace" has a significance only if it leads to a knowledge of the Divine which touches, and hence transforms, his experience of the world around him in some tangible way. It is a knowledge which does not solve all of his problems or obliterate his frustrations. But he expects his religion to help him transcend these problems, to conquer his frustrations, and to look to the future in the confidence that in spite of life's baffling ambiguities this evil world is also his Father's world. This, of course, has been a prominent part of Pietism's traditional message, expounded in a myriad number of sermons, hymns, and other devotional guides.

That American Protestantism has traditionally been given to a strong biblical emphasis in theology as well as in ethics needs no demonstration. Whatever original impulses in this direction may have come from the Puritan beginnings in New England it was the Pietist tradition of the eighteenth century which reinforced them in a way which made biblicism a dominant characteristic of a very large section of Protestantism in America. America's early frontier situation became fertile soil for the Bible-centered theology of Halle, of Bengel, of the Moravians, as well as the Reformed and radical Pietists. It spoke to the need of those early settlers in a way in which a more sophisticated theology or ethic could never have done. Nor has the biblicism of an earlier day ever been outgrown even by substantial segments of the larger denominations. Among the smaller Protestant groups it is today as sure-footed and as untouched by hermeneutical uncertainties as when it came from the hands of its eighteenth-century advocates.

In speaking about ethics it is necessary also to mention Pietism's considerable sensitivity to social need and of the impact of this sensitivity on the American churches. Too little has been made thus far of the fact that it was Pietism on the Continent, and its first cousin, namely Wesleyan evangelicalism in England, which first began to call attention to the needs of orphans, of prisoners, of the aged, of the sick, of slaves, and of all manner of suffering humanity. Thus were established not only institutions for the needy, but schools for the children of the poor who had hitherto been economically exploited. It was this sensitivity to human need which Pietism helped transmit to the American churches and which has remained a widely acknowledged element of American Christianity.

The connection between Pietism and the development of the Protestant hymnody in America is very striking. In the foregoing essays only a few indications of this relationship are indicated. Much more could presumably be made of the power of Pietist hymnody and its role in undergirding and transmitting the message of the American churches. It is a moot question, indeed, whether it was the pulpit, the church school, or the typical hymnal with its manifestly Pietist leanings which communicated most effectively the traditional insights and values of American Protestantism.

The origin of the relatively pronounced role of the laity within American Protestantism remains somewhat problematical. There can be no doubt about the fact that it is related to all those economic, social, and cultural factors in early American life which tended to make for the democratization of

American society. In this connection it should not be forgotten, however, that Martin Luther's insistence on the priesthood of all believers, together with that same insistence among radical Reformers on the Continent, began to lay a theological foundation for a broader participation of the laity in the affairs of the church. And it is a matter of record that the sixteenth-century doctrine of the priesthood of all believers was dramatically implemented on the pragmatic level within Pietism, both church related and radical. Thus, the impulses toward lay participation which came out of Continental Pietism helped to reinforce democratic attitudes latent in early American Protestantism.

From the beginning Pietists were interested in the new being and the quality of life in which this newness comes to expression. For that reason they always sat relatively lightly on such matters as doctrinal purity, exaggerated confessional loyalty, ecclesiastical polity, and liturgical refinements. By and large they regarded these as the external forms in which "true religion" must necessarily appear. At the same time, however, they were profoundly given to the conviction that authentic Protestantism must emphasize the substance rather than the form. No one could have stated more succinctly the general Pietist openness in the realm of interconfessional (interdenominational) relations than did John Wesley when he said: "If your heart is as my heart, give me your hand." If this is the beginning of the ecumenical vision then Pietists must be credited with a prominent part in its rise. Again it should be pointed out, therefore, that whatever social and cultural factors may have moved American Protestantism in an ecumenical direction Pietism's contribution to the rise of ecumenical understanding in America must be taken far more seriously than it has been. It is significant that it was Zinzendorf who first de-emphasized publicly denominational rigidity in America when he projected his scheme for a "Fellowship of God in the Spirit" in Pennsylvania.

On the other side of the ledger, it should also be pointed out that Pietism has contributed its share to some of those features of American Protestantism which are widely regarded as less admirable. If certain segments of American Protestantism have sometimes been escapist in their theology, putting the emphasis on blessedness in the hereafter rather than justice for all in the here and now, the Pietist influences which came from the Continent are not wholly unrelated to this development. Nor can Pietism entirely escape the blame for a certain anti-intellectual atmosphere which has traditionally permeated large segments of American Protestantism. The pronounced tendency toward sectarian fragmentation among American Protestants must probably also be seen, in part at least, against the background of the Pietist influence on Protestant life in the new world. Here again it must be granted, of course, that the sources of church life in America are many-faceted and that Pietism is simply one of these facets, though a rather important one.

If there is truth in what has been said above, it should also be mentioned that the Pietist tradition, along with others, has not only influenced the American churches, but through them American life and institutions in general. No longer can Puritanism be regarded, for instance, as the major source of democratic ideas. Along with the Enlightenment, Pietism has also made its contribution in this direction. It is indeed a question whether the clerocracies of New England contributed as much to this end as the Pietist sectarianism of the Middle Colonies. The same could be said about whatever social concern we have in American society. A case could even be made to the effect that the Pietist understanding of life, which regards every fellow believer as "sister" or "brother," helped to begin the process of breaking down the rigid barriers associated with ethnic origin, race, and sex, which Americans originally inherited from Europe.

In closing it should be reiterated that the authors of the foregoing articles are aware of the fact that it was a whole spectrum of economic, social, intellectual, and religious forces which have worked together to fashion American Christianity into the kind of historical entity it became. The attempt here has been to lift up one of these forces, namely, the Pietist movement, and to indicate in an initial way its contribution to American Protestantism, and through it to American life and institutions in general.

INDEX

Albright, Jacob 217
American Bible Society 38
American Philosophical Society 262
American Revolution 28, 57, 58, 75,
    155, 156–159, 160, 161, 256–264
Ames, William 35, 36
Antes, Henry 135, 136, 139
Arminianism 51, 56
Arminius, Jacobus 40, 56
Arndt, John 9, 20, 79, 203, 204, 218
Arnold, Gottfried 9, 90, 108, 167,
    168, 169, 171, 242
Asbury, Francis 72, 160, 211, 214,
    215, 216, 217, 218
Augustine 180

Bancker, Willem 45
Bangs, Nathan 210
Bartholf, Guiliam 43, 44, 45, 47
Barton, Thomas 27
Bäumeler, Joseph 174
Becker, Peter 228, 233, 239, 240
Beissel, Conrad 64, 140, 213, 240,
    241, 243, 244, 246, 252, 253
Benezet, John Stephen 139, 143
Bengel, Johann Albrecht 9, 168,
    171, 198, 199, 200, 201, 204, 211,
    269
Berkenmeyer, William Christopher
    15, 18, 23

Bertholet, Jean 140
Boehler, Peter 133, 134, 136, 137,
    138, 142, 145, 147, 190, 192, 194,
    195, 208, 209
Boehm, Anthony William 204
Boehm, Henry 214, 215
Boehm, Johann Philip 63, 64, 65,
    141, 237, 248
Boehm, Martin 74, 75, 78, 79–87,
    88, 91, 92, 93, 96, 98, 99, 100, 101,
    102, 103, 104, 105, 106, 107, 110,
    111, 120, 214, 215, 216
Boehme, Jacob 80, 86, 186, 235, 242
Boehnisch, George 132, 133, 135
Boel, Henricus 47
Bogatzky, C. H. von 20
Boltzius, John Martin 27, 31
Brakel, Theodorus à 50, 61, 70
Brakel, Willem à 50, 51, 52, 70
Brothers of the Common Life 36
Bruce, David 147
Brunnholtz, Peter 22
Buddeus, Johann Franz 134
Burkholder, Christian 102, 104,
    105, 106

Cabet, Etienne 170, 179
Calvin, Jean 36, 37, 40, 51, 71, 124,
    147
Campanus, Johannes 167

Cassel, Abraham Harley 224
Cave, William 168
Charity Schools 251
Chelcicky, Peter 156
Cherbury, Edward Herbert 184
Clarke, Adam 203
Coccejus, Johannes 49, 50
Coetus 66, 67, 70, 71, 84, 86
Coke, Thomas 160
Collins, Nicholas 29
Comenius, John Amos 126, 130
Cyprian, Ernest S. 16

Danckaerts, Jasper 41, 42, 43
Davenport, James 63
David, Christian 126, 127
Davis, Samuel 215
Deism 184
Dieterici, Wilhelm 47, 48
Dippel, Konrad 8
Dock, Christopher 256
Doddridge, Philip 198
DuBois, Gualtherus 39, 47
DuBois, Pieter 39
Duché, Jacob 243

Eckstein, Johannes 239
Edwards, Jonathan 49, 234
Edwards, Morgan 232, 233, 238, 244, 256, 263
Eliot, John 42
Embury, Philip 214
Engle, Jacob 88, 92, 93, 94, 100
Engle, John 88, 94, 100
Engle, Ulrich 88
Ephrata 64, 119, 140, 145, 146, 172, 213, 236, 238–253, 261–263
Ettwein, John 156, 157, 158, 159, 160

Fahnestock, William 245
Falckner, Justus 15, 23, 213
Finley, Samuel 65
Flory, John 225, 226, 254
Franck, Sebastian 167
Francke, August Gotthilf 128, 134
Francke, August Hermann 8, 15, 31, 32, 115, 125, 128, 171, 204, 206, 225
Frantz, Michael 116, 253

Freeman, Bernhardus 45, 46, 47, 48, 53
Frelinghuysen, John 58
Frelinghuysen, Theodorus Jacobus 39, 43, 45, 47, 48, 49, 50, 53, 54, 55, 56, 57, 58, 59, 61, 213, 234
Frey, Andreas 246, 247
Freylinghausen, Johann Anastasius 207

Gargon, Mathias 46
Garrison, Nicholas 138
Geeting, George Adam 100, 101, 216
German Society of Pennsylvania 32
Germantown Academy 256
Gersdorf, Henrietta von 125, 127
Gichtel, Johann Georg 242
Goetschius, Henricus 54, 55
Göttingen, University of 178
Greider, John 88
Gruber, Jacob 214
Gruber, Johann Adam 239
Guldin, Samuel 60, 61, 62, 63, 65, 72, 213
Gumre (Gomorry), John 232, 233
Guyse, John 198

Hagen, John 136
Hagerty, John 214
Halle 8, 15, 16, 17, 18, 31, 60, 61, 68, 98, 125, 127, 128, 131, 132, 134, 171, 204, 205, 206, 209, 211, 212, 236, 269
Handschuh, John F. 20
Hardenbergh, Dinah 57, 58, 59
Hardenbergh, Jacob Rutsen 58
Harvard University 34, 171, 178
Hasidism 9
Heck, Barbara 214
Heidelberg, University of 63
Heitz, John George 127
Hellenbroek, Abraham 50, 51, 52
Helmstedt, University of 15
Helmuth, J. C. H. 20, 212
Henkel, Anthony Jacob 213
Herborn, University of 47, 67, 69, 70, 80, 217
Heylin, John 198
Hildebrand, Johannes 252

Hochenau, Ernst Christoph Hochmann von 89, 91, 95, 98, 108, 110, 111, 117, 118, 225, 227
Höcker, Ludwig 245, 252, 253
Holmes, Benjamin 253
Hooker, Thomas 43
Horneck, Anthony 185, 186, 187, 196, 206
Huber, Samuel 100
Huguenots 35, 36, 37, 38, 39, 47, 63, 139
Hussites 124
Huter, Jakob 167

Jablonsky, Daniel Ernst 130
Jansenism 9, 186
Jay, John 38
Jena, University of 134, 141
Joachim of Fiore 168
Jung-Stilling, Johann Heinrich 9

Keil, Wilhelm 173, 174, 176, 178, 179
Kelpius, Johannes 169, 240
Koch, Stephan 238, 239
Koelman, Jacobus 43, 48, 50, 54
Krahn, Cornelius 74
Kulenkamp, Gerardus 65
Kunze, Johann Christoff 254
Kurtz, John Nicholas 29, 30

Labadie, Jean de 41, 42, 43, 47, 185, 187
Labadism 41, 42, 43, 44, 48, 51, 185, 186, 187
Lampe, Friedrich Adolph 46, 50, 216
Landmann, Barbara Heynemann 173
Lange, Friedrich Adolph 171
Lavater, Johann Caspar 9
Law, William 186, 191, 195
Lawrence, John 112, 186
Lee, Jesse 202, 205
LeMercier, Andrew 37, 38, 63
Leon, Maximilian De 178
Leydt, Johannes 57
Liebe, Christian 233
Lingen, University of 48, 66
Linner, Michael 194

Lischy, Jacob 67
Locke, John 185
Lodenstein, Jodocus van 43, 47, 54
Lowe, Petrus 52
Luther, Martin 21, 171, 196, 209, 270

Mack, Alexander ("Sander"), Jr. 228, 238, 239, 253, 254
Mack, Alexander, Sr. 90, 91, 213, 228, 229, 230, 238, 241, 254
Mallot, Floyd E. 224
Mann, Thomas 244
Marck, Johannes à 46, 48, 53, 57
Marpeck, Pilgram 167
Marx, Karl 168
Mather, Cotton 37, 168
Meiners, Eduard 48
Metz, Christian 173
Meyer, Hans Heinrich 60
Meyer, Hans Jacob 60
Miller, Johann Heinrich 250
Miller (Müller), Johann Peter 63, 64, 67, 242, 245, 252, 253, 262, 263
Miller, Simon 214
Minuit, Pieter 38
Mosheim, Johann Lorenz von 168
Muhlenberg, Henry Melchior 13–32, 68, 69, 145, 213, 236, 248, 250, 258
Muhlenberg, Peter 27
Müller, Joseph 246, 247
Mysticism 14, 34, 36, 186, 191, 195, 204, 235, 252

Neidig, John 101, 102
Nevin, John 83
Newcomer, Christian 100, 101, 102, 112, 216
Nitschmann, David 130, 133, 136, 137, 138, 141, 147
Noble, Thomas 138
Nordhoff, Charles 175
Noyes, John Humphrey 172

Order of the Four Brethren 127
Orosius, Paulus 166, 180
Orthodoxy 9, 22, 40, 64, 169
Otterbein, Philip Wilhelm 67, 69,

70, 71, 72, 74, 75, 78, 79–87, 88, 91, 92, 93, 96, 98, 99, 100, 101, 102, 103, 105, 106, 107, 110, 111, 112, 113, 120, 215, 216
Outrein, Johannes d' 49, 50
Oxford Movement 27

Paracelsus (Theophrastus Bombast von Hohenheim) 167
Pennsylvania Synods 62, 139, 141, 142–145, 148, 149, 162, 246
Perkins, William 35, 43
Peterson, P. J. 231
Pfautz, John Eby 222, 223
Phillipsz, Dirck 167
Post, Frederick 152
Preiss, Johannes 253
Primitivism 166, 167–171, 173, 175
Princeton, University of 69
Puritanism 9, 10, 11, 34, 35, 37, 38, 48, 54, 55, 165, 179, 186, 187, 191, 210, 211, 218, 257, 266–271
Pyrlaeus, John Christopher 141

Rabenhorst, Christian 26
Ramus, Petrus 55
Rankin, Thomas 202
Rapp, Georg 174, 178
Rationalism 9, 32, 184–185, 201
Rauch, Christian Henry 148
Reuss, Erdmunthe Dorothea von 126
Riegel, Adam 217
Rock, Friedrich 173, 235
Rothe, John 127, 128
Russell, Charles Taze 167
Rutgers University 57, 58, 59

Santvoort, Cornelius van 39, 45, 46, 47, 57
Sauer Family 142, 239, 248–251, 255–256, 258–260
Schaeffer, Melchior 127
Schlatter, Michael 24, 64, 65, 66, 67, 68, 69, 72, 145, 216
Schuurman, Anna Maria van 57, 185
Scougal, Henry 186, 191
Seabury, Samuel 160
Seiffert, Anton 136, 147

Simons, Menno 167
Skippack Brethren (Associated Brethren of Skippack) 135, 136, 138, 139, 140
Sluyter, Peter 41, 42
Smith, Samuel 230
Smith, William 251
Society for Propagating Knowledge of God among the Germans 67, 77
Society for the Promotion of Christian Knowledge 15
Society for the Propagation of the Gospel 26
Spangenberg, Augustus Gottlieb 132, 133, 134, 135, 138, 144, 147, 149, 151, 152, 153, 154, 157, 190, 194, 239
Spanheim, Friedrich (the Younger) 185
Spener, Philipp Jakob 8, 15, 115, 125, 225
Stähelin, Christof 64
Starck, Johann Jacob 218
Stoll, Jacob 253
Stollberg-Wernigerode, Count von 132
Synod of Dort 23, 24, 35, 36, 56, 169

Taffin, Jean 35, 39, 40, 41, 48
Taylor, Jeremy 195
Teellinck, Willem 34, 35, 43, 50
Tennent, Gilbert 49, 52, 55, 63, 65, 138
Tennent, William 28
Thurnstein (see Zinzendorf) 139

Udemans, Godefridus Cornelisz 35, 50, 60
UnderEyck, Theodor 64
Urlsperger, Samuel 15
Urner, Martin 240
Utopian Socialism 165
Utrecht, University of 34, 35, 39, 47, 57, 58

Velthusen, John C. 15
Verschuir, Johan 48, 49
Visscher, Hendrik 49, 52, 54, 55, 56, 57, 59

Voetius, Gysbertus 34, 35, 36, 39, 41, 43, 47, 49, 50, 64, 70

Walch, John 16, 35
Warburton, William 201
Watterville, Frederick de 127, 128
Weiser, Conrad 148, 149, 252
Weiss, Georg Michael 60
Wenger, J. C. 106
Wesley, Charles 9, 59, 133, 184, 186, 187, 188, 189, 190, 191, 192, 194, 206, 207–212, 216, 217, 218
Wesley, John 9, 59, 133, 162, 167, 168, 184–212, 216, 217, 218, 270
White, William 28, 160
Whitefield, George 16, 27, 37, 39, 49, 55, 61, 69, 136, 137, 147, 184, 215
Wiedner, Henry 214

Wiegner, Christopher 132, 135, 136, 139
Wilhelmius, Johannes 48, 66
Williams, Robert 202
Winger, John 88
Witsius, Herman 50
Wittenberg, University of 125
Witzel, Georg 167
Wohlfarth, Michael 253
Wolff, Christoph W. 178
Wrangel, Charles Magnus 16, 17

Zeisberger, David 152, 154, 155, 156
Zinzendorf, Nicholas Ludwig von 22, 62, 65, 68, 78, 123–162, 195, 206, 209, 213, 246, 248
Zubly, John J. (Züblin) 69, 72
Zwingli, Huldreich 36

DATE DUE

JAN 03 2017			